With this book, Dr. Gentry has throw
pecially for evangelicals, including Re
churches. This challenge confronts th
creation account that choose for the li̶̶̶̶̶y̶ a̶g̶a̶i̶n̶s̶t̶ t̶h̶e̶ l̶i̶t̶e̶r̶a̶l̶,
for poetic metaphor instead of historical sequence. The argu-
ments are lawyer-like in their cumulative force, and prophetic in
their call to listen to the Bible's very text. The author has served
us well with his clearheaded writing and broad-based defense of
the traditional understanding of God's creation of the world in
six sequential 24-hour days.

— Dr. Nelson D. Kloosterman

Dr. Kenneth Gentry has taken a scholarly approach in dealing
with the subject of creation as expressed in Genesis 1. This book,
As It Is Written, is designed in particular to contrast the differences between the "Framework Hypothesis" interpretation of
the Genesis account in light of a "Literal six, twenty-four hour
Creationist" interpretation. Dr. Gentry masterfully explains the
theories, concedes areas of agreement in order to rightfully present each view faithfully and establish the objectionable areas of
conflict that are key to understanding Genesis 1. This polemic is
designed to reject that system of interpretation which allows for
reconstructing various texts to support alternative renderings of
the Geneses account that rejecting a literal six day, twenty-four
hour interpretation which is the historical orthodox view of Geneses, especially as maintained in the historical church based on
the grammatico-historical method of interpretation. This book
is a must-read by scholars, pastors, students, and laymen alike.
If there is one book you need to read in a time when the literal
interpretation of the Scripture, and in particular Geneses 1, has
come under attack, this is that book!

— Dr. Kenneth Gary Talbot

As It Is Written: Dismantling the Framework Hypothesis is a book
that helps guide readers across the debate between the traditional,

six-day creation view, and the framework hypothesis or literary framework theory, which attempts to create a bridge between the Genesis account and modern secular science. Kenneth Gentry provides a detailed analysis and powerful refutation to the arguments in favor of the framework hypothesis, while clarifying the exegetical reasoning to defend the literal interpretation of these passages of Genesis. Clear, concise, and thought-provoking!

— Dr. Kevin Clauson

Kenneth Gentry provides a powerful response to the revisionist views of the Genesis creation narrative that arose as rebuttals to evolutionist attacks on Scripture. *As it Is Written* is a succinctly documented, logically flowing work for the layperson and scholar alike, focusing on the issues of the foundational truth of God's Word from the first pages, and defending their literal nature over the literary structure that others are trying to impose. These are subjects of great concern, with a growing number of well-meaning biblical scholars yielding to the temptation to submit Scripture to a modernist view of science rather than letting its authority stand on its own.

— Dr. Geoff Downes

As It Is Written is a superb defense of 6-day creation by one of the finest Bible scholars of our time. Dr. Gentry demonstrates that the text of Scripture is clear about the timescale of creation and that non-literalist views, such as the framework hypothesis, collapse under careful scrutiny.

— Dr. Jason Lisle

Dismantling the Framework Hypothesis

AS IT IS
Written

The Genesis Account
Literal or Literary?

"...Christ died for our sins..."
1 Corinthians 15:3

Kenneth L. Gentry, Jr., Th.D.

First printing: February 2016

Master Books®, P.O. Box 726, Green Forest, AR 72638

Master Books® is a division of the New Leaf Publishing Group, Inc.

ISBN: 978-0-89051-901-1
Library of Congress Number: 2015919231

Cover by Diana Bogardus

Unless otherwise noted, Scripture quotations are from the New American Standard Bible.

Please consider requesting that a copy of this volume be purchased by your local library system.

Printed in the United States of America

Please visit our website for other great titles:
www.masterbooks.com

For information regarding author interviews,
please contact the publicity department at (870) 438-5288.

Master
Books®
A Division of New Leaf Publishing Group
www.masterbooks.com

Dedicated to:
Al Miller

A good friend I have never met
A great encourager I will never forget

CONTENTS

Preface

Since ancient times, men have been literally star-struck at the majesty of the sky above. Around 1000 B.C., King David expressed this awe when he contemplated the stars and considered the universe and man's place in it:

> When I consider Your heavens, the work of Your fingers,
> The moon and the stars, which You have ordained;
> What is man that You take thought of him,
> And the son of man that You care for him? (Ps. 8:3–4).

Our earliest records show men attempting to understand the origin and structure of the world and the universe — at least that portion that could be seen without the aid of the telescope (which was not invented until 1608 by Hans Lippershey).[1] German

---

1. Based on his observations made between 1922 and 1924, Edwin Hubble (1889–1953) was the first astronomer to provide substantial evidence that galaxies exist beyond our own. Until then astronomers believed that what we know as the Milky Way Galaxy was the entirety of the universe. Now we know that billions of other galaxies exist. According to one of the most popular astronomy websites, *Universe Today*: "The most current estimates guess that there are 100 to 200 billion galaxies in the Universe, each of which has hundreds of billions of stars." Fraser Cain, "How Many Galaxies in the Universe." May 4, 2009. http://www.universetoday.com/30305/howmanygalaxiesintheuniverse/.

philosopher Martin Heidegger (1889–1976) famously declared that the fundamental question of metaphysics should be: "Why is there something instead of nothing?"[2] And that certainly is an important question for any comprehensive worldview.

Indeed, there are several compelling reasons Christians ought to study the issue. Evangelical theologian Millard Erickson presents the case for our study of creation in the following: (1) The Bible stresses this doctrine. (2) The Church has included the doctrine of creation in its creeds. (3) The unity of biblical doctrine requires the doctrine of origins. (4) The biblical doctrine of creation is distinctively different from other religions and philosophies. (5) It confronts modern secular, naturalistic science.[3] In the final analysis, the doctrine of creation is essential to the ultimacy of God, for it shows that God alone is the Creator of the entire universe and the temporal order. Therefore, "the Book of Genesis is a record of the highest interest . . . because it is the foundation upon which the whole Bible is built."[4]

In the 17th and 18th centuries, the study of geology began to suggest a long course of development of the earth. Then with the 19th-century work of Charles Darwin (1809–82) and the publication of his *On the Origin of Species* (1859), the matter of (biological) origins became a universally debated question. The debate accelerated by Darwin involves not only biological origins but the very origin of the universe itself. Today, of course, the prevailing "mainstream" view of cosmic and life origins is some form of evolutionary theory. Cosmic evolution teaches that the universe is ultimately self-creating and self-organizing, without need of an intelligent Creator.

---

2. Martin Heidegger, *An Introduction to Metaphysics* (New Haven, CT: Yale University Press, 1959), p. 7–8.

3. Millard Erickson, *Christian Theology* (2d. ed.: Grand Rapids, MI: Baker, 1998), p. 392–93.

4. R. Payne Smith, "Genesis" in Charles John Ellicott, ed., *Ellicott's Commentary on the Whole Bible* (Grand Rapids, MI: Zondervan, rep. 1954), 1:3.

The rise of evolutionary theory with its rapid and widespread acceptance presented a strong intellectual and cultural challenge to Christianity. For the Christian, evolutionary theory impacts such issues as the integrity of the Bible as God's revelation to man, the legitimacy of the Christian faith that is rooted in that Bible, and the integrity of the comprehensive worldview erected from the Bible. That debate has certainly risen to a boiling point in the last half century, with evolution dominating government policy, scientific research, educational theory, media reporting — indeed, all areas of modern life. Unfortunately, too many Christians have either become wholly dispirited by the culture-wide challenge to their faith or have removed the challenge by attempting to adapt the Bible's message to the evolutionary outlook.

In response to the evolutionary assault on our faith, new views of the Genesis creation narrative have arisen in an attempt to reduce the conflict. Tremper Longman (2005, 104) observes that the Christian understanding of the creation days changed because of "the discoveries of modern science. Scientific research concluded that the world is old, the process that brought the cosmos into being took huge amounts of time." B.A. Robinson (2014) highlights several views of creation that developed in response to the evolutionary hegemony that rejects a literal six-day creation. Those views include the following: theistic evolution, indefinite age, gap theory, revelatory day, revelatory device, intermittent day, days of divine fiat, expanding time, replicated earth, analogical day, progressive creation, and the framework hypothesis. On page 2 of his report, Robinson suggests that there are four main views in this list: calendar interpretation, day-age, framework, and analogical day. Theologian Vern S. Poythress (2013) presents ten views of the interpretation of Genesis 1 and includes the following: young-earth creationism, mature creation theory, revelatory day theory, gap theory, local creation theory, intermittent day theory, day age theory, analogical day theory, framework view, and religion only theory. While presenting the 24-hour day view as an option, Kenneth D.

Keathley and Mark F. Rooker (2014, Part 2) reduce the remaining field to the gap theory, day age theory, temple inauguration theory, and historical creationism theory. Zondervan's CounterPoint series, Moreland and Reynolds (1999) reduces the options to three basic positions: young-earth creationism, old-earth (progressive) creationism, and theistic evolution.

In addition, many Christians have turned to one of the newer approaches to the creation-evolution debate that has gained national media attention since the mid-1990s: intelligent design. This view teaches that "certain features of the universe and of living things are best explained by an intelligent cause, not an undirected process such as natural selection."[5] Though challenging evolutionary theory, its advocates clearly state that the view is not rooted in Scripture, nor is it a creationist viewpoint. As the leading intelligent design website (just cited) puts it: "Creationism typically starts with a religious text and tries to see how the findings of science can be reconciled to it. Intelligent design starts with the empirical evidence of nature and seeks to ascertain what inferences can be drawn from that evidence." This view is causing controversy not only among evolutionists, but even among traditional, biblical creationists.[6]

A further example of a popular view is the progressive creation approach, which has been rejuvenated and promoted most recently and most effectively by Christian astrophysicist Hugh Ross. Progressive creationism is a form of old-earth creationism that accepts mainstream scientific estimates of the age of the universe.

---

5. "Definition of Intelligent Design," http://www.intelligentdesign.org/whatisid.php. Center for Science and Culture.

6. See, for example, the debate in Tony Carnes, "Design Interference" *Christianity Today*, 44:14 (December 4, 2001): 20; Alan G. Padgett, "Creation by Design," in *Books & Culture*, 6:4 (July/August, 2000): 30; Scott Swanson, "Debunking Darwin," *Christianity Today*, 41:1 (Jan. 6, 1997): 64; John G. West, "Intelligent Design and Creationism Just Aren't the Same," Center for Science and Culture (Dec. 1, 2002), http://www.discovery.org/a/1329; Henry Morris, "Intelligent Design and/or Scientific Creationism," Institute for Creation Research (Apr. 2006), http://www.icr.org/article/2708/.

It holds that God created new forms of life gradually over long periods of time by means of occasional bursts of new life forms. These "bursts" are instances of God Himself creating new types of living organisms by direct divine intervention. This allows its adherents to deny the biological evolution of all life forms from simpler ancestors. Hence its name: *progressive* creationism.[7]

Another new perspective is the framework hypothesis, a view of biblical origins that has been around the evangelical world since introduced to it by the Dutch biblical scholar Arie Noordtzij in 1924. It seems to have first appeared, however, almost 150 years earlier in the writings of the liberal[8] German romanticist philosopher, Johann Gottfried von Herder (1744–1803).[9]

I will define the framework view more fully later in this book, but for now one of its leading contemporary evangelical proponents, Lee Irons, provides us with a succinct definition suitable for a general introduction: "It is that interpretation of Genesis 1:1–2:3 which regards the seven-day scheme as a figurative framework. While the six days of creation are presented as normal solar days, according to the framework interpretation the total picture of God's completing His creative work in a week of days is not to be taken literally. Instead, it functions as a literary structure in which the creative works of God have been narrated in a topical order. The days are like picture frames. . . . There are two essential elements of the framework interpretation: the nonliteral element and the nonsequential element" (Irons and Kline 2001, 219). The evangelical formulation of this view is enjoying a growing

---

7. See, for instance, Robert C. Newman, "Progressive Creationism," in Moreland and Reynolds 1999: 105–06.

8. Elgin S. Moyer, *Who Was Who in Church History* (Chicago, IL: Moody, 1962), p. 194. In his *On the Spirit of Hebrew Poetry* (1782–83), Herder argued that we must accept falsehood and inconsistency in the Bible. In *On the Spirit of Christianity* (1798) he described God as a mind.

9. Marc Kay (2007a: 73) cites von Herder's *The Spirit of Hebrew Poetry* as stating that the "history of the creation [account] is entirely a sensuous representation arranged by days' work and numbers; in seven pictures of the separate portions of the created universe; and placed with reference to their parallel or corresponding relations."

influence among evangelical theologians and commentators, but it is also influencing an increasing number of average Christians in the pews.

Though having its genesis (pun intended) in the writings of the liberal theological scholar von Herder, I should note up front that contemporary evangelical proponents of the framework hypothesis hold a high view of Scripture, as well as a devout and reverential view of God as the Creator. Two of its leading spokesmen, Lee Irons and Meredith G. Kline (2001, 220), clearly declare that "we do not equate a nonliteral interpretation with a nonhistorical interpretation of the text." Another framework proponent, Mark Ross (1999, 114–115), states as the first of his "working boundaries" in dealing with creation that "the Bible is without error in all that it teaches." He goes on to declare another boundary by noting that the framework interpretation does "not aim to call into question the whole historical character of the Genesis narrative." Even its most vigorous opponents recognize that it is an "in-house" debate among Bible-believing scholars. Framework critic Joseph A. Pipa Jr. (Pipa and Hall 1999, 151) states that advocates of the framework do not "have a weak view of Scripture or deny the historicity of Genesis 1." Thus, evangelical framework theologians believe both in the inerrancy of Scripture and the creation of the universe by the God of Scripture, even while disagreeing on what Scripture teaches in Genesis 1–2 and the method whereby God created the world.

Nevertheless, it does seem rather odd that neither historic Judaism nor Christianity properly understood the first chapter of the first book of their Bible for over 3,000 years (from Moses in 1450 B.C. until von Herder in the late 18th century). That it does not leap out from the text may explain why it lay hidden from the greatest rabbinic scholars of Israel and the brightest minds of the Church for so long. Intelligent Christians, however, ought to keep abreast of such issues — issues impacting the integrity of the Christian faith in the modern world and the Christian apologetical enterprise. After all, we are obliged to bring "every thought captive to the obedience of Christ" (2 Cor. 10:5). And we must be always "ready to make a defense" of our positions as Christians (1 Pet. 3:15).

Within this work the reader will discover solid exegetical arguments for the traditional understanding of creation: the literal, sequential, six-day creation viewpoint. In addition, he or she will discover a thorough presentation, analysis, and rebuttal to the leading arguments of the framework hypothesis. These will not only rebut the framework view as such, but more fully elucidate the implications of the literal viewpoint.

I would like to thank Mischelle Sandowich for looking over the manuscript in a never-ending quest to uncover typos, grammatical errors, and such. Her keen eye is much appreciated and very helpful. Two sets of eyes reading over a manuscript are better than one. Especially when that second set is owned by an excellent proofreader.

So then, I present this work to the evangelical theological world in the hope of furthering the debate, while at the same time providing material to assist intelligent lay-Christians and ordained ministers committed to the literal view. As Winston Churchill once observed, "Men occasionally stumble over the truth, but most of them pick themselves up and hurry off as if nothing ever happened."[10] I pray that this careful presentation of the traditional view of six-day creation over the innovative framework hypothesis might confirm the historic position of the Church in the modern world.

Kenneth L. Gentry Jr., Th.D.

---

10. This Churchill quote is variously attributed on the Internet to Churchill. Apparently it went through several versions, in that he used this in several contexts, including a speech to the House of Commons. This version is from *Reader's Digest*, Volume 40, April 1942, http://quoteinvestigator.com/2012/05/26/stumble-over-truth/.

Part I

The Framework /
Literalism Debate

Chapter 1

Introduction and Definition

Introduction

The Christian is confronted with the fundamentally import-ant matter of creation immediately upon opening his Bible to its first chapter. In Genesis 1, we possess the direct revelation of God through Moses[1] regarding the divine origin of the material universe and the temporal order, the divine filling of the earth with all its flora and fauna, and the creation of man as the special image of God and high point of creation. Consequently, "As the first book of the OT, Genesis provides the foundation for the Pentateuch and for the rest of Scripture" (Turner 2003, 350). This is especially significant in that, as Currid (2007, 49) has aptly noted, "Creation constitutes a unique feature of the biblical worldview, and along with the existence of God comprises the very first worldview issues that a person confronts in reading the Bible." And as such it "provides the context out of which the

---

1. In this book I accept the traditional Mosaic authorship of Genesis 1 and 2, as per many conservative scholars. See Young 1964, 67 n59; Collins 2006, 37; Currid 2003, 28–31), including some framework advocates (Kline 1970, 79). I accept this over the doubts of some framework advocates (e.g., Ridderbos 1957, 17, 28). Even some scholars who stop short of a dogmatic conviction, can conclude that "the principal inspired, purposeful, and creative mind behind Genesis was Moses" (Walton 2001, 42).

rest of the biblical narrative, with all of its many dimensions, develops."

The Christian Church has historically — though not universally — understood the Genesis account as revealing that God created the world according to the chronological order of the narrative of chapter 1.[2] And until 1869 when the day age theory first appeared,[3] the traditional exegesis also held that the duration of the creative process transpired "in the space of six days," as stated, for instance, in the 17th-century Westminster Standards (WCF 4:1; LC 15, 120; SC 9). Noted 19th-century theologian Charles Hodge (1973, 1:570) recognized this when he wrote that "according to the generally received interpretation of the first chapter of Genesis, the process of creation was completed in six days." Thus, the "generally received interpretation" of Genesis 1 understands the creation narrative as presenting a series of successive divine fiats resulting in the sequential progress of creation over the span of six days of 24 hours' duration each. B.A. Robinson (2014, 2), writing for the Ontario Consultants on Religious Tolerance, states that "this is the historical belief taught by the Christian religion."

Indeed, even framework advocates admit that six-day creation is the "traditional view," as we may see in the following statements:

- Henri Blocher (1984, 46): It is "the reading that enjoys the support of the majority throughout church history, notably that of the Reformers."
- Meredith Kline speaks of the chronological sequence view that has "long been traditional." He notes that "these traditional interpretations continue to be dominant in orthodox circles" (Kline 1996, 11). He also speaks of "the more traditional types of exegesis" (1996, 11). Even some 40

---

2. See for example the following ancient writers (references to Ante-Nicene Fathers): Barnabas (1:146); Irenaeus (1:551, 557); Theophilus (2:9); Victorinus (7:341); Methodius (6:333); Disputation of Archelaus and Manes (6:203).
3. Blocher 1984, 43; Ramm 1944, 211.

years later, he lamented: "Advocacy of the literalist tradition, however, is as clamant as ever" (1995, 2).

- Lee Irons (1998, 23) refers to the "more traditional interpretations," which are "time-honored exegetical options."
- Bruce K. Waltke (2012, 3, 9): "Straightforward readings of the two creation accounts of Genesis 1 and 2 respectively lead to the traditional beliefs that the creation of all things took place in six consecutive twenty-four hour days." He later states that "a traditional reading of Genesis 1 and 2, is the largest hindrance to narrowing the gap between biblical faith science and secular science."

Unfortunately, these "time-honored exegetical options" (Irons 1998, 23), which represent the traditional position of historic Christianity, are derided by some framework advocates as "biblicist" (John R. Muether and Bruce K. Waltke), "anti-scientism" (Blocher 1984, 22, 48, 224, 227), "a deplorable disservice to the cause of biblical truth" (Meredith G. Kline), "extreme" (J.A. Thompson), and "folk-science" (Van Till).[4]

Non-framework advocates mention this fact when responding to framework advocacy:

- Carl F.H. Henry: "It is fair to say that six-day creationists, and not theistic evolutionists, reflect what may be taken as the Christian tradition before the rise of modern science."[5]
- Frances Young (DBI 147): "Before the development of modern geology and evolutionary theory, it was normal for Christians and Jews to understand the account in Gen. 1 as a literal description of the creation of the world."
- James Bibza and John Currid (1986, 44): "This interpretation has had the greatest support throughout the history

---

4. See Muether 1990, 254; Waltke 1975d, 338–39; Kline 1996, 15 (n 47); Thompson 1968, 20; Van Till 2006, 6.

5. Carl F.H. Henry, *God Who Stands and Stays* (Part Two), Vol. 6 of *God, Revelation and Authority* (Waco, TX: Word, 1983), p. 142. Henry criticizes Noordtzij, Ridderbos, and Kline on pages 134–35.

of the church. The majority of the Reformers, for example, held this view."

- A.W.H. Curtis (DBI 147): "These indications of the thought of the Reformation period underline an attitude to Genesis which prevailed until the nineteenth century. . . . The factual basis of the earlier chapters [of Genesis] in particular was challenged by modern scientific thinking about the origins of the universe and the evolution of the animal kingdom."
- Douglas Kelly: "Simply stated, the writer of Genesis meant to say what the historic Christian Church (until the mid-nineteenth century) believed he said."
- David W. Hall (1990, 267): "The long history of biblical interpretation, and specifically the Westminster divines' written comments, endorse only one of the major cosmological views considered today: *They thought creation happened neither in an instant nor over a long period, but in the space of six normally understood days.*"

Otto Zöckler explains the change of views regarding the creation process that was effected after the Reformation period during the Enlightenment:

> In the period of the Reformation . . . the commentators began to keep more closely to the words of the biblical narrative, and to avoid more carefully any trace of allegorization. But there came a time when natural science felt called upon to construct a doctrine of creation; and from that moment, the middle of the eighteenth century, until our time, a more or less noisy controversy has gone on between the orthodox party of the Church and the radical students of natural philosophy.
>
> It was, in the beginning, chiefly from the science of geology that the arguments against the biblical representation were drawn. Evidences derived from the most authentic

document (the earth itself), and by the most infallible method (scientific observation), were marched up to show, that, instead, of a creation in six days, there was, indeed, a progressive development through huge periods. The scriptural narrative was ridiculed as childish; and captious questions were put to those who still adhered to its very letters. (SHERK 1, 569)

Today, evangelicalism is witnessing the growing influence of the "framework hypothesis," which readily admits its non-traditional standing. What are the distinctives of this approach to Genesis? What are its problems that many traditional Christians deem of great concern? Is the hypothesis a tolerable option on the crowded scene of approaches to biblical origins?[6] These are a few of the questions that I hope to answer in this work.

Much of my early work for this study arose in the context of an ecclesiastical debate within a conservative, evangelical denomination of which I was a ministerial member, the Orthodox Presbyterian Church. This debate came to a head in the mid-1990s and resulted in the 1998 establishment of a Special Committee to Study the Framework Hypothesis, to which I was appointed as a defender of six-day creation. In 1999, the committee's rather detailed and extensive report was published. I will refer often to this Majority Report (1999) due to its clear and focused presentation of both sides of the debate.

So now, let us begin.

Working Definition of the Framework Hypothesis

A framework proponent, Mark Ross (1999: 113), provides the following succinct definition: "The Framework Hypothesis is a view of Genesis 1:1–2:3 which claims that the Bible's use of the seven-day week in its narration of the creation is a literary (theological) framework and is not intended to indicate the chronology

---

6. For a survey of the options, see: Poythress 2013. Robinson 2014.

or duration of the acts of creation." Howard Van Till (1986, 84) concurs: "The seven-day chronology that we find in Genesis 1 has no connection with the actual chronology of the Creator's continuous dynamic action in the cosmos. The creation-week motif is a literary device, a framework in which a number of important messages are held."

In the Special Committee "Report," the framework members presented a fuller definition of the hypothesis. And although the definition "evolved" (!) over the course of the Special Committee's labors, both sides to the debate agreed upon a definition that was acceptable for framing (no pun intended) the issue:

> The Framework Interpretation of Genesis 1:1 through 2:3 is the view which maintains that, while the six days of creation are normal solar days, the total picture of God's completing His creative work in a week of days is not to be taken literally, but functions as a literary framework for the creation narrative; and that the eight creative historical works of God have been arranged according to other than strictly sequential considerations, and that where there is sequential order it must be determined by factors other than the order of narration alone.[7]

In his own explanation, framework theologian Henri Blocher (1984, 50) draws a clear distinction between a *literary* approach to Genesis 1 and a *literal* approach. He does this while providing what he deems to be the theological reason why the author of Genesis expresses the manner of creation as he does:

> The literary interpretation takes the form of the week attributed to the work of creation to be an artistic arrangement, a modest example of anthropomorphism that is not

---

7. The original definition we used for a year in our deliberations read in part: "The Framework Interpretation of Genesis 1:1 through 2:3 is the view which maintains that the days of the creation week are not normal solar days, but function as part of a literary framework for the creation narrative. . . ."

to be taken literally. The author's intention is not to supply us with a chronology of origins. It is possible that the logical order he has chosen coincides broadly with the actual sequence of the facts of cosmogony; but that does not interest him. He wishes to bring out certain themes and provide a theology of the sabbath. The text is composed as the author meditates on the finished work, so that we may understand how the creation is related to God, and what is its significance for mankind.

Chapter 2

Problematic History and Traditionalist Concerns

Historical Issues

Framework theologian Henri Blocher (1984, 50; compare Young 1964, 44, 55) lists "the main proponents" in the historical outworking of the framework hypothesis among evangelicals: "The pioneer, around 1930, was A. Noordtzij of the University of Utrecht, and since World War II the main proponents have been N.H. Ridderbos of Amsterdam, B. Ramm of California, M.G. Kline of New England, D.F. Payne of Britain and J.A. Thompson of Australia." Wayne Grudem (1994, 301 n67) adds Ronald Youngblood to the list of influential framework advocates. Of course, there are many more, some of whom I will cite in my analysis and rebuttal.

Despite the long-standing tradition of orthodox exegesis and the deeply held convictions of Christian devotion, Genesis 1 is a flashpoint of debate in the evangelical world as the pressures of modernity weigh upon the Church. In fact, in 1958 Meredith Kline (1958, 146), the putative mentor of American framework advocacy, observed that "there are no signs that the debate over the chronological data of Genesis 1 is abating." There he noted that the debate's "flames have recently been vigorously fanned by the bellows of the dissenters." The "dissenters" cited by Kline

were framework theologians Bernard Ramm and N.H. Ridderbos, whose "discussions in particular have evoked animated reac-
tions among evangelicals" (Kline 1958, 146 n1).

Although some framework advocates propose that we aban-
don the label "framework *hypothesis*" in favor of "framework
interpretation," I will continue employing the more widely recognized designation. This choice of labels may seem to be little
more than a quibble, but I maintain it for the following reasons:
(1) This is the familiar designation that has prevailed at least since
Ridderbos' seminal work defending it and E.J. Young's classic refutation.[1] (2) Many recent framework advocates employ it without hesitation, for example, Tremper Longman, Henri Blocher,
Mark E. Ross, and Jeffrey Niehaus,[2] as do most contemporary
critics.[3] (3) The Special Committee itself arose from an ecclesiastical appointment to "evaluate the conformity of the Framework
Hypothesis to the teaching of Scripture."[4] In fact, the Majority
Report of the Special Committee itself spoke of the framework
triad structure as a "hypothesis."[5] So then, at best, it is a working
hypothesis that is set against the "traditional" exegesis, as admitted by framework advocates themselves.

I must point out at this early stage in my presentation that
I am not tenaciously holding to an approach to Scripture more
in keeping with a "naive fundamentalism," as some might complain. Rather, the six-day creationist view that I hold, and which

---

1. Ridderbos 1957, 36, 38, 40, 41, 42, 45, 54, 56, 68, etc. Young 1964, 44, 55.

2. Tremper Longman III, "Literary Approaches to Biblical Interpretation," in
   Moises Silva, ed., *Foundations of Contemporary Interpretation* (Grand Rapids,
   MI: Zondervan, 1996), p. 130. Blocher (1984, 50, 53). Blocher also calls it
   the "framework theory" (49). Mark Ross (1999, 113–114, 117, 119). Niehaus
   (2014, 39).

3. Weeks (1988, 104, 108, 115): "hypothesis" and "theory" (105, 112). Currid
   (2007, 46). Grudem (1994): "hypothesis" (301), "theory" (302). See also Pipa
   and Hall (1999): passim.

4. "The Report of the Committee to Study the Framework Hypothesis, presented to
   the Presbytery of Southern California (OPC) at its Meeting on October 15–16,
   1999," 1.

5. Ibid., p. 6–7.

I will present and defend, stands upon the exegetical observations of well-argued, long-standing, traditional orthodoxy — an orthodoxy including many noteworthy biblical and exegetical scholars from the past and the present.

Older noteworthy scholars include the following:

- Martin Luther (1483–1546): "Moses spoke in the literal sense, not allegorically or figuratively, i.e., that the world, with all its creatures, was created within six days, as the words read."[6]
- John Calvin (1509–64): "God himself took the space of six days" to create; "six days were employed in the formation of the world."[7]
- The Westminster Standards (1643–49): God created the world "in the space of six days" (WCF 4:1; LC 120; SC 9), "within the space of six days" (LC 15).
- Francis Turretin (1623–87): "The simple and historical Mosaic narration . . . mentions six days and ascribes a particular work to each day."[8]
- John Gill (1697–1771): "Though God took six days for the creation of the world and all things in it, to make his works the more observable, and that they might be distinctly considered, and gradually become the object of contemplation and wonder; yet the work of every day, and every particular work in each day, were done in a moment, without any motion and change, without any labour and fatigue, only by a word speaking, by an almighty *fiat*, let it be done, and it immediately was done."[9]

---

6. Martin Luther, *Lectures on Genesis: Chapters 1–5*, George V. Schick, trans., Vol. 1 of *Luther's Works*, Jaroslav Pelikan, ed. (St. Louis, MO: Concordia, 1958), 1:5. Cited from Hyers 1984, 5.

7. John Calvin, *Commentaries of the First Book of Moses Called Genesis*, John King, trans. (Grand Rapids, MI: Eerdmans, 1948), 1:78, 105.

8. Francis Turretin, *Institutes of Elenctic Theology*, George Musgrave Giger, trans., James T. Dennison Jr., ed. (Phillipsburg, NJ: P & R Publishing, rep. 1992), 1:444.

9. John Gill, *A Body of Divinity* (Grand Rapids, MI: Sovereign Grace, 1971 [rep. 1769]), p. 261.

- Heinrich Heppe (1820–79): "God completed the creation of matter and of the creatures made from it in the course of six successive days; not as though God could not have called every item into existence in one moment, but in order to manifest the variety and wise ordering of His creatures."[10]

- C.F. Keil (1807–88) and Franz Delitzsch (1813–90): "If the days of creation are regulated by the recurring interchange of light and darkness, they must be regarded not as periods of time of incalculable duration, of years or thousands of years, but as simple earthly days" (Keil and Delitzsch 2001, 32). In their footnote they add: "Exegesis must insist upon this, and not allow itself to alter the plain sense of the words of the Bible, from irrelevant and untimely regard to the so-called certain inductions of natural science. Irrelevant we call such considerations, as make interpretation dependent upon natural science, because the creation lies outside the limits of empirical and speculative research, and, as an act of the omnipotent God, belongs rather to the sphere of miracles and mysteries."

- Robert L. Dabney (1820–98): "The sacred writer seems to shut us up to the literal interpretation," noting that "the natural day is its literal and primary meaning" (Dabney 1973, 255).

More recent advocates of six-day creation include the following:

- Geerhardus Vos (1862–1949): "The days of creation were ordinary days."[11]

- Louis Berkhof (1873–1957): "The literal interpretation of the term 'day' in Gen. 1 is favored" (Berkhof 1941, 154).

---

10. Heinrich Heppe, *Reformed Dogmatics: Set Out and Illustrated from the Sources,* Ernst Bizer, ed., G.T. Thomson, trans. (Grand Rapids, MI: Baker, 1978 [rep. 1950]), p. 199.

11. From his *Gerreformeerde Dogmatiek,* as cited in Berkhof 1941, 154.

- H.C. Leupold (1891–1972): "When the verse [Gen. 1:5] concludes with the statement that the first 'day' (*yôm*) is concluded, the term must mean a twenty-four hour period" (Leupold 1970, 1:56).
- Jack B. Scott (1928–2011), Professor of Old Testament: The days of Genesis are in "the Biblical order of the 24 hour period."[12]
- John MacArthur (1939–), pastor and scholar: "I am convinced that Genesis 1–3 ought to be taken at face value — as the divinely revealed history of creation. Nothing about Genesis suggests that the biblical creation account is merely symbolic, poetic, allegorical, or mythical."[13]
- Douglas F. Kelly, Professor of Systematic Theology: "Genesis 'days' as plain, solar days" (Kelly 1997, 109).
- Robert L. Reymond (1932–2013), Professor of Systematic Theology: "[I] can discern no reason, either from Scripture or from the human sciences, for departing from the view that the days of Genesis were ordinary twenty-four-hour days" (Reymond 1998, 392).
- R.C. Sproul (1939–) of Ligonier Ministries: "For most of my teaching career, I considered the framework hypothesis to be a possibility. But I have now [2006] changed my mind. I now hold to a literal six-day creation."[14]
- Morton H. Smith (1923–), Professor of Systematic and Biblical Theology; Joseph A. Pipa, Professor of Systematic and Historical Theology; Benjamin Shaw, Professor of Old Testament; Sid Dyer, Professor of Greek and New Testament; and W. Duncan Rankin, Professor of Systematic Theology, are contributors to a book-length defense of the historical exegesis of Genesis 1 (Pipa and Hall 1999).

---

12. Jack B. Scott, *God's Plan Unfolded* (n.p., 1976), p. 9.
13. John F. MacArthur, *The Battle for the Beginning: The Bible on Creation and the Fall of Adam* (Nashville, TN: Thomas Nelson, 2005), p. 9.
14. R.C. Sproul, *Truths We Confess* (Phillipsburg, NJ: P&R, 2006), 1:127.

Traditionalist Concerns

In chapters 4–5 below I will summarize the exegetical evidence
for a literal, 24-hour, sequential, six-day creation, as long held in
the history of Christianity. Then in chapters 6–9 I will critique
the leading arguments buttressing the framework hypothesis.
But now at this point I will briefly list a few of the concerns
that traditionalist interpreters have with non-literal approaches
to Genesis 1, such as the framework hypothesis. Due to my concern for evangelical orthodoxy, I will limit my interaction with
overtly liberal advocates of the framework hypothesis, such as
Conrad Hyers and Howard Van Till.[15]

Exegetical Concerns

The framework hypothesis discounts obvious textual indicators. Though
prima facie considerations may often collapse upon closer analysis,
the fact is that most evangelicals admit the first-impression impact
of the historically accepted exegesis of Genesis 1. We may at least
argue that such *prima facie* evidence places the burden of proof on
those who would discount it, especially when set within the context of long-standing traditional exegesis.

In the 19th century, Charles Hodge (1973, 1:570–71) con-
fessed that "it is of course admitted that, taking this account by
itself, it would be most natural to understand the word [*yom*]
in its ordinary sense." Only a little later, theologian Robert L.
Dabney (1973, 255) observed that "the plain reader has no trouble with it." More recently, framework critic and renowned Old
Testament scholar E.J. Young (1964, 66) notes that "if we read
Genesis 'without prepossession or suspicion' we receive the impression that the author meant to teach a creation in six ordinary

---

15. Hyers 1984, see especially Parts II and IV. Evangelical commentator Kenneth
Mathews (1996, 107 n206) lists Hyers along with Blocher as advocates "for the
Framework' ('Literary') view." See Hyer's triad chart: "Problem, Preparation, Pop-
ulation" (1984, 69); see also Van Till (1986). Van Till started out as a conservative
scholar but later developed into an advocate of free thought (Van Till 2006).

days and, more than that, to teach that the earth was created before the sun, moon, and stars. This impression, apparently, is to be considered naive." Young well notes that such charges of naivete "prove too much, for it could be applied to other passages of Scripture as well. One who reads the Gospels, for example, is likely to receive the impression that they teach that Jesus rose from the dead. But can we in this day of science seriously be expected to believe that such an event really took place?" (Young 194, 67).

Against various non-chronological views, including J.A. Thompson's framework perspective, Derek Kidner (1967, 54–55) objects: "Yet to the present writer the march of the days is too majestic a progress to carry no implication of ordered sequence; it also seems over-subtle to adopt a view of the passage which discounts one of the primary impressions it makes on the ordinary reader." Day age proponent R.L. Harris (1999, 21) "will freely admit, that the view that the days were 24-hour days is a natural first reading of the chapter, especially in English."

Indeed, framework advocates themselves admit this. Ridderbos (1957, 29) confesses that "one who reads Genesis 1 without prepossession or suspicion is almost bound to receive the impression that the author's intent is to say that creation took place in six ordinary days." Mark Ross (1999, 118) agrees: "It is admitted by all that the first impression of Genesis 1:1–2:3 is of a sequential, chronological account of a six-day creation with a seventh day of rest."

Nevertheless, against not only the admitted historical tradition, the universally acknowledged first impression, the careful, numerical succession of days defined by "evening and morning" — and many other such exegetical observations (see chapter 4) — framework theologian Blocher declares: "The text gives not the slightest hint" of the literal interpretation! Not the "slightest hint"? Remarkably, he asserts that "there is no reason to suppose it" (Blocher 1984, 52, 53)! "No reason?" Thompson (1986, 22) agrees: "It is difficult to see how this great chapter was ever intended to become anything other than a tremendous affirmation of the fact that God is the creator of all things." Irons (1998, 53) concurs: "The text contains so many indications that its chronological data are *not* to be taken literally that it truly puzzles us that we non-literalists are always having to shoulder the *onus probadi*. In all candor we believe that the literalist interpretation has the burden of proof in this case." Niehaus (2014, 46) adds: "The 'days' are not literal days. They are structuring devices. . . . Genesis 1:1–2:3 gives us no 'timeline.' The world could be four billion years old and the universe could be seventeen billion years old, and that would present no problem for the truthfulness of Genesis 1, which is in fact not designed to tell us anything about the age of the world or the cosmos."

With such strong assertions, one must wonder why the sequential interpretation enjoyed, as Blocher (1984, 46) informs us, "the support of the majority throughout church history, notably that of the Reformers." Why, asks Irons (1998, 23), are *sequential* approaches "the traditional interpretations." Standing on the framework view, we should stand amazed that Hebrew scholar Young (1964, 100) could declare: "It is questionable whether serious exegesis of Genesis one would in itself lead anyone to adopt a non-chronological view of the days for the simple reason that everything in the text militates against it." But strangely, it would appear from the observations of Blocher, Thompson, and Irons that the *one and only* temporal conclusion we may draw from the text is that it does *not* teach that God created the world in the space of six days — despite the express, vivid, chronological, enumerated order of the narrative. This conclusion is incredible, and fuels the burning suspicions of many regarding the danger of the framework hypothesis method for other historical texts. Or to use Ridderbos's phrase, it seems framework advocates *are* in fact reading Genesis 1 *with* "prepossession or suspicion."

But as Kenneth Keathley and Mark Rooker (2014, 165) argue, "The burden of proof, however, is on those who do not attribute to *yom* in Genesis 1 its normal and most common interpretation, especially when *yom* is always described as being composed of an evening and morning." Even evangelical, non-literalist commentator John Walton (2001, 81) states that "it is extremely difficult to conclude that anything other than a twenty-four-hour day was intended."

The framework hypothesis relies on extravagant theological analysis. In discounting the *prima facie* impression of the Genesis 1 account of creation, the framework hypothesis establishes in its place a complex, counter-intuitive hermeneutical approach. I will provide a much fuller critique of the framework methodology in chapters 6–9; here I simply highlight the *prima facie* difficulty of the framework method.

In 1996, Old Testament scholar Meredith Kline, the leading evangelical advocate of the framework hypothesis,[16] published an important article titled "Space and Time in the Genesis Cosmogony." He wrote it because "an apologia is needed for addressing again the question of the chronological data in the Genesis creation account." This article presents his "two-register cosmological concept," which has "developed into the main point and has become the umbrella under which the other, restated arguments are accorded an ancillary place here and there" (Kline 1996, 2). According to framework advocate and Kline disciple Lee Irons, "Kline's 1996 article is the most comprehensive and convincing exegetical defense of the framework interpretation available" (1998, 36).

But what do we discover upon reading Kline's presentation? What does this Old Testament scholar offer in the place of the historic, confessional, *prima facie* impression of Genesis 1? Jack Collins, associate professor of Old Testament at Covenant Theological

---

16. Framework theologian Niehaus (2014, 41) states that "Kline has given the form its most mature and best articulation to date."

Seminary, a competent Hebraist, an expert in discourse analysis and language theory, and himself a non-literalist, complains that Kline's article is "quite complicated and hard to follow, even for the biblical specialist" (1996, 141). And this is despite Kline's (1996, 1) presenting it as a "more accessible statement" of his "exegetical arguments"! Kelly (1997, 119) does not exaggerate when he declares such exegesis "a tortured mode of interpretation." Yet, such is the necessity in rebutting six-day creation that scholars will go to great lengths in their efforts.

If Kline's extravagant presentation is an accurate assessment of Genesis 1–2, we must conclude that the ancient Jews held highly sophisticated and intricate theories of literary expression — hidden beneath the veil of simple historical narrative. But as Jewish Old Testament scholar Umberto Cassuto (1998, 12) observes regarding Genesis 1, it "was not intended for the thinkers and the elect few only, but for the people as a whole, including also its common folk." Even framework advocate Thompson (1968, 14; cp 22) writes: "If such a book is to find acceptance among all peoples (which, incidentally, it does), its language in regard to natural phenomena must be simple, popular, and understandable to all." He further warns, "One must always avoid the temptation of forcing the symbols into a complex maze of theological speculations" (Thompson 1968, 15). Well stated — though he rejects it in practice by affirming the framework hypothesis.

Anyone who has labored through Kline's prior *Images of the Spirit* (1980) knows the chore before him. His "Space and Time in the Genesis Cosmogony" provides further evidence that Kline, as Blocher puts it, is "not afraid to leave the beaten track." This is just the latest in a series of unique arguments for the framework hypothesis, for as Blocher (1984, 53) also notes of Kline's 1957 article based on Genesis 2:5, he "has thrown into the arena a new argument." Kline disciple and theologian Mark Futato (1998, 1–2), confesses that he himself offers "new insights" that have "not yet been set forth." The hypothetical nature of the framework approach is evidenced in its "progressive creation" (pun intended) of new insights never before seen in the history of biblical exegesis or literary analysis. Interestingly, Kline disciple Niehaus (2014, 252) speaks of Kline's "own brilliant (but perhaps not always rightly guided) imagination." On the same page he even confesses, "We find his arguments attractive but also sometimes questionable."

Furthermore, some advocates of the framework hypothesis assert that Genesis employs images from ancient cosmogonies, effectively picking up on the errors of antiquity and reporting them as truth. For instance, Ridderbos (1957, 44) writes, "And with regard to verses 6ff, one can say that the author expresses himself in terms derived from the world-picture of the ancient Orient, or to put it differently, in the terminology current in his day. The ancient orient generaly [sic] held to the concept of a celestial arch which separated the waters above, the heavenly ocean from the waters beneath (cf. also Gen. 7:11, 8:2, Ps. 148:4, Isa. 24:18)."[17]

By applying literary analysis based on the opposition between ancient pagan and the Jewish cosmogonies, evangelical scholar, Hebrew authority, and framework advocate Bruce K. Waltke[18] promotes a flawed and dangerous view of Genesis 1:2 when he declares that it represents the "situation prior to the creation" (1975b, 28). He argues of the "primeval, dark, watery, and formless state prior to creation" that Genesis does not attribute "this state to the Creator/creator" (1975d, 329). And "*bara* in Genesis 1:1 does not include the bringing into existence of the negative state described in verse 2" (1975d, 336). He continues:

---

17. See also Hyers 1984, 39. As noted above, Hyers is a liberal proponent of the framework hypothesis.

18. Waltke designates the six days of creation as a "temporal framework" with the first three days paralleling the last three (Waltke 1975d, 29-31). He is deemed a framework proponent by analogical day advocate Collins (2005, 146). In his commentary he writes, "Following Henri Blocher, we can describe the creation account as an artistic, literary representation of creation intended to fortify God's covenant with creation" (Waltke 2001, 78).

But what about the uncreated or unformed state, the darkness and the deep of Genesis 1:2? Here a great mystery is encountered, for the Bible never says that God brought these into existence by His word. What, then, can be said about them?

First, it can be said that the Book of Genesis does not inform us concerning the origin of that which is contrary to the nature of God, neither in the cosmos nor in the world of the spirit. . . .

The biblicist faces a dilemma when considering the origin of those things which are contrary to God. A good God characterized by light could not, in consistency with His nature, create evil, disorder, and darkness. On the other hand, it cannot be eternally outside of Him for that would limit His sovereignty. The Bible resolves the problem not by explaining its origin but by assuring man that it was under the dominion of the Spirit of God" (Waltke 1975d, 338–39).

Later he surmises:

Moreover, to show His sovereign dominion over His creation, God gave names to the light, to the darkness, to the firmament, to the dry land, and to the gathered waters. He called them Day, Night, Heavens, Earth, and Sea, respectively. To understand the significance of this act of naming the parts of the creation it must be realized that in the Semitic world the naming of something or someone was the token of lordship. . . . Is it not significant that God gave names precisely to those features that belonged to the precreated situation? In so doing He showed that He was Lord of all" (Waltke 1975d, 341).

Still later, in his study of the wisdom analysis of creation in Proverbs 8, Waltke (1976, 38) muses:

Many commentators assume that the "depths" spoken of in verse 24 refer to the *tᵉhôm* mentioned in Genesis 1:2. If this is so, then wisdom is including the state mentioned in Genesis 1:2 as among God's creative acts, and the present writer's analysis of Genesis 1:1–3 must be wrong.

The framework hypothesis promotes a risky hermeneutic. The framework hypothesis approaches the foundational chapter of Genesis, which is the cornerstone of all Scripture, in a way that *can* easily lead to dismissing it from the realm of historical factuality. The historicity of the Genesis creation narrative is held on a tenuous basis *given the tolerances within their literary theory*. I will present one sample from a noted framework proponent to illustrate my concern (other illustrations may be found later in this book).

While dealing with "history recording in the Bible" as an introduction to his framework analysis of Genesis 1, Thompson (196: 17) writes:

> The point should be clear. Within the pages of the Old Testament there are many ways of recording historical events. To be sure, the normal method of recording history is either the annalistic or the selective with interpretive comments. But there are a significant number of cases where the language is figurative or symbolic enough indeed to show that the figurative, the symbolic, the descriptive form of presentation was an acceptable medium in Israel for recording the historical events, particularly when it was not so much the intimate details of the event that mattered, but some broad, underlying issue which could be emphasized and highlighted by a parable, a fable, or a vivid presentation in highly figurative language.
>
> I have laboured this point because it is important for the proposition that *in Genesis 1–3 we are dealing with events*, the exact nature of which may escape us as to detail, but the fact of which, and the import of which for all

future generations of men, are by no means obscured by the symbols, and by the figurative and descriptive language used in their presentation.

There is another important aspect of this argument. It is that, while men might freely use symbolism and figurative language for events which were well known and for which the details could be obtained from written records or from eye-witnesses, it was impossible to call on witnesses or written records either for the dawn of human history or for its end. In the realm of the *proton* or the *eschaton*, the use of symbolic and figurative language was the only possible way of approach."

On what necessary principle may we declare that when dealing with matters regarding the original creative activity of God that "the use of symbolic and figurative language was the only possible way of approach" (Thompson 1968, 17)? The "only possible way"? Certainly when dealing with cosmic origins, the only sure insights we may gain will be from divine revelation, since, as a matter of fact, man was not present. Would God's challenge to Job not remain valid today: "Where were you when I laid the foundation of the earth? Tell Me, if you have understanding" (Job 38:4). But since God created the orderly, rational, physical world, why is a figurative approach the *only* possible approach? This simply does not make sense. This is a non sequitur of the most glaring sort, despite it being an "important aspect" of the framework hypothesis according to Thompson. If God created the world either in an instant, or in six days, or over billions of years, why is it not "possible" for Him to so inform us? These and other results of the literary approach to Genesis 1 alarm interpreters committed to the inspiration of Scripture and to the traditional and historic exegesis of the text. Such seems not only unnecessarily extravagant but exegetically unwarranted and theologically perilous.

To underscore the risky character of the framework's interpretive method, we even have noteworthy examples of men who have fallen away from their evangelical convictions through the instrumentality of the framework hypothesis. While serving as professor of physics at Calvin College, Howard Van Till wrote a significant and controversial book on science and creation from the framework perspective in 1986. That book is titled *The Fourth Day: What the Bible and the Heavens are Telling Us about the Creation*. In that work he affirmed both the Bible and evolution. Eventually, though, he began to have doubts about his previous theological convictions.

In a 2006 speech to the Freethought Association of West Michigan, Van Till (2006, 10) states: "What about today, forty years later? There's no going back now. I have embarked upon a journey that brings me into new conceptual territory. I continue to have high respect for my former colleagues, my friends, and family members who remain loyal to the Calvinism with which I was once comfortable. They are good people, and what they hold dear I will not dismiss lightly or disrespectfully, whether I can agree with it or not. And most of them have been exemplary in their willingness to maintain a friendly relationship with me in spite of the changes in my belief system. A column in the *Grand Rapids Press* focuses on Van Till's recent work. There we read, "His concept of God and God's role in creation has changed since his Calvin crucible — and remain 'a work in progress,' Van Till says."[19] The article continues by noting as a consequence that he now worships at an "independent and theologically liberal" church.

The influence through Van Till's book eventually led a minister into atheism. Noted atheist John W. Loftus originally earned a master's degree in theology from Trinity Evangelical Divinity School and was eventually ordained to the gospel ministry.[20] After about 20 years, he began to doubt his Christian convictions.

---

19. Charley Honey, "Scientist Still Explores 'Mystery' of God," *Grand Rapids Press* (Feb. 2, 2008), Web: Michigan Live.
20. "John W. Loftus," Wikipedia, Mar. 21, 2015.

On his blog "Debunking Christianity," Loftus published an article titled "Howard Van Till's Intellectual Journey." There Loftus states:

> Howard Van Till wrote the book *The Fourth Day,* which was one of the books that put me on a course of study that eventually led me away from the Christian faith. On page 79 in a footnote he listed several works on Genesis 1–11 that I proceeded to read. These initial books led me to still others, and others. After reading them I came to deny Genesis 1–11 was historical. I concluded these chapters were mythical. Anyway, Van Till has now been led down the same path as I. He has moved away from his Calvinism, and taken a much more ambiguous position on religion. That too is where I was for a time in my intellectual journey. But it eventually led me to atheism. I wonder where he will eventually end up?[21]

Fortunately, such testimonies are rare, but unfortunately, they do occur. Historian and six-day creationist Weeks (1978, 13) highlights a significant concern in this regard when he writes, "It is nonsense to speak of the unique and total authority of Scripture at the same time as we change our interpretation of Scripture to accord with theories drawn from outside Scripture."

Theological Concerns

The framework hypothesis reinterprets implications of divine Curse. The framework hypothesis demands a creational process that allows for a longer period of time than recorded in Genesis 1, even allowing for billions of years. For as Kline (1996, 2) argues, "With respect to both the duration and sequence of events, the scientist is left free of biblical constraints in hypothesizing about cosmic origins." Not only does this require that God has only "recently"

---

21. John W. Loftus, "Howard Van Till's Intellectual Journey," web: Debunking Christianity," Feb. 12, 2007.

completed His creation,[22] but according to framework advocate Ridderbos (1957, 70), a consequence of this is that "according to natural science there were great catastrophes, caused by movements of the earth-crust, there was cruelty and the 'struggle for life' long before man appeared and hence *a fortiori* before the fall."[23] Thus, disarray, destruction, and death precede by countless eons the Curse of God. In fact, they are actually features of God's creative activity — which He declared as "good" along the way (Gen. 1:4, 10, 12, 18, 21, 25). Indeed, when the Lord looked back over His entire creation process after the creation of man (Gen. 1:31), He ultimately declared it to be "very good."

What is more, Kline states that "the Bible does not require us, therefore, to think of the character and working of man's natural environment before the Fall as radically different from what is presently the case."[24] This effectively discounts (or at least downgrades through massive reinterpretation) the enormity of God's Curse that prevails over all creation and explains death in the animal and human kingdoms. Despite Kline, Genesis clearly indicates that the animals were subjected to the Curse. In Genesis 3:14, God curses the serpent: "Because you have done this, cursed are you more than all cattle, and more than every beast of the field." In fact, numerous arguments demand that animal death results from God's Curse on creation after Adam's Fall, rather than being a feature of God's original creational activity. Consider the following evidence in this regard.

---

22. The universe is supposedly 13.8 billion years old; man (the last created entity during the original period of divine creative activity, Matt. 19:4; Mark 10:6) is no more than 3 million years old. On Kline's assumptions, the Second Coming of Christ could end temporal history at (in Kline's view) "any moment." Oddly then, were Christ to return today, 13.8 billion years would have expired in the creation process, and *at the most* 3 million years since the end of God's original creational activity (but really much, much less, according to natural science estimations). That is, less than .002 percent of earth's history would involve man, God's highest creature!

23. See also: Blocher (1984, 42) and Thompson (1968, 34).

24. Meredith G. Kline, *Kingdom Prologue* (S. Hamilton, MA: self-published, 1991), p. 81.

First, by divine decree, man and animals were originally created as exclusively herbivorous. In Genesis 1:29–30, God grants only vegetation for food — for *both* man *and* animals: "Then God said, 'Behold, I have given you every plant yielding seed that is on the surface of all the earth, and every tree which has fruit yielding seed; it shall be food for you; and to every beast of the earth and to every bird of the sky and to every thing that moves on the earth which has life, I have given every green plant for food'; and it was so." As Hamilton (1990, 139) notes regarding man's dominion over the animals, "Such dominion does not allow him to kill these creatures or to use their flesh as food. Only much later (9:3, post-Flood) is domination extended to include consumption." There we read: "Every moving thing that is alive shall be food for you; I give all to you, as I gave the green plant. Only you shall not eat flesh with its life, that is, its blood" (Gen. 9:3–4). Hamilton (1990, 140) continues commenting on the original creation situation: "Man is to have as his food the seed and fruit of plants. Animals and birds are to have the leaves. . . . At no point is anything (human beings, animals, birds) allowed to take the life of another living being and consume it for food. . . . What is strange, and probably unexplainable (from a scientific position), is the fact that the animals too are not carnivores but also vegetarians."[25] Despite this, framework advocates do not suggest that animals were vegetarians for hundreds of millions of years.

Second, the "death" of vegetation is of a qualitatively different order, and not as a result of divine Curse. We may discern this from the following: (1) God expressly designs vegetation alone for food consumption (Gen. 1:29–30). (2) Plants lack a *nephesh* ("breath, desire, inner person"), unlike animal and man (Gen.

---

25. Compare Wenham 1987, 33. That today's carnivorous animals were once herbivorous is no more strange than bears with their gaping jaws and crushing teeth live largely on vegetation. More than 90 percent of the Eastern Black bear's diet is plants. "Black Bear Diet," by Mary Holland, web: Audubon Guides (June 28, 2006).

1:20, 24, 30, 2:7). In fact, both animal (Gen. 1:20–21, 24, 9:10) and man (Gen. 2:7) are called "living creatures" (*nephesh hayah*), whereas plants are not. Of Genesis 1:20–24, Waltke (TWOT 2:590) explains of man's sharing a *nephesh* with animals: "Man is here being associated with the other creatures as sharing in the passionate experience of life and is not being defined as distinct from them." (3) Plants do not possess the "breath (*ruach*) of life," as do animals and man (Gen. 6:17; 7:15, 22). (4) Scripture never ponders the loss of a plant's *ruach*, as it does animal's and man's: "All [man and beast] go to the same place. All came from the dust and all return to the dust" (Eccles. 3:20). In fact, a similarity exists between man's *ruach* and animal's: "For the fate of the sons of men and the fate of beasts is the same. As one dies so dies the other; indeed, they all have the same breath" (Eccles. 3:19). (5) When animal life "returns to the dust" it is because God "hides his face" (see Ps. 104:29). Scripture does not present God responding to plant death in any similar manner whatsoever.

Third, the creation account does not record God's "blessing" on creation until he creates *sentient* life on day 5 (Gen. 1:22). By this act of blessing, God draws a distinction between the zoological and the botanical branches of life. In that "blessing" involves fecundity — which *plants* also have (Gen. 1:11–12): the lack of God's "blessing" on plant life indicates this divine benediction is *more* than simply endowing living organisms with the capacity to multiply (contra Irons and Kline 1996, 6; Irons 1998, 28).

Fourth, Paul relates the effects of the Curse upon the creation in such a way that surely implies the post-Fall creation must be quite different from the original, uncursed world. He even strongly suggests that animal death is a consequence of it: "For the creation was *subjected to futility*, not willingly, but because of Him who subjected it, in hope that the creation itself also will be set free from its *slavery to corruption* into the freedom of the glory of the children of God. For we know that *the whole creation groans and suffers* the pains of childbirth together until now" (Rom. 8:20–22, emphasis added). Note that this "slavery to corruption" and "groaning and suffering" result from God's "subjecting creation to futility" — obviously by divine Curse. According to Murray, the bondage of corruption in the creation itself (Rom. 8:21) "must be taken in the sense of the decay and death apparent even in non-rational creation."[26] (For more information on this matter see later arguments.)

This is in keeping with what we expect from reading about God's Curse in Genesis 3. In Genesis 3:14, we read of God's Curse on the serpent: "The LORD God said to the serpent, 'Because you have done this, cursed are you more than all cattle, and more than every beast of the field.' " As framework advocate and Kline student Niehaus (2014, 120) observes of this statement: "The comparative ['more'] makes it clear that the animals are also cursed — otherwise, the serpent could not be more cursed than they." Therefore, he breaks with Kline and states on the same page, "God subjected the whole creation, including the animals, to frustration . . . and He has done so even as He also subjected humanity to frustrations." That God's curse involves the non-rational, sub-human creation is held by many scholars.[27]

Interestingly, this matter may be irrelevant as an *historical* issue. It seems likely that the Fall occurred not long after creation week, before an animal would have had time to die. We may discern this from God's command to Adam and Eve to be fruitful and multiply (Gen. 1:28). Thus, as a matter of obedience and in a perfectly healthy situation, Eve would probably have conceived fairly soon after creation and during her first menstrual cycle. And since they were expelled from Eden before she conceived her first child (Gen. 4:1) after being commanded to "be fruitful

---

26. John Murray, *The Epistle to the Romans* (Grand Rapids: Eerdmans, 1965), 1:304.
27. See Thomas R. Schreiner, *Romans* (BECNT) (Grand Rapids, MI: Baker, 1998), p. 432, 437; Douglas J. Moo, *The Epistle to the Romans* (Grand Rapids, MI: Eerdmans, 1996), p. 514; William Hendrikson, *Romans* (NTC) (Grand Rapids, MI: Baker, 1981), p. 266; Leon Morris, *The Epistle to the Romans* (Grand Rapids, MI: Eerdmans, 1988), p. 321; R.C.H. Lenski, *Interpretation of St. Paul's Epistle to the Romans* (Columbus, OH: Wartburg, 1945), p. 537.

and multiply" (Gen. 1:28), we may suspect a very early date for the Fall.[28]

Fifth, prophetic images picture animals living in peace as symbols of the eschatological victory of God's Kingdom. In our fallen world, the lion's deadly and terrifying power even serves as a proverbial image in the Old Testament (Num. 23:24; Ps. 7:2, 17:12; Prov. 19:12, 20:2, 28:15; Isa. 38:13). But gentle carnivores are images of the fullness of God's Kingdom. For instance, carnivores are seen living in harmony with herbivores, though herbivores are their natural prey in Moses' and our post-Fall world (Gen. 49:9, 27; Deut. 33:20; Ps. 104:21; Isa. 5:29; Nah. 2:12). And in Isaiah 11:6–7 we read that "the wolf will dwell with the lamb, and the leopard will lie down with the young goat, and the calf and the young lion and the fatling together; and a little boy will lead them. Also the cow and the bear will graze, their young will lie down together, and the lion will eat straw like the ox" (see also Isa. 65:25). Prophecies of God's victory often reflect pre-Fall, Edenic conditions (e.g., Ezek. 36:35, 47:1–12; Isa. 51:3; Rev 2:7, 22:2). If such reflect the actual historical reality of Eden, then peaceable conditions prevailed in the pre-Fall world and were radically changed upon the Fall.

Framework advocates disagree with any original passivity of such beasts. For instance, Kline argues, "Psalm 104:21 seems to indicate clearly that the Creator had from the outset granted to predatory beasts to feed on other animals."[29] That verse reads: "The young lions roar after their prey and seek their food from God." But this does not speak of the lion's original behavior. It is speaking in the present, and highlighting God's governance of all of life in that "the earth is full of Your possessions" (Ps. 104:24).

28. It is even possible that they sinned on the eighth day, the day following God's seventh day of rest. This may have given rise to the significance of the eighth day, as in circumcision (Gen. 17:12), the giving up of the firstborn animals to God (Exod. 22:30), and other eighth day rituals (Lev. 14:10, 23, 15:14, 29, 22:27, 23:36, 29, etc.).

29. Meredith G. Kline, *Kingdom Prologue: Genesis Foundations for a Covenantal Worldview* (Overland Park, KS: Two Age, 2000), p. 35.

Neither does Psalm 104:26 imply of the seas in creation week that "there the ships move along."

Kline also points to 1 Timothy 4:3–4 as evidence for animal death from the beginning of creation: ". . . false teachers who were forbidding some of them to marry and others forbidden to eat various kinds of foods and meats. Paul says it's all wrong thinking here, because God made these things, all of them to be received with thanksgiving. They're all good. So, here's the language of God's intention from the beginning in creating them."[30] There Paul states: ". . . men who forbid marriage and advocate abstaining from foods which God has created to be gratefully shared in by those who believe and know the truth. For everything created by God is good, and nothing is to be rejected if it is received with gratitude." How shall we reply?

Paul is dealing with Gnostics who believe the material realm is in itself evil. As the *Dictionary of Paul and His Letters* (DPL, 661) notes regarding the mission works of Timothy and Titus: "They were increasingly endangered by a Judaizing-Gnostic countermission (1 Tim. 1:3–7, 19–20, 4:1–2, 6:20; 2 Tim. 4:3–4; Titus 1:10–16) . . . that included church leaders and probably former coworkers (2 Tim. 1:15–18, 2:16–17, 3:6–9, 4:10; Titus 3:9–14)." An "essential feature of Gnosticism" was "an opposition between the spiritual world and the evil, material world" (DPL, 350), which led them to abstain from meat as a feature of their "Gnostic asceticism" (DPL, 353). Paul's fundamental point against these false teachers is that "everything created by God is good" (1 Tim. 4:4). Yet the Gnostics are declaring certain foods to be evil *in themselves* — despite the fact that God created them.

Interestingly, in 1 Timothy 4:3, Paul uses the generic word "food" (*brōma*) rather than the specific word for "meat" (*kreas,* "flesh"). Consequently, he is referring to "foods which God has created to be gratefully shared in" (1 Tim. 4:3). Clearly, he is not

---

30. Kline, "Dr. Meredith Kline, Prologue, Lecture 17," Web: Faculty.Gordon.edu (8/14/2012), 1.

declaring all God-created foods to be always received and "gratefully shared in" throughout all times from the beginning of time. After all, Adam was forbidden to partake of the fruit of the tree of the knowledge of good and evil (Gen. 2:15–17, 3:11). Though it was food that God created (Gen. 1:11, 3:6), it could not be taken and "gratefully shared in." Nor could faithful saints under the old covenant partake of unclean animals (Lev. 11:4ff; Deut. 14:7ff; Acts 10:14). Though God created them, they could not be taken and "gratefully shared in." And though in Paul's context regarding eating he declares that "everything created by God is good," surely he does not allow for cannibalism to supply food to be "gratefully shared in."

Calvin notes that here in 1 Timothy 4 the "creatures are called pure not just because they are God's works, but because they are given to us with His blessing. We must always have regard to God's appointment, both what He commands and what He forbids."[31] After all, our food "is sanctified by means of the word of God and prayer" (1 Tim. 4:5). This requires a directive from God (through His Word) along with prayer. In fact, God does not allow man to eat meat until after He establishes His covenant with Noah: "Every moving thing that is alive shall be food for you; I give all to you, as I gave the green plant" (Gen. 9:3). So likewise, before the Fall man was directed only to eat vegetation (Gen. 1:29) — which could be taken and "gratefully shared in."

The framework hypothesis allows for evolutionary theory. Many framework advocates clearly disavow the evolution of humans. I applaud their public stand against this naturalistic theory that reduces man to an animal. Nevertheless, we must be concerned over the theoretical tolerance of evolution that the framework hypothesis clearly allows — and which cannot be resisted on the principles inherent in the hypothesis.

---

31. John Calvin, *The Second Epistle of Paul the Apostle to the Corinthians and the Epistles to Timothy, Titus, and Philemon*, David W. Torrance and Thomas F. Torrance, eds. (Grand Rapids, MI: Eerdmans, 1964), p. 241.

Our concerns illustrated: Early on in the American spread of the framework hypothesis, an uneasy suspicion arose that it was generated to allow for the "assured results" of naturalistic scientific theory. Young (1964, 44) expresses his concern thus: "Recently there has appeared a recrudescence of the so-called 'framework' hypothesis of the days of Genesis, an hypothesis which in the opinion of the writer of this article treats the content of Genesis one too lightly and which, at least according to some of its advocates, seems to rescue the Bible from the position of being in conflict with the data of modern science." Later, he writes that "some of those who espouse a nonchronological view of the days of Genesis are moved by a desire to escape the difficulties which exist between Genesis and the so-called 'findings' of science" (Young 1964, 51). After considering the wealth of exegetical evidence for the traditional view of Genesis 1, he writes under the heading "The Real Problem in Genesis One": "It is questionable whether serious exegesis of Genesis 1 would in itself lead anyone to adopt a nonchronological view of the days for the simple reason that everything in the text militates against it. Other considerations, it would seem, really wield a controlling influence. As it stands Genesis might be thought to conflict with 'science' " (Young 1964, 100).

This suspicion continues today. Weeks (1988, 96–97) expresses his alarm: "While some authors claim to be interpreting Genesis with never a thought about the views of dominant secular science, such claims are rather unconvincing. Obviously a conviction that the majority of scientists cannot be wrong must lead to a disposition towards nonliteral interpretations." Traditionalist theologian Douglas Kelly (1997, 119) surmises that "it must be some factor from outside the Scripture itself that has caused distinguished Christian exegetes to bring in such a tortured mode of interpretation." We see this clearly displayed in the complaint by framework theologian Henri Blocher (1984, 50): "The rejection of all the theories accepted by the scientists requires considerable bravado." Wayne Grudem (1994, 302) notes that "one aspect of the attractiveness of this theory is the fact that it relieves evangelicals of the burden of even trying to reconcile scientific findings with Genesis 1." But more appropriately, Weeks (1978, 16) urges Christians to look for scriptural arguments regarding how to interpret Genesis 1, *not* evolutionary science or natural revelation. As I point out elsewhere, Jesus, Paul, and the New Testament clearly understand Genesis 1 as historical, chronological fact.

Regarding the question of our (potentially) rejecting natural revelation by rejecting evolutionary theory, we must recognize the following: (1) Natural revelation will not contradict special revelation. After all, both natural and special (Bible) revelation are from the same God. (2) By the very nature of the case, special revelation should control natural revelation as being more direct, clear, and authoritative as propositional. This is especially true when we read Paul speaking about natural revelation: he points out the sad fact that men suppress the truth in unrighteousness (Rom. 1:18) so that they "have no excuse" (Rom. 2:1).

Our concerns justified: Ridderbos' title certainly suggests such a motive: *Is There a Conflict Between Genesis 1 and Natural Science?* This is especially significant in that we realize that evolution is a major conclusion of contemporary "natural science," indeed, the controlling principle guiding virtually all scientific endeavor today. A leading problem Ridderbos (1957, 46) has with a literal construction of Genesis 1 is that there "arise grave difficulties with respect to natural science." Kline (1958, 157) accepts the conclusions of naturalistic scientific inquiry as a given when he sympathizes with Ridderbos' concerns: "Surely natural revelation concerning the sequence of developments in the universe as a whole and the sequence of the appearance of the various orders of life on our planet (unless the revelation has been completely misinterpreted) would require the exegete to incline to a not exclusively chronological interpretation of the creation week."

In fact, more recently Kline (1996, 13) complains: "I am unable to accept the strictly chronological interpretation of Genesis 1 when I take account of the light of natural revelation concerning the sequence of the primordial events"; and "the more traditional interpretations of the creation account are guilty not only of creating a conflict between the Bible and science but, in effect, of pitting Scripture against Scripture." He speaks of the "aeons of creation" as a given fact (Kline 1958, 115). As noted framework scholar and Hebraist Bruce K. Waltke (2012, 9) admits, the "framework theory" is "promoted to reconcile the Genesis account of creation with evolution." Indeed, he states that "this hypothesis in fact aims to support the theory of creation by evolution" (2012, 6).

Framework advocate Blocher (1984, 22, 48, 224, 227, etc.) criticizes the traditionalist view of a literal six-day creation as engaging in "anti-scientism." Of course, by that he actually means anti-evolutionism. He queries: "How are we to compare the assertion of the seven days with the billions of years, at the lowest estimate, which current scientific theory attributes to the origin of the universe?" He tries to avoid the implications of our concerns by noting the great advantage of adapting to contemporary scientific conclusions: "So great is the advantage, and for some the relief, that it could constitute a temptation." And yet he confesses that the framework hypothesis provides a positive benefit in relieving us of "the confrontation with the scientific vision of the most distant past." Of the six literal day view of Genesis 1, framework exegete Wenham (1987, 39)[32] laments "the result that science and Scripture have been pitted against each other instead of being seen as complementary."

---

32. Collins (2005, 146) classifies Wenham as a framework advocate. Irons (1998, 3) states regarding the framework definition: "I would argue that anyone who holds to a position that meets these two criteria holds to the framework interpretation." Wenham (1987, 7, 39) holds that the days are a part of a literary "framework" allowing a "six-day schema" designed simply to "stress the system and order that has been built into creation."

Even more pointedly Kline (1995, 15 n47) confesses, "In this article I have advocated an interpretation of biblical cosmogony according to which Scripture is open to the current scientific view of a very old universe and, in that respect, does not discountenance the theory of the evolutionary origin of man." Fortunately, he holds that Genesis 2:7 discourages an evolutionary view of human origins (though this is an anti-scientific view to hold). Nevertheless, in Kline's own words he has "advocated an interpretation of biblical cosmogony" that allows "the evolutionary origin of man." And since he hesitates here solely on the basis of his exposition of Genesis 2:7 and Luke 3:38, and since these verses do not refer to animal origins, obviously he himself is very much open to biotic evolution short of man.

Even here with Genesis 2:7 serving as an exegetical brake, we must wonder — given Kline's literary approach — if this verse could simply be informing us of nothing more than God's special interest in and intimate concern for man, and not meant to provide us with a literal description of man's origin. Blocher (1984, 50) surmises that in composing Genesis, Moses merely "wishes to bring out certain themes and provide a theology of the sabbath." Thompson (1968, 17) informs us that historical narratives such as Genesis 1 can be presenting "some broad, underlying issue which could be emphasized and highlighted by a parable, a fable, or a vivid presentation in highly figurative language." Therefore, *conceivably* upon the framework hermeneutic, Moses could be providing us a more general, theological explanation of man's origin in Genesis 2:7. After all, current scientific theory teaches that man *ultimately* derives from the "dust," tracing his ancestry back to single-celled, land-based organisms evolving into more complex entities.

Thompson (1968, 21), however, is not as cautious as Kline. He claims ignorance regarding the possibility of the evolutionary origin of man: "The picture of man is a noble one. But despite the nobility of the picture, all that we are told about the origin of man is that God 'made' him and God 'created' him. How

God performed His work is not declared. Hence, provided that we are persuaded of the fact that man, like everything else in the universe, is the work of God, it would seem that in our present state of knowledge, we must allow for diversity of opinion among Christians. So far as I am aware, the scientists do not know the origin of man. An attitude of reverent agnosticism is the only reasonable attitude to adopt."

Thus, we see the wisdom of Weeks' (1978, 13) observations regarding the influence of prevailing scientific theories:

> We are not the first Christians to be troubled by the teaching of Genesis. Simply because the Bible has a different view of origins to those put forth in human philosophy there is a period of conflict whenever the church comes under the influence of a human philosophical system. Thus any defender of neo-Platonism in Augustine's day or of Aristotelianism in the late Middle Ages found himself in trouble with Genesis. It is a gross oversimplification to act as though we alone face a problem here. Nevertheless the problem for most Christians today is generated by a specific challenge, namely that of biological evolution and related theories. I believe that there are deeper problems than merely the problem of Genesis. If we take the theory of evolution as established and modify our interpretation of Genesis accordingly, then we introduce a problem for the doctrine of Scripture. It is nonsense to speak of the unique and total authority of Scripture at the same time as we change our interpretation of Scripture to accord with theories drawn from outside Scripture. Hence evangelicals have tended to seek for principles within Scripture itself which will allow them to interpret Genesis in a way that is compatible with evolution. If Scripture itself forces us to such an interpretation then we are not subjecting Scripture to evolutionary theory. It is with these attempts to find such principles within Scripture that this paper is mainly concerned.

After all, Copernicus was initially fearful of publishing his research because it contradicted the dominant, prevailing position of Aristotelian science of the day. "The Earth-centered Universe of Aristotle and Ptolemy held sway on Western thinking for almost 2000 years. Then, in the 16th century a new idea was proposed by the Polish astronomer Nicolai Copernicus (1473–1543)."[33] As Al Van Helden of Rice University notes:

> It is believed by many that his [Copernicus'] book was only published at the end of his life because he feared ridicule and disfavor: by his peers and by the Church, which had elevated the ideas of Aristotle to the level of religious dogma. . . .
>
> European learning was based on the Greek sources that had been passed down, and cosmological and astronomical thought were based on Aristotle and Ptolemy. Aristotle's cosmology of a central Earth surrounded by concentric spherical shells carrying the planets and fixed stars was the basis of European thought from the 12th century CE onward. . . .
>
> The reason for this delay was that, on the face of it, the heliocentric cosmology was absurd from a common-sensical and a physical point of view. Thinkers had grown up on the Aristotelian division between the heavens and the earthly region, between perfection and corruption. In Aristotle's physics, bodies moved to their natural places. Stones fell because the natural place of heavy bodies was the center of the universe, and that was why the Earth was there. Accepting Copernicus's system meant abandoning Aristotelian physics.
>
> The Copernican system simply did not fit into the Aristotelian way of thinking.[34]

---

33. "The Copernican Model: A Sun-Centered Solar System," published by the University of Tennessee Physics Department. http://csep10.phys.utk.edu/astr161/lect/retrograde/copernican.html (1/16/2015).
34. Al Van Helden, "Copernican System," Web: Galileo. http://galileo.rice.edu/sci/theories/copernican_system.html (April 09, 2015).

Furthermore, perhaps the rather unscientific view of Eve's origin in Genesis 2 might merely be a literary device instructing us of the divinely blessed *unity* between husband and wife. Perhaps the origin of *both* Adam and Eve are literary artifices teaching this, and nothing more. We must remember the "genius" of Moses in composing Genesis 1, according to framework advocates: "The text is composed as the author meditates on the finished work, so that we may understand how the creation is related to God, and what is its significance for mankind" (Blocher 1984, 50). Framework proponent Thompson[35] agrees: "The primary importance of Genesis 1–3 lies not in any specific historical or scientific value, but in their theological value; that is, in their great assertions about the nature of God, man, and the world" (1968, 13). Why should not the exegetico-theological method of the framework hypothesis surmise a related rationale for these — unusual and primitive? — features of Genesis 2? Especially since both Adam's and Eve's creation involve an "unnecessary supernaturalism," to use Kline's surprising concept (1958, 150). And perhaps Paul was just kidding when he mentions that Adam was created first (1 Cor. 11:8–9; 1 Tim. 2:13).

In addition, what are we to make of the record of Eve's temptation by the serpent in Genesis 3? Surely *here* we have some sort of parable, it would seem! After all, does not framework advocate Thompson (1968, 17) instruct us: "But there are a significant number of cases where the language is figurative or symbolic enough indeed to show that the figurative, the symbolic, the descriptive form of presentation was an acceptable medium in Israel for recording the historical events, particularly when it was not so much the intimate details of the event that mattered, but some broad, underlying issue which could be emphasized and highlighted by a parable, a fable, or a vivid presentation in highly figurative language." But Moses presents this as an historical event that literally transpired

---

35. Thompson's (1968, 20) work is clearly a framework analysis: "The scheme was, after all, literary and artistic, not chronological and scientific." Irons (1998, 81) lists him as a framework advocate, as does Blocher (1984, 50).

in time and on earth. And in the New Testament, Paul affirms this (2 Cor. 11:3).

Framework advocate Mark Ross (1999, 114) confesses that "as adherents of the Framework Hypothesis have come from divergent theological persuasions, including some who do reject the historical character of the Genesis narrative, this suspicion seems to be confirmed. Given this diversity, it is easy for confusion to arise over just what the Framework Hypothesis is claiming and what it is denying."

Blocher (1984, 226) chastises adherents to the traditional exegesis of Genesis, in that "to talk about the alternative as 'evolution or creation,' as though they were two concepts of the same order, is an unfortunate beginning. Nothing in the idea of creation excludes the use of an evolutionary procedure. Why must we tie God to one single method of action?" He continues in the next paragraph: "If the unmodified concept of God's creative action does not exclude evolution, what are we to say about the teaching of Genesis? At this point our study again requires that we question anti-scientism. A reading which respects the forms of the language of Genesis can find no clear indication in the text for or against transformism,[36] except in the case of the creation of mankind in his unique position. . . . Thus it is at least incautious to reject the idea of an evolving creation *a priori*. There is, of course, no suggestion that the Bible positively supports an evolutionary model. The question is whether it does or does not leave the method of creation and the time scale of creation much more open than anti-scientism claims" (Blocher 1984, 227). Consequently, the framework hypothesis by necessity is open to evolution, even if some of its advocates do not fully accept it themselves.

Furthermore, Blocher (1984, 50) designates Bernard Ramm as a framework advocate, and according to the definition given

---

36. This is Blocher's term for upward evolutionary development of biotic systems to higher forms. It allows him to urge an evolution-like transformation over time without employing the weighted term "evolution."

above, he meets the requirements.[37] Ramm (1955, 113) holds that Genesis 1 provides us an artistic expression rather than an historical sequence, for "in *art* the pattern is from unformed materials to artistic creation."[38] Of the six days of Genesis, he observes that it is "apparent that the six days are *topically* ordered or *logically* ordered, not only *chronologically* ordered" (p. 221). "The order of this communication is partially a topical arrangement" (p. 223). "The days are means of communicating to man the great fact that *God is creator*, and that *He is Creator of all*" (p. 222). This last assertion is virtually identical to the conclusions of Blocher and Thompson as cited above in this section.

Ramm is a progressive creationist, allowing for a fiat-punctuated evolution of living organisms, whereby God "pushes" the evolutionary process over natural roadblocks imposed by the limits of natural variation: "*We believe that the fundamental pattern of creation is progressive creation.* . . . Progressive creationism tries to avoid the arbitrariness [!] of fiat creationism and preserve its doctrine of the transcendence of God in creation; and it has tried to avoid the uniformitarianism of theistic evolution and preserve its sense of progress or development" (p. 113). His view holds, in part, that "the movement in Nature comes from the law of cosmical evolution which is the principle of continuity" (p. 115).

Waltke (1976, 33) distinguishes the creation of man from that of animal by noting that "the vegetation sprang from the earth, the sea creatures originated out of the sea, and the beasts likewise trace their origin back to the earth. All these were created through the mediacy of other agents. But *not* man."[39] This must involve some form of theistic evolution or progressive creationism, which is evolution with God starring (anthropomorphically speaking, of course!) as the *deus ex machina*. Waltke's observation,

---

37. Irons (1998, 3) states regarding the Framework definition: "I would argue that anyone who holds to a position that meets these two criteria holds to the framework interpretation."
38. The following parenthetical pagination points to Ramm's work.
39. This perspective fits within the vaguely announced scheme of Kline as cited previously.

though, is mistaken. For we read that man also arises from the earth: "The Lord God formed man of dust from the ground, and breathed into his nostrils the breath of life; and man became a living being" (Gen. 2:7).

Thompson (1968, 14) is expressly open to evolutionary theory: "As far as the Bible is concerned, it has the broad view that God is the 'Ground' of all nature. He was at its beginning, He will be at its end. He is both *above* nature, and *in* nature. That is, if you like an all-embracing theory. But it can never be proved wrong. Whatever the scientist discovers about God's world can be accommodated to such a concept." Speaking of the creation process: "Was it by the separate instantaneous creation of each and every creature? Or was it by some process which, in the case of living things, began with some simple organism and arrived finally under the hand of God at the completed product, that is by some evolutionary process? In my view, the narrative in Genesis 1 yields no information about the divine method, only that, whatever the method, it was divine, so that any concept of a purely naturalistic evolution without God is ruled out. But there are alternatives to the two extreme positions of fiat creationism and naturalistic evolution, and men of deep Christian conviction can be found who hold such intermediate positions as *theistic evolution or progressive creationism*" (Thompson 1968, 20). Here, we could also rehearse Thompson's (1968, 21) statements cited previously, urging that we "must allow for diversity of opinion among Christians" over how man was created by God.

My concerns with the framework hypothesis appear to be well justified. Thompson (1968, 20) urges our tolerant acceptance of men who hold some forms of evolution: "There are alternatives to the two extreme positions of fiat creationism [i.e., the traditional, six-day creation approach] and naturalistic evolution, and men of deep Christian conviction can be found who hold such intermediate positions as *theistic evolution or progressive creationism*." Here fiat creation is declared an "extreme" position, whereas tolerance of the basic evolutionary principle may be held by "men of deep Christian conviction." Irons (1998, 72) widely misses the mark when he responds to the concerns of adherents to the traditional view of creation. He is chagrined that we often charge that "nothing in the theory" (i.e., the framework hypothesis) prevents "one from believing that man evolved from lower animals." I believe the theory *does* allow for the evolution of man — even though some framework advocates deny such. This is not my only concern, though. I also deny that animal species evolved from lower order creatures, a position upon which most published framework hypothesis proponents are strangely silent (e.g., Kline, Blocher, and Thompson). Irons (1998, 72) makes the incredible and mistaken counter-claim against the literal approach to Genesis: "There is nothing in the literal interpretation that deals directly with this issue either." How in the world (I ask this very literally!) could a system that claims animals were created early on day 6 and man a few hours thereafter *on the same literal day* allow for evolutionary development from those animals into man or even between animal "kinds"? The very nature of the system forbids such.

Conclusion

Though framework advocacy is making much progress among many biblical scholars, it is a position that deserves the evangelical's concern. In this chapter I have pointed out concerns that arise from three different areas of the debate: The historical genesis (pun not intended) of the hypothesis that has been prompted by evolutionary theory; the exegetical issues surrounding the discussion, both the strong evidence against it and the questionable exegesis in favor of it; and the theological matters that arise as the framework view submits itself to evolutionary pressures.

Part II

The Traditional Interpretation of Genesis 1

Chapter 3

Establishment of Genre Type

Importance of Genre

Those who hold to a high view of Scripture believe that it is, as Jesus declares, "the word of God," which "cannot be broken" (John 10:35). The Lord was so confident of the abiding authority of God's Word that He taught: "If they do not listen to Moses and the Prophets, they will not be persuaded even if someone rises from the dead" (Luke 16:31). This confidence in God's Word is due to the fact that "no prophecy of Scripture is a matter of one's own interpretation, for no prophecy was ever made by an act of human will, but men moved by the Holy Spirit spoke from God" (2 Pet. 1:20–21). Therefore, even today we are to receive it as the early Christians themselves did: with entire submission and humble respect. Paul thanked God and praised his converts because "when you received the word of God which you heard from us, you accepted it not as the word of men, but for what it really is, the word of God" (1 Thess. 2:13). Because of this high view of Scripture, we must make every effort to avoid "adulterating the word of God" (2 Cor. 4:2).

Since Scripture is God's authoritative revelation to man, evangelical Christians should agree with Kaiser (1970, 48) that "the primary task of the Biblical scholar is to unfold the meaning of the text of Scripture as it was originally intended to be understood by the writer of that text." This certainly is the task before us in the debate over the creation narrative in Genesis 1–2. In order to do this, we must recognize with Boyd (2010, 163, 168) that "the starting point for understanding any text is to read it according to its *genre*," for "if we get this wrong, we *will* misinterpret the text." Or as the *Dictionary of Biblical Interpretation* (256) puts it: "Recognition of the genre, therefore, brings with it expectations about content, style, and structure, in the service of a coherent meaning. Mistaking the genre, for example mistaking a novel for history, can lead to complete misunderstanding." A genre error will cause us to be like the man who read the dictionary thinking it was a crime novel, only to be surprised at the end when he concludes that the zebra did it. Therefore, "The writer's intention must be the first order of business if we are going to make any progress in locating the literary form for this section [Gen. 1–11]" (Kaiser 1970, 59). This is especially important because, as Keil and Delitzsch (2001, 24) note, Genesis "is accepted as the pedestal throughout the whole of the sacred Scriptures. This is not the case with the Old Testament only; but in the New Testament also it is accepted and taught by Christ and the apostles as the basis of the divine revelation."

As Bruce (1984, 565) notes, the need for genre determination is accentuated by "the multifaceted character of the Bible" so that when dealing with any given biblical text "one must ask whether it is prose or poetry, history or allegory, literal or symbolic." Indeed, Scullion (1992, 956) lists various literary forms that different scholars apply to Genesis: legend, folktale, myth, narrative, novella, saga sage, and story. The problem of genre-determination is very real in such a massive work as the Bible due to the "wide range of genres in biblical literature" (DBI, 256). This is because, as Osborne (2005, 673) observes: "Truth is derived differently depending on the genre employed in Scripture."

That is, historical narrative presents facts to us more directly than poetic imagery, which does so indirectly. Consequently, he continues: "Genre plays an important role in interpretation" in that "it is a classification device" that "provides the framework for understanding the intended meaning of a text" (p. 679). As such, it "communicates to the reader a set of conventions that controls the understanding of the whole intention" (p. 680).

Unfortunately, "for all their talk of genre and devices, literary theorists pay significantly less attention to the historical milieu of Genesis 1's origin than would be expected. . . . In other words, they have ignored the type of literature that [it] really is representative of, namely historiography" (Kay 2007b, 99). This is especially frustrating in that "were it not for the unproven and unprovable theories of evolutionary biology, geology, and cosmology, and the faulty but rarely challenged assumption of radioisotope dating, no one would be questioning what kind of text this is" (Boyd 2010, 169). In fact, acceptance of the literal, six-day creation process was the generally prevailing view throughout Christian interpretive history, as even framework advocates admit. We should recall that Blocher (1984, 46) confesses that the literal-historical view enjoys "the support of the majority throughout church history, notably that of the Reformers." This is enormously significant in that the creation narrative "is a magisterial literary composition; it is a foundational theological treatise; and it is a literal historical account" (Boyd 2010, 164). Indeed, according to the *Dictionary of the Old Testament: Pentateuch* (357), in Genesis itself "the primeval history [Gen. 1–11] provides a significant theological backdrop for understanding the blessings and promises that dominate the ancestral history [Gen. 12ff]."

In this chapter I will discuss the genre of Genesis 1 by demonstrating the historical interests of the Jews in antiquity, the historical concerns of Moses in Genesis, the chronological structure of Genesis by Moses, and the general style of the creation narrative and its intended purpose. These will underscore the wisdom of the traditional understanding of Genesis 1, thereby confirming the six-day creation viewpoint. We roundly reject the liberal notion that "the stories of Genesis 1–11 . . . are properly termed 'myths' " (ABD 2, 935).

Sailhammer (1990, 3) wisely notes that "in the final analysis, an understanding of the book [of Genesis] and its message comes from reading the book itself. No amount of historical and literary scholarship can replace the simple reading of the text as the primary means for determining the book's nature and purpose." This is significant in that as Westermann (1984, 5) notes, "The average reader who opens his Bible to Genesis 1 and 2 receives the impression that he is reading a sober account of creation, which relates facts in much the same manner as does the story of the rise of the Israelite monarch, that is, as straightforward history." He adds that this is because Genesis 1:1–2:4 is a narrative that "is characterized by its onward, irresistible, and majestic flow" (p. 80). Leupold (1942, 104) agrees, noting that "the account as it stands expects the impartial reader to accept it as entirely literal and historical." We will see how and why this is so.

Interests of the Jews

Genesis was written by Moses, a well-educated Jew in ancient Israel. As the New Testament notes, "Moses was educated in all the learning of the Egyptians" (Acts 7:22). Ancient Jews had a strong interest in history because it was created by God in the beginning and is in the process of being redeemed by Him in the present. Thus, in their worldview, the God of Israel was not only the transcendent Creator over history, but also the immanent Redeemer within history. Israel understood that she had an important role to play in God's world as the conduit of His redemptive grace. This conviction arises from God's pre-covenantal promise to Abraham, which states, "In you all the families of the earth will be blessed" (Gen. 12:3). Because of these truths "a biblical, Hebraic mindset was deeply and inextricably attached to 'the march of time' " (Kay 2007b, 97). With their interest in the historical process, we discover that "chronological sequence is the backbone of the Bible's narrative books, their most salient and continuous organizing principle" (DOTH, 82). Interestingly, we must understand that "although historiographical materials are preserved from Egypt, Mesopotamia, and the Hittites, Van Seters concluded that true history writing developed first in Israel and then in Greece, where its closest analogs are found" (DOTH, 419).

Not only was Israel deeply interested in history and historical writing and records (Exod. 17:14, 24:7; Num. 21:14; Deut. 28:58; Josh. 10:13; 1 Kings 11:41, 14:19), but the Jews were committed to a particular approach to history that distinguished them from most of the peoples of antiquity. As Currid (2007, 62) points out, "The Hebrews held to a linear history. They believed there was a beginning to time and creation (cosmogony) and a movement to a consummation (eschatology)." Of course, it is especially in Genesis that we find the most information on creation.[1] And in an important sense the consummation begins at creation; thus, protology (the study of the beginning) entails eschatology (the study of the end). By that is meant that "immediately after the fall, God spoke to the serpent and pronounced the first prophecy of the Bible," which leads us to recognize that "the prophets of the Old Testament further anticipated this future redemption by the work of the Messiah" (Currid 2007, 59, 61). Westermann (1984, 90) argues that the author of Genesis "is concerned throughout his work with linear time and the celebration of the holy and the goal to which they are directed." Therefore, ancient Judaism "was a highly teleological faith: it rejected the cyclical views of time which dominated pagan thought,

---

1. Ps. 104 is a praise based on Gen. 1. Many passages of Scripture reflect on Gen. 1, such as Exod. 20:9–11, 31:17; Ps. 8; Matt. 19:4–6, 11; Luke 3:38; John 1:3; Col. 1:16; 2 Pet. 3:5.

seeing history instead as a linear progression, in which God's design gradually unfolded and his people were led towards a predetermined end."[2] Or as Kennard expresses it, "A linear view of history is dependent upon the Jewish construct of creation unto Kingdom or more microscopically: exodus to Promised Land as a stage on the way to Kingdom (Exod. 1–19; Deut. 1–4)."[3] In fact, Cahill argues that a linear conception of history was one of the great *Gifts of the Jews* to mankind.[4]

Bringing this Jewish concern with linear history to bear on the creation narrative, Sproul puts the matter well: "Unlike beginning with the words 'once upon a time,' the Bible begins with the words, 'In the beginning God. . . .' This statement, at the front end of the entire Bible, introduces the Pentateuch or the first five books of the Old Testament, and it sets the stage for God's activity in linear history. From the opening chapters of Genesis to the end of the book of Revelation, the entire dynamic of redemption takes place within the broader setting of real space and time, of concrete history."[5] As we will see, the Genesis creation narrative presents a literal, historical understanding of the world's origin. And it even opens with a statement regarding the establishment of time: ("And there was evening and there was morning, one day," Gen. 1:5) and the appointment of the sun and moon to measure the passing of time ("Let there be lights in the expanse of the heavens . . . and let them be for signs and for seasons and for days and years" Gen. 1:14).

Of course, by itself the argument for the Jewish interest in history does not prove Genesis 1 is historical narrative. After all,

---

2. Neil Faulkner, *Apocalypse: The Great Jewish Revolt Against Rome AD 66–73* (Gloucestershire, Eng.: Tempus, 2002), p. 123.

3. Douglas Kennard, "Method of Philosophy, Theology, and Science," Web: http://www.hgst.edu/wp-content/uploads/Kennard-MethodPhilTheoSci.pdf (7/22/2011): 15.

4. Thomas Cahill, *The Gifts of the Jews* (New York: Doubleday, 1998), p. 18–19, 125–31.

5. R.C. Sproul, *An Historic Faith*, 1 Web http://www.ligonier.org/learn/articles/historicfaith/ (Tabletalk 2/1/2006).

the Jews also wrote abundant poetry — as the third largest book in the Old Testament demonstrates: the Book of Psalms.[6] But it is the first step in that direction. I will now make a second step toward the conclusion.

Concerns of Moses

Moses writes Genesis for Israel before she enters the Promised Land — and in anticipation of her entering it. This is important for us to establish as we consider Genesis. It is the opening book of the Pentateuch, the five books of Moses. The Pentateuch prepares Israel for her life as a national people in a new land — a land populated by people who held a mythological view of origins that led them to practice astrological worship (Deut. 4:19, 5:8–9, 8:19, 11:16, 17:2–3, 29:26, 30:17–18; compare 2 Kings 17:16, 21:3). The Pentateuch states near its conclusion: "Then Moses called to Joshua and said to him in the sight of all Israel, 'Be strong and courageous, for you shall go with this people into the land which the LORD has sworn to their fathers to give them, and you shall give it to them as an inheritance. The LORD is the one who goes ahead of you; He will be with you. He will not fail you or forsake you. Do not fear or be dismayed'" (Deut. 31:7–8). Deuteronomy is Moses' last book, which is given not long before Israel enters Canaan (Deut. 34:1–5). In it he continually warns against following after the false gods of the land (Deut. 10:17, 11:16, 28, 12:2, 3, 30–31, 13:2, 6–7, 13, 17:3, 18:20, 20:18, 28:14, 36, 64, 29:18, 26, 30:17, 31:16, 18, 20, 32:16–17, 37).

In this regard, we should note what he writes in Leviticus 18:1–3, 24–25: "Then the LORD spoke to Moses, saying, 'Speak to the sons of Israel and say to them, "I am the LORD your God. You shall not do what is done in the land of Egypt where you

---

6. According to Hebrew scholar David J. Reimer, the Psalms happen to be the third largest collection of material in the Old Testament. It is third behind Jeremiah (1st) and Genesis (2nd) in both "graphic units" and "morphological units." Interestingly, three other books of Moses are in the top ten: Exodus (6), Numbers (7), and Deuteronomy (8). Cited by Justin Taylor 2015.

lived, nor are you to do what is done in the land of Canaan where I am bringing you; you shall not walk in their statutes. . . . Do not defile yourselves by any of these things; for by all these the nations which I am casting out before you have become defiled. For the land has become defiled, therefore I have brought its punishment upon it, so the land has spewed out its inhabitants." ' " His warning against adopting the ways — the worldview — of the Canaanites is serious. Their false gods and false worldview must be avoided. Moses therefore reminds Israel of the true God and the true worldview rooted in Him.

Genesis is an important and foundational book for the Pentateuch that is inextricably bound up with it. As Alexander (2002, 97) notes, "The Pentateuch consists of five books which have been composed in the light of each other to form a single unit. . . . [As we see in] the plot which begins in Genesis and flows logically through to the end of Deuteronomy." McClintock and Strong put the matter well: "We must bear in mind that Genesis is, after all, but a portion of a larger work. The five books of the Pentateuch form a consecutive whole: they are not merely a collection of ancient fragments loosely strung together, but . . . a well-digested and connected composition" (CBTEL, 3:777). Leupold (2009, 721, 723) adds: Genesis "was written to lay the groundwork for the remaining books of the Pentateuch" and that "the material from Exodus to Deuteronomy demands some such substructure as Genesis."

Because of this, in the Pentateuch we see that the "adjacent books are also linked closely together" in many ways (Alexander 2002, 97). For instance, at the end of Genesis, in 50:24, Joseph is about to die in Egypt. His death is recorded in the next book (Exod. 1:6), along with the arising of a new king over Egypt "who did not know Joseph" (Exod. 1:8). At the end of Exodus we read of the erection of the Tabernacle (Exod. 40:17–18) and the cloud glory filling it (Exod. 40:34–35). Then the next book, Leviticus, opens with God speaking from the Tabernacle in order to instruct Moses regarding sacrifices: "Then the LORD called to Moses and spoke to him from the tent of meeting, saying, 'Speak to the sons of Israel and say to them, "When any man of you brings an offering to the LORD . . ." ' " (Lev. 1:1–2).

Leviticus is given to Israel while she is at Sinai. It ends with these words: "These are the commandments which the LORD commanded Moses for the sons of Israel at Mount Sinai" (Lev. 27:34). The next book, Numbers, links to this by opening with: "Then the LORD spoke to Moses in the wilderness of Sinai, in the tent of meeting" (Num. 1:1). And it contains preparations for leaving Sinai (Num. 1–10; cf. 10:12). The date given in the opening of Numbers is one month after the Tabernacle is erected, for we read of its date of erection in Exodus: "Now in the first month of the second year, on the first day of the month, the tabernacle was erected" (Exod. 40:17).

Deuteronomy (which means "second law") is a summary and reminder of God's laws, with an exhortation to keep the laws of Exodus through Numbers (Deut. 1:1, 5). Numbers ends with, "These are the commandments and the ordinances which the LORD commanded to the sons of Israel through Moses in the plains of Moab by the Jordan opposite Jericho" (Num. 36:13). Then Deuteronomy opens with, "These are the words which Moses spoke to all Israel across the Jordan in the wilderness, in the Arabah opposite Suph, between Paran and Tophel and Laban and Hazeroth and Dizahab" (Deut. 1:1).

So now, in the opening of the historically rooted Pentateuch, Moses presents an account of origins that "has a dimension very different from the comparable literature of the ancient Near East" (A. Ross 2007, 23). Hoffecker (2006, 4–5) explains the difference between the cosmologies in Canaan and that which Moses presents in Genesis: "Ancient cosmologies from Egypt, Mesopotamia, and Canaan are among the oldest written documents in the world. Their cosmologies are mythical accounts of a polytheistic universe. Each myth ties the origin and meaning of the cosmos to forces of nature that personify the gods." But he adds that "the Bible describes a cosmos that sprang not from a battle among many gods or from abstract rational principles but from creation out of nothing by an absolutely sovereign God. Biblical cosmology is historical, moral, and revelational. The cosmos had a distinct beginning; it provides the time and space framework in which God's sovereign plan is worked out (the fall and redemption); and it is moving toward a glorious consummation" (p. 5–6). Consequently, "Genesis 1 betrays a totally different notion about time. Here time is conceived as linear and events occur successively within it" (TWOT, 1:371). This is evident in the majestic march of days in Genesis 1, as one day progressively succeeds another. Or again, as Westermann (1984, 80) notes, the creation narrative "is characterized by its onward, irresistible, and majestic flow."

We find in the Genesis creation narrative numerous subtle testimonies against the pagan creation myths dominating Canaan and the Ancient Near East. As Hamilton (1990, 127) observes, "Few commentators deny that this whole chapter has a strong anti-mythical thrust." He continues, "Gen. 1 could not be written with a more antimythical basis" (p. 130). For instance, Moses chooses a word for the "deep," *tͪhōm*, in Genesis 1:2 that probably intentionally reflects Tiamat, the primordial goddess of chaos that was prominent in creation myths. But Moses shows that God created the "deep," and that His Spirit governed it. The six days of creation show an orderly creation process rather than a chaotic one. In fact, all along the way, God issues the divine appreciation formula "it was good" (1:4, 10, 12, 18, 21, 25, 31) rather than leaving any impression that it was a chaotic struggle. Also, we should note that the "expanse" created on day 2 is a peaceable action of the one true God (Gen. 1:6–8). It does not result from the violent tearing apart of the dead body of Tiamat to form the ceiling of the sky.

On day 4, Moses avoids calling the sun by its proper name *šemeš* or the moon by its name *yārēah*. This is almost certainly because these were the names of pagan deities. Rather, he presents the sun and moon in terms of their God-ordained and God-controlled *function*: they are to serve as luminaries; they are (literally) "places of light" (*māʾôr*). Then on day 5, God creates the "sea monsters," the *tannînim*. These are not the terrifying dragons of ancient myth that were supposedly involved in the struggle of creation. God creates and controls them, and declares them "good" (Gen. 1:21) and even blesses them (Gen. 1:22). In fact, later in the Psalms they are presented as God's playthings for His pond, the sea: "There the ships move along, and Leviathan [*tannînim*], which You have formed to sport in it" (Ps. 104:26).

Furthermore, in pagan lore many gods were hybrid creatures, especially those in Egypt, where Israel was in the days near the time Moses wrote Genesis. We think of such Egyptian gods as Anubis, who was part jackal, part man, and Ammit, who was part crocodile, lion, and hippopotamus. And in Canaan (where Israel was headed) perhaps Dagon, who (in some constructions) was the "fish-god" responsible for creating swarming abundance. Thus, he was part fish, part man. Later in Assyro-Babylonian religious art, we find Shedu, who was sometimes depicted either as a winged bull or winged lion with a human head. Genesis presents Moses' subtle rejection of such gods in that these hybrids are impossible. After all, God creates living creatures to reproduce "after their kind" (Gen. 1:21). In fact, He seems to go out of His way to emphasize this with the land animals by wearisome repetition: "Then God said, 'Let the earth bring forth living creatures *after their kind*: cattle and creeping things and beasts of the earth *after their kind*'; and it was so. God made the beasts of the earth *after their kind*, and the cattle *after their kind*, and everything that creeps on the ground *after its kind*; and God saw that it was good" (Gen. 1:24–25, emphasis added).

ISBE (3:741) lists the basic themes of the Pentateuch, then makes an important observation on its historical nature:

The nine basic pentateuchal themes mentioned above are tied to movement and involvement in God's created world, to history. They are not timeless abstract ideas but deal with particular theological or historical realities that exist when God relates to His image-bearing creatures. So the religious-moral message of the Pentateuch cannot be divorced from the fact that God has given his message through events in history to mankind, which is encased in history and meets God in history. Mankind is part of creation; the speaking of God to mankind through the created orders in an ongoing way is historical revelation. Thus if the historical bedrock of God's dealings with mankind is dissolved, then the message of God evaporates into thin air (or at best into abstract religious concepts). It is, in short, not possible to hold to the religious-moral message of the Pentateuch without holding to its basic historicity, which constitutes a necessary but a sufficient condition for its truth. Hence, in the Pentateuch we understand that, because of the nature of God, mankind, and the world, we are not dealing with myth, fable, mere astrological tales, or literary creations, but with the truth communicated by God to mankind through history in concrete word and concrete event.

Reymond (1998, 383) aptly encourages us in this regard: "Because the first eleven chapters of Genesis figure so significantly in biblical teaching on the origin and nature of the universe, biblical anthropology, and salvation itself, it is necessary to say something about their integrity as reliable, trustworthy history over against the modern view which treats them as religious *saga*, that is, as a mythical story which, while not actually historical, nevertheless intends to convey religious truth." In fact, Kaiser (1970, 59) notes that in these chapters "there are 64 geographical terms, 88 personal names, 48 generic names, and at least 21 identifiable cultural items." Thus, the fundamental problem with views like the framework hypothesis is that "it divorces the Genesis creation account from actual history" (Kuliovsky 2004, 61). Clearly, Genesis is an historical book relating historical reality by means of historical genre.

We see this further emphasized in the overarching structure discussed next.

Structure of Genesis

We can see Moses' interest in writing Genesis as historical genre by noting the book's most basic structuring device: the *tôlĕdōt* formula. This formula appears ten times in Genesis and introduces material of longer and shorter lengths (2:4, 5:1, 6:9, 10:1, 11:10, 11:27, 25:12, 25:19, 36:1, 37:2). The Hebrew word *tôlĕdōt* can be translated "account" (NASB, NIV), "generations" (NRSV, ESV), "history" (NKJV), or "descendants, generations" (DOTTE, 4:280). As Kaiser (1970, 59) well observes regarding this formula, "The writer's intention must be the first order of business if we are going to make any progress in locating the literary form for this section [Gen. 1–11]. We believe such an indication is given to us by the recurring heading, 'These are the generations of.' "

The *tôlĕdōt* formula emphasizes the historical character of Genesis by referring to temporal events resulting from prior narrative movement. Because of this formula, "Genesis consists of narrative sections that are linked together by genealogies" (Alexander 2002, 101). This is because *tôlĕdōt* "serves as a kind of link between what precedes and what follows" (BEB, 2:852). In Genesis, "ten histories are offered by the book, some dealing with important characters (Terah, Isaac, Jacob, Joseph), some dealing with important categories, like heaven and earth or the sons of Adam and of Noah; others with minor characters, like Ishmael and Esau" (Leupold 2009, 2:721). The many genealogies in the Old Testament clearly reflect historical matters of deep interest to the Jews. Scullion (1992, 935) points out that Genesis is organized "as a genealogical document, from the generations of heaven and earth (Gen 2:4) to the genealogical descent of Israel's ancestors." Even more pointedly, Alexander (2002, 101) argues that we should understand that "the book of Genesis has been carefully composed to focus on a unique family line, starting with Adam and continuing down to the twelve sons of Jacob. . . . The present text [of Genesis] has been carefully shaped to highlight the importance of a family lineage that begins with Adam and is traced through the sons of Jacob." Few issues are of more historical and religious significance to the Jews than Abraham's lineage, a lineage that is rooted in history. In Genesis, his lineage begins in its first chapters as we see in his genealogical descent from Adam to Shem (Gen. 5:32), then from Shem to Abram/Abraham (Gen. 11:10–27; compare Luke 3:34–38).

DOTP (356) puts this in its wider historical context, highlighting its theological implications for the world through Israel's redemptive-historical role in history: "The basic structural division of Genesis into primeval (Gen. 1:1–11:26) and ancestral (Gen. 11:27–50:26) histories shows the book's overarching theological interests. The primeval history, which takes the reader from the creation of the universe (Gen. 1:1) and humanity (Gen. 1:26–27, 2:7, 21–22), by way of a universal Flood (e.g., Gen. 6:17, 7:19), through to the dispersal of the nations at Babel (Gen. 11:9), indicates its universalistic preoccupations. . . . This global focus in Genesis 1–11 provides a significant theological preface to the call of Abraham (Gen. 12:1–3), which governs the ancestral history. The universalism of the primeval history is adopted as the subtext of the ancestral history, in which the one family in focus will be the agent for the blessing 'all the families of the earth' (Gen 12:3)."

Thus, "the primeval history provides a significant theological backdrop for understanding the blessings and promises that dominate the ancestral history" (DOTP, 357). As a result, "The biblical text of Gen 1:1–11:25 is Israel's statement on the universe and the human race" (Scullion 1992, 949). Leupold (2009, 721) well summarizes Genesis' impact as giving "a basically adequate answer to the question how the world originated, how humankind originated, how sin came into the world, how man and woman fell from grace, how God gave the hope of redemption to fallen sinners, how sin spread, how a great judgment was visited upon the sinful world in the flood, how a remnant of the human race was providentially saved, how the human race again spread abroad still proudly asserting itself." History — not myth, not poetry, not metaphor, not analogy — is the foundation and structuring device that presents Israel to the world.

The *tôlĕdōt* that interests us appears in the context of the creation narrative. In Genesis 2:4 we read: "This is the account [*tôlĕdōt*] of the heavens and the earth when they were created, in the day that the LORD God made earth and heaven." It appears where it does for a significant reason: it announces "as the subject of the section which it introduces . . . an account of the offspring of heaven and earth" (Green 1910, 11, 12). Consequently, "It is obvious that the heaven and the earth must first be brought into existence before the generations of the heaven and the earth can be spoken of, just as Adam and Noah must precede the generations of Adam and the generations of Noah" (Green 1910, 13). Thus, it introduces the account of the next "generation," and does not simply restate that of the previous generation. It connects the first narrative (the creation of the world) with the second narrative (the creation of the Garden).[7]

The Genesis 2:4 *tôlĕdōt* provides the *historical* backdrop for an *historical* Adam and his *historical* testing. It sets him in history following upon the *historical* creation of the world by God. And this requires that the record of creation be literal, historical narrative. If we are to believe in an historical Adam — as do Luke (Luke 3:38) and Paul (1 Cor. 15:45; 1 Tim. 2:13) — we must

---

7. See Cassuto 1998, 101–02; Pipa 1999, 156.

accept the setting of his creation as historical, at the very beginning of history. After all, Jesus does when He links Genesis 2 with Genesis 1: "But from the beginning of creation, God made them male and female. For this reason a man shall leave his father and mother, and the two shall become one flesh" (Mark 10:6–8).

These observations on the historical character of Genesis now lead us to the following considerations.

Style of Genesis

The literary structure of a passage is obviously significant for its proper interpretation. So in addition to that which we have already seen, I would note that the very style of Genesis also demonstrates that it is historical narrative genre. Though the Old Testament is written in many styles, Kaiser (1970, 59) reminds us regarding Genesis 1: "Basically, there are two broad categories for arranging the material: poetry or prose." And we will see that Genesis 1 is most definitely not poetry, which would allow somewhat open-ended poetic license in dealing with the material it presents. Had Moses presented his creation account poetically it would more suitably lend itself to the framework understanding.

Hebrew poetry has a characteristic style involving several distinctive elements, including especially parallelism, terseness, and ellipsis. *Parallelism* presents two lines of thought that correspond either synonymously, antithetically, or synthetically. Parallelism "is generally recognized as *the* characteristic feature of Hebrew poetry" (DOTW, 521) so that it actually stands as "fundamental to Hebrew poetry" (DBI, 553). *Terseness* presents poetic statements by means of a noticeable economy of words. Hebraist and Guggenheim scholar Adele Berlin sees terseness combining with parallelism to produce its distinctive poetic impact. She states that "it is not parallelism per se, but the predominance of parallelism, combined with terseness, which marks the poetic expression of the Bible." And she adds that this "factor of the terseness . . . tends to produce phonetic and syntactic balance in parallel lines."[8] *Ellipsis* involves the omission of a word (usually a verb in the second line) where it would normally be expected. Thus, parallelism is the controlling feature of poetry, with terseness and ellipsis supplementary to it.

Hebrew scholar E.J. Young (1976, 13) points out that "Hebrew poetry had certain characteristics, and they are not found in the first chapter of Genesis." Even framework theologian Blocher (1984, 32) admits that Genesis 1 "contains no rhythms of Hebrew poetry or synonymous parallelism." Thus, biblical scholars recognize Moses' genre as prosaic rather than poetic. Moses writes in an elegant style, but Young (1964, 82) notes that "Genesis one is written in exalted, semi-poetical language; nevertheless, it is not poetry." Collins (1999, 82; compare 2006, 71) calls it "exalted prose"; Wenham (1987, 19) "elevated prose." Boyd deems it "magisterial" prose (2010, 164–165) that presents "a *literal historical account*" (Boyd 2010, 166; compare 174). But the fact remains: it is *not* poetic.

As the introduction to an extremely historical book, we should expect Genesis 1 to present historical narrative itself. Indeed, Hasel (1984, 11) argues that "from a purely comparative approach of the literature structures, the language patterns, the syntax, the linguistic phenomena, the terminology, the sequential presentation of events in the creation account, Genesis 1 is not different from the rest of the book of Genesis or the Pentateuch for that matter." As a result, "the non-poetic nature of Genesis 1 shows that its intention is to take it in its plain sense as a straightforward and accurate record of creative events" (Hasel 1984, 12).

Framework scholars, however, often wrongly present the matter in the debate over Genesis 1. For instance, Hiebert states, "The framework of the week of creation is an artistic one designed to convey primarily theological, rather than purely scientific, information." This woefully misconstrues the matter. No six-day

---

8. Adele Berlin, *The Dynamics of Biblical Parallelism* (Bloomington, IN: Indiana University Press, 1985), p. 5–6.

creationist believes Moses is giving a "scientific" statement. And certainly not a "purely scientific" one. Rather he is giving a theologically informed *historical* account, as we are seeing. Kaiser (1970, 59–60) states the technical matter powerfully: "Genesis 1–11 is prose and not poetry. The use of the *waw* consecutive with the verb to describe sequential acts, the frequent use of the direct object sign and the so-called relative pronouns, the stress on definitions, and the spreading out of these events in a sequential order indicates that we are in prose and not in poetry."

The *waw* consecutive is perhaps the most significant feature of Moses' historical style in Genesis 1. *Waw* is the sixth letter of the Hebrew alphabet and is often used as the primary conjunction "and" or "then." The construction known as the "*waw* consecutive" involves a verb that has been prefixed with *waw*, and it is known as the "narrator's tense" (Keathley and Rooker 2014, 131). It generally functions in the sense of "then x." It appears 55 times in the 34 verses of the creation narrative (Gen. 1:1–2:3). On the same page Keathley and Rooker note that "this high frequency of the occurrence of other *waw* consecutive verbs is completely consistent with the other narrative passages in the book of Genesis."

The *waw* consecutive is characteristic of historical genre. As McCabe (2010, 216) observes, "Though the *waw* consecutive may appear in poetic literature, it is not a defining characteristic of Hebrew poetry. However, it is a significant component of Hebrew historical narrative and generally provides an element of sequence to past time narrative." Indeed, "the use of *waw* consecutive to communicate sequential, past tense material is the expected style for a historical book like Genesis." Given the Jews' linear conception of time and their interest in historical occurrence (see earlier discussion), we are not surprised to discover the abundant use of this grammatical feature in Genesis 1.

So then, when the first verb in a narrative context appears in the perfect tense and is followed by a series of imperfects, this presents the reader "a series of past events" (Kuliovsky 2004, 62). This is quite significant for the debate over the genre of Genesis 1, for Genesis 1:1 has the word "created" (*bārā*) in the qal perfect followed by a long series of qal imperfects beginning in 1:3, such as "then God said," "and God saw," "and God called," etc. As we learn from *Gesenius' Hebrew Grammar*: "The imperfect with *waw consecutive* serves to express actions, events, or states, which are to be regarded as the temporal or logical sequence of actions, events, and states mentioned immediately before."[9] Thus, Genesis 1 is presenting chronological history.

Moses is certainly familiar with poetry and could have easily structured this passage in poetic style had he so desired. Indeed, he wrote large poetic sections in the Pentateuch, most significantly in Exodus 15:1–18 ("The Song of Moses and of Israel") and in Deuteronomy 32:1–43 ("The Song of Moses"), as well as numerous other places (Exod. 15:21; Num. 6:24–26, 10:35–36, 12:6–8, 21:27–30, 23:7–10, 18–24, 24:3–9, 15–24; Deut. 33:2–29; Ps. 90). Indeed, brief poetic statements appear in many passages in the historical narrative of Genesis itself (Gen. 4:23–24, 8:22, 9:6–7, 25–27, 12:1–3, 14:19–20, 15:18, 16:11–12, 17:1–5, 24:60, 27:27–29, 39–40, 35:10–12). Genesis even records for us a quite sizeable poetic section (Gen. 49:2–27).

Moses even employs poetry when writing the primeval history of Genesis. For instance, many scholars deem Genesis 1:27 to be a poetic statement:

> So God created man in his own image,
> in the image of God he created him;
> male and female he created them.[10]
> (ESV; compare NRSV, NIV)

---

9. A.E Cowley, ed., Wilhelm Gesenius, *Gesenius' Hebrew Grammar* (Oxford, UK: Clarendon, 1910), par. 111a.

10. "The statement about recreation in v 27 is best set out in rhythmic form." Scullion 1992, 943.

Genesis 2:23 is most definitely poetry:

> This is now bone of my bones,
> And flesh of my flesh;
> She shall be called Woman,
> Because she was taken out of Man. (NASB; compare
> ESV, NIV, NKJV, NRSV)

Immediately after the creation narrative, God's declaration of the Curse at the Fall of Adam appears in poetic structure:

> The LORD God said to the serpent,
> "Because you have done this,
> Cursed are you more than all cattle,
> And more than every beast of the field;
> On your belly you will go,
> And dust you will eat
> All the days of your life;
> And I will put enmity
> Between you and the woman,
> And between your seed and her seed;
> He shall bruise you on the head,
> And you shall bruise him on the heel." (Gen. 3:14–15).

This poetic structure continues with the curse on Eve (Gen. 3:16) and on Adam (Gen. 3:17–19). But again, Moses avoids poetic devices in structuring the Genesis 1 narrative.

Interestingly, various poetic portions in later passages of Scripture reflect on creation. We see this when God speaks to Job out of the whirlwind (Job 38). Or when he speaks to Israel through Isaiah (Isa. 40:21–31). Psalm 104 is loosely a hymn written while reflecting on Genesis 1, and sometimes following its chronological order. Kidner writes, "The structure of the psalm is modeled fairly closely on that of Genesis 1, taking the stages of creation as starting-points for praise."[11] He points to the following flow:

---

11. Derek Kidner, *Psalms 73–150* (TOTC) (Downers Grove, IL: InterVarsity, 1973), p. 368.

Psalm 104:2a = day 1 (light)
Psalm 104:2b–4 = day 2 (firmament)
Psalm 104:5–9 = day 3 (land and water distinguished)
Psalm 104:14–17 = day 3 (vegetation)
Psalm 104:22–33 = day 4 (luminaries to divide days)
Psalm 104:25–26 = day 5 (sea and air creatures)
Psalm 104:21–24 = day 6 (land animals and man)
Psalm 104:27–28 = day 6 (food for creatures)

But these poetic reflections on creation do not present the numbered days, or report sequencing by use of the *waw* consecutive, as does the historical narrative of Genesis 1. Rather, these are hymnic and theological reflections on the original historical fact of creation, not re-tellings of those facts for instruction and reminder.

Yet we must recognize that even poetry *can* present true history. It can do so in a memorable and aesthetic fashion (e.g., Exod. 15:1–18; Deut. 32:1–43). Newling's comment is worth citing at length: "Poetry is not the opposite of historicity. Poetry is a literary form, and historicity is a comment on the content and purpose of a text. To conclude that something didn't happen on the basis of poetics is to confuse categories. . . . This confusion between literary genre and history-as-event needs to be reiterated. "Poetry" and "narrative" are general comments about types of literature. Historical poetry is as much in evidence throughout the ages as narrative fiction. It's in the Bible, too; Philippians 2:5–11 is poetry, but it certainly is history too. To label a text as "poetry" is to say nothing of its historical value. In other words, the tension that people are trying to alleviate by calling Genesis 1 "poetry" or "poetic" is not alleviated; it is simply a confusion of categories. What they are doing is something else entirely, which gets hidden by the terminology (Newling 2011).

Even more significantly, elements of the creation record (including from the lifetime of Adam) are referred to as historically trustworthy in the New Testament — for instance, all of the following:

> The first stage of creation involving a water-covered earth (2 Pet. 3:5; compare Gen. 1:2, 6–9).
>
> God's command that "light shall shine out of darkness" (2 Cor. 4:6; compare Gen. 1:3).
>
> The creation of two individuals (Adam and Eve) "from the beginning of creation" whom God joined together in marriage (Mark 10:6; Matt. 19:4; compare Gen. 1:27; 2:24).
>
> The creation of Adam as a "living soul" (1 Cor. 15:45; Gen. 2:7).
>
> Adam's creation before Eve (1 Cor. 11:8; 1 Tim. 2:13; compare Gen. 2:20–22).
>
> The sin and Fall of Adam (Rom. 5:12–14; compare Gen. 3:17–19).
>
> The prior temptation and sin of Eve (2 Cor. 11:3; 1 Tim. 2:14; compare Gen. 3:1–5).
>
> The genealogies of Adam, Seth, and Enosh (Luke 3:38; Jude 14; compare Gen. 5:1–11).
>
> The rejection of Cain's sacrifice and the acceptance of Abel's (Heb. 11:4; Gen. 4:3–5).
>
> Cain's murder of his brother Abel (Matt. 23:35; Luke 11:51; 1 John 3:12; compare Gen. 4:8).
>
> Man's seeing God's "eternal power and divine nature" in the world ever "since the creation of the world" (Rom. 1:20), which requires that man has been around "since the creation of the world."

As Weeks (1978, 17) perceptively observes regarding the New Testament's use of Genesis 1–3 specifically, "The form which the original creation took is made the basis of theological and/

or ethical teaching." As a consequence, if the events cited were not historically factual, then the ethical and religious arguments would collapse.

Young (1964, 105) concludes his work on Genesis 1 by forthrightly stating: "Genesis 1 is not poetry or saga or myth, but straightforward, trustworthy history, and, inasmuch as it is a divine revelation, accurately records those matters of which it speaks." An older work by McClintock and Strong states: "Not the least trace of mythology appears in it. Genesis plainly shows how very far remote the Hebrew mode of thinking was from mythical poetry, which might have found ample opportunity of being brought into play when the writer began to sketch the early times of the Creation" (CBTEL, 3:780).

So now let us turn to the next facet.

Purpose of Moses

Today we have the Bible in completed form. We might easily apply Jude's declaration and note that we have the finalized Scriptures "once for all handed down to the saints" (Jude 3). Because of our late place in Christian history, we tend to assume Scripture as a given, and therefore tend to overlook *why* the books of the Bible were written. Moses did not compose Genesis *solely* for the sake of instruction — though it does provide us with vitally important historical instruction. We must recognize Moses' place in redemptive-history in order to better discern the *reason* he wrote Genesis. Wisdom teaches us that "if we would judge of the work as a whole we must not forget the evident aim of the writer" (CBTEL, 3:776). In this regard, we should remember that "the message of Genesis was originally a message for Israel in Egypt. It told that community who they were, why they were there, and what future God had promised to them" (EDBT, 285).

So then, what was Moses' rationale in writing Genesis? For what purpose was he providing Israel with this particular instruction — an instruction beginning as far back as creation?

Most scholars would agree that it is quite clear that "the 'Primeval History' (Gen. 1:1–11:26) sets the stage for the whole of the book," and as such, "sets the stage for the emergence of Israel among the nations" (EDBT, 285). Indeed, "the book of Genesis has been carefully composed to focus on a unique family line, starting with Adam and continuing down to the twelve sons of Jacob" (Alexander 2002, 101). Thus, "Genesis i–xi in general, and the first section in particular, are a broad introduction to the history which commences with Abraham" (Speiser 1964, 9). More narrowly, as Collins (2006, 33, 34) explains regarding the first four chapters of Genesis, "We must first clarify their literary relation to the rest of the Pentateuch, to which these chapters are the front end" — and "the Pentateuch is about the Mosaic covenant." He continues, "The Mosaic covenant carries forward the covenants made with the patriarchs."

As we enter Genesis, we must understand the big picture presented, then the specific flow to Abraham. The big picture laying the foundation for the rest of Genesis is this: the God of Israel created the world and everything that is in it (Gen. 1:1; compare Ps. 8:3, 102:25, 104:1ff; Isa. 40:22; Neh. 9:6). That world was originally "very good" as it came about at his behest (Gen. 1:31; compare Ps. 33:6–9, 148:5). But the world in which all men now live (in the days of Moses) is quite different, having been corrupted by the alien intrusion of sin (Gen. 3:1–13). Consequently, God's righteous character requires that He judge sin, which He does at the Fall in the Garden (Gen. 3:14–24), and which gives rise to His judgment at the Flood throughout the world (Gen. 6–9) and at the Tower in the land of Shinar (Gen. 11). Yet His gracious mercy leads Him to engage redemption in calling man back to Himself, beginning at the Fall with Adam (Gen. 3:14–15), continuing through the Flood with Noah (Gen. 6:13, 18–19, 9:1, 8–11), and following after the Tower with Abraham (Gen. 11:27–12:3). In the *Baker Encyclopedia of the Bible* (2:852) we read, "Genesis relates the beginning of the history of redemption with the announcement of a Redeemer who was to come (Gen. 3:15). It names the early progenitors in the lineage of the Messiah and the beginning of the Hebrew people through whom the Bible and the Savior came."

Thus, Harrison (1969, 553) well states, "The prolouge [to Genesis] is cast in universal terms suitable to the subject-matter, and depicts the creative activity of God in fashioning the cosmos and placing man upon the earth. The universality of sin is depicted, along with the fact that, as rebellion against God, it must always stand under divine judgment, a situation exemplified by the account of the deluge." Wenham (1987, li.) discerns an important matter in the early plot-line of Genesis: "Gen. 1–11 gives the background to the call of Abraham in two main ways. First, it discloses the hopeless plight of mankind without the gracious intervention of God. Second, it shows how the promises made to the patriarchs fulfill God's original plans for humanity." Unfortunately, Wenham leaves out the ultimate backdrop to all of this: Genesis 1 and 2 shows that man's hopeless plight was not his original condition, for God created the whole world in which man lives in an originally happy and glorious condition as "very good" (Gen. 1:31).

Alexander's (2002, 98) lengthy statement of the Genesis plan will be relevant to the argument that the creation account is historical genre. He states:

> The basic plot of the Pentateuch may be outlined as follows. At the outset human beings are created to enjoy a special relationship with God and to exercise authority on his behalf over the earth. However, the disobedience of Adam and Eve alienates them from God, and as a result they are punished through divine curses and expelled from Eden. While the early chapters of Genesis concentrate mainly on the terrible consequences of these initial

developments, the rest of Genesis, from chapter 12 onwards, moves forward with the hope that humanity may yet be reconciled to God.

He adds further (2002, 114):

> Although the first chapter of Genesis affirms that human beings were created in the divine image and blessed by God, the subsequent disobedience of Adam and Eve in the Garden of Eden resulted in a series of divine curses that radically affected human existence. The tragic events that resulted from the broken relationship between God and humankind are highlighted in Genesis 4–11. After the division of humanity into different people and nations, Abraham is introduced as the one through whom God's blessing will once again extend to human beings.

Now, since "Gen. 1–11 serves simply as the background to the subsequent story of the patriarchs, and their history is in turn background to the story of Israel's exodus from Egypt and their lawgiving at Sinai which form the subject matter of Exodus to Deuteronomy" (Wenham 1987, xlv), we should expect that the creation story itself is historical, not myth, metaphor, or poetry. If the creation account is not factual history, then it is not actually relevant. As Kulikovsky (2004, 61) suggests, "The 'patriarchal' history is generally regarded as an accurate historical record, therefore, there is no reason why the 'primeval' history should not also be accepted as an accurate historical record."

Conclusion

It would be absolutely incongruous for Moses to lay a foundation for primeval history in poetic metaphor, especially given Israel's historical interests, Genesis' grammatical structure, and Moses' instructional purpose. As Keil and Delitzsch (2001, 23) comment, "The account of the creation, its commencement, progress, and completion, bears the marks, both in form and substance, of a historical document in which it is intended that we should accept as actual truth ... the description of the creation itself in all its several stages. If we look at the *form* of the document, its place at the beginning of the book of Genesis is sufficient to warrant the expectation that it will give us history." Genesis 1 is clearly written as historical genre. And it presents us with a clear sequential process of six successive 24-hour days.

Chapter 4

Survey of Exegetical Arguments

Advocates of the framework hypothesis hold that the days of Genesis 1 are actually "normal solar days," yet they interpret these days neither in the traditional manner nor in a *prima facie* fashion. This is indicated in their general tendency to put the word "day" in quotation marks.[1] Consequently, though some framework proponents decry such (Irons 1998, 53), the burden of proof is on their position. After all, why would the "historic" (Blocher 1984, 46), first "impression" (Ridderbos 1957, 29; compare M. Ross 1999, 113) view have to shoulder the burden against a view supported by "new" (Blocher 1984,

---

1. As seen, for example, in Kline's and Irons' writings. Kline (1958): "These may disagree as to the duration of the 'days' of Genesis 1" (146); "within the era of the 'six days'" (147); "this closed era of the 'six days' was characteristic" (147); "which terminated the era of the 'six days'" (147 n3); "originated with the 'six days'" (147 n3); "the Sabbath of the seventh 'day'" (147 n4); "the world during the 'six days' era" (148); "providence during the 'six days' accords well with the analogy of subsequent divine providence" (150 n8); "the work of the 'third day'" (151); "even if the 'days' are regarded" (152); "on the 'fourth day'" (153); "the rest of the 'seventh day'"; "the contents of 'days' one to three" (154); "the 'days' are not of equal length"; "in terms of six 'days' of work followed by a seventh 'day' of rest" (155). See also: Kline (1996): "providence was in operation during the creation 'days'" and "the sequence of the 'days' is ordered" (13); "the first three 'days' of creation" (14); "made during the 'six days' includes" (14 n33). Irons (1998): "we will then return to the 'days' of creation" (37); "the 'days' of Gen. 1 are not literal" (37); "what do these 'days' refer to?"

53), "recently developed" (Irons 1998, 6) and "quite complicated and hard to follow" exegesis (Irons 1998, 12 n85)? Even
Hebrew scholar and analogical day advocate John Collins (Collins 1996, 141) complains that Kline's article is "quite complicated and hard to follow, even for the biblical specialist." This
is all the more necessary since Kline (1958, 156) himself admits, "It also needs considerable emphasis, even among orthodox exegetes, that specific evidence is required for identifying
particular elements in the early chapters of Genesis as literary
figures. The semi-poetic form of Genesis 1 does not make it an
exception."

Rather than literally signifying that creation occurs "in six
days" (Exod. 20:11, 31:17), Blocher (1984, 45) argues, "It is possible to treat the terminology of the week as figurative language,
but at that moment 'day' has its ordinary meaning and with that
meaning plays a figurative role." Kline (1995, 7) contends that
"when we find that God's upper level activity of issuing creative
fiats from his heavenly throne is pictured as transpiring in a week
of earthly days, we readily recognize that, in keeping with the
pervasive contextual pattern, this is a literary figure, an earthly,
lower register time metaphor for an upper register, heavenly reality." Irons (1998, 3) agrees, proposing that the days of Genesis
"are part of an extended metaphor that functions as a literary
framework for the creation narrative."

Despite framework arguments, the historical understanding
of the days of creation as actual calendrical time-coordinates covering a temporal space of "six days" is not only the clear first
impression that Moses' reader receives from the passage, but the
proper exegetical conclusion that Moses placed in the passage.
Later, in chapters 6–9, I will expose some of the exegetical errors
inherent in the foundation stones of the framework hypothesis.
But here in the present chapter I will survey the exegetical argument for interpreting the days of Genesis 1 in a straightforward
manner that demands both their chronological succession and

24-hour duration. Then I will briefly respond to certain objections charged against this exegesis.

Below I will present the abundant evidence for the 24-hour day view of the traditional approach to Genesis 1. I offer this argument despite being criticized by one six-day creationist for offering such in a debate against the framework hypothesis. Kulikovsky (2004, 61) deems my "detailed exegetical defence of the traditional 24-hour interpretation of the creation days" as "rather pointless given that Framework advocates do not deny that the days refer to normal 24-hour days." What he means is that they agree that Moses actually presented normal days, but that he intended them to serve as a figurative time frame for God's creative activity. For as frameworkers Irons and Kline (2001, 85) put it, "All believe that the days, with their evening-morning refrain, have a very specific meaning as part of the picture of a divine workweek of six days followed by a seventh day of rest." Yet, if we are to debate the framework proponents, we must present our own reasoning regarding why we believe that the days are literal — reasoning which demands that Moses was emphasizing this fact. My argument would be hobbled if I offered no evidence for my own view, the view of the traditional exegesis. This is made all the more important since framework proponents recognize, as does M. Ross (1999, 113) immediately after defining the literary function of the Genesis days, that "admittedly, this is not the first impression one gets from the text."

The very historical character and foundational necessity of Genesis 1, not only to the Book of Genesis but to all of Scripture, compels us to adopt the literal, sequential nature of the six days. In fact, the chronological progression of the days provides an obviously logical sequence: the days progress from creating the foundational structure for the biosphere as a habitat for life (days 1, 2, 3, 4) to the formation of living organisms within that realm (days 3b, 5, 6). It moves from the creation of *immobile* aspects of creation (days 1, 2, 3) to the *mobile* features of creation (days 4, 5, 6).[2]

1. Argument from Primary Meaning

The Hebrew word for "day" is *yôm*. This is a very common word, appearing 2,304 times in the Old Testament (the fifth most frequent noun), 668 times in the Pentateuch, and 152 times in Genesis (Hasel 1984, 16). The preponderant usage of the word *yôm* in the Old Testament is of the well-known temporal period. The *Theological Lexicon of the Old Testament* notes that there are two primary meanings of *yôm*: (1) "The basic meaning of *yôm* is 'day (from sunrise to sundown)'" and (2) "in the sense of the astronomical or calendrical unit" (TLOT 2:537 538).

In Genesis 1:1–2:3, *yôm* appears 13 times in the singular. As McCabe (2010, 226) notes, "The noun *yôm* ('day') always refers to a normal day when it is used as a singular noun and is not found in a compound grammatical construction." It also appears one time in the plural in Genesis 1 so as to require its literal meaning: "Then God said, 'Let there be lights in the expanse of the heavens to separate the day from the night, and let them be for signs and for seasons and for *days* and years'" (Gen. 1:14, emphasis added). Clearly, the "days" here mark out our naturally created, short-term time measure, just as "years" speaks of our naturally created, long-term time measure.

In fact, the *Theological Dictionary of the Old Testament* (6:23, 22) defines *yôm* as used in the creation narrative thus: "from its outset at creation (Gen. 1:3–5), *yôm* as 'full day' had the same beginning as *yôm* in the narrower sense," i.e., the "daylight period in contrast to night." It continues: "If we start from the observation that *yôm* refers in the first instance to 'daylight,' the meaning 'full day' (twenty-four hours) is itself an extended temporal sense" (TDOT, 6:25). The *Theological Lexicon of the Old*

---

2. Some scholars deny this for day 4, which has the sun being created after light. I will respond to this objection later.

Testament (2, 528) defines the day of Genesis 1 as "a day of 24 hours in the sense of an astronomical or calendrical unit of time."

The overwhelming majority of the appearances of *yôm* in the Old Testament clearly refer either to a normal, full day-and-night cycle, or to the lighted portion of that cycle. And both of these directly related options would be easily understood without any difficulty by the casual reader both in antiquity and today.[3] In fact, on day 1 God Himself "called" the light "day" (Gen. 1:5), establishing the commonly understood, temporal significance of the term in the creation week. The daylight hours being the most important portion of the day (in that they are the time of man's productive labors, normal travel, and so forth[4]), the designation "day" can apply to the full cycle that brings the daylight back around.

Interestingly, the Jewish Mishnah refers to the creation days as literal: "The one day spoken of in the law 'It and its young' means the day together with the night that went before. This was expounded by Simeon b. Zoma: In the story of Creation it is written 'one day'; and in the law of 'It and its young' it is written, 'one day': as the 'one day' spoken of in the story of Creation means the daytime together with the night that went before" (Hullin, 5:5). The first-century Jewish historian Josephus does, as well. He states that God "separated the light and the darkness; and the name he gave to one was Night, and the other he called Day: and he named the beginning of light, and the time of rest, The Evening and The Morning, and this was indeed the first day. But Moses said it was one day. . . . Accordingly Moses says, That in just six days the world, and all that is therein, was made" (*Antiquities*, 1:1:1).

---

3. "As in most languages, this basic meaning broadens to 'day (of 24 hours)' " (TDOT 2: 528). "As in other Semitic and Indo-European languages, 'day' is understood both in contrast to 'night' and as a term including both daytime and nighttime" (TDOT 6:6).

4. Judg. 19:9, 11; Neh. 4:22; Ps. 104:23; Luke 21:37; John 9:4; Rom. 13:12; 1 Thess. 5:5–7.

As conservative theologian Berkhof (1941, 154) declares in defending the historic exegesis of a six-day creation: "In its primary meaning the word *yom* denotes a natural day; and it is a good rule in exegesis, not to depart from the primary meaning of a word, unless this is required by the context." Dabney (1973, 254–55), a well-known theologian from the late 19th century, points out:

> The narrative seems historical, and not symbolical; and hence the strong initial presumption is, that all its parts are to be taken in their obvious sense. . . . It is freely admitted that the word day is often used in the Greek Scriptures as well as the Hebrew (as in our common speech) for an epoch, a season, a time. But yet, this use is confessedly derivative. The natural day is its literal and primary meaning. Now, it is apprehended that in construing any document, while we are ready to adopt, at the demand of the context, the derived or tropical meaning, we revert to the primary one, when no such demand exists in the context.

Why would Moses employ a temporal term ("day") in an (allegedly) anthropomorphic context (Ridderbos 1957, 30; Kline 1996, 14 n24; Majority Report 1999, 8–9)? The use of this mundane term in this (supposedly) highly stylized and sophisticated passage would generate unnecessary trouble for Moses' readers who are supposed to think of "upper register realities" (Irons 1998, 37). They know their God inhabits eternity and cannot be measured by days — as per Moses' own statement in Psalm 90:2–4: "From everlasting to everlasting, You art God. . . . For a thousand years in Your sight are like yesterday when it passes by."

This periodical time measurement was established directly by God on the first day of creation to lock in the *temporal pattern* for all earth history (Jer. 33:20, 25; compare Gen. 8:22; Ps. 74:16–17; Jer. 31:35). "The two divisions of time known to us as Day and Night are precisely the same as those that God established at the time of creation, the *light* being the Day, and the *darkness* the Night" (Cassuto 1998, 27). But it also provides the *temporal measure of God's creative activity* as a pattern for man's workweek. Calvin explains: "God himself took the space of six days, for the purpose of accommodating his works to the capacity of men." And, "I have said above, that six days were employed in the formation of the world; not that God, to whom one moment is as a thousand years, had need of this succession of time, but that he might engage us in the consideration of his works. He had the same end in view in the appointment of his own *rest*, for he set apart a day selected out of the remainder for this special use."[5] I will have more to say about this in Point 6 below.

2. Argument from Explicit Qualification

So that we not miss his point, Moses relentlessly qualifies each of the six creation days by the phrase "evening and morning:" *wāy⁻ehiy ʿereb wāyᵉhiy bōqer*, "and it was evening and it was morning."[6] Although this exact expression "evening and morning" only occurs in Genesis 1, outside this chapter the singular words *eber* ("evening") and (*bōqer*) "morning" appear together 30 times in the Old Testament and denote a normal day.[7] In those passages the terms are either presenting the two elements marking off a 24-hour day or speaking of the opening and closing limits of the daylight portion of a normal day. And the word "morning" and the word "evening" occur alone with *yôm* 17 and 19 times (respectively) outside of Genesis 1. And as Stambaugh notes, "With

---

5. John Calvin, *Commentaries of the First Book of Moses Called Genesis*, trans. John King (Grand Rapids, MI: Eerdmans, 1948), 1:78 (at Gen. 1:5), 107 (at Gen. 2:3).

6. The seventh day does not involve God's creative activity and does not have the qualifiers (Gen. 2:1–3). See later discussion on this matter.

7. Gen. 49:27; Exod. 16:8, 13, 18:13–14, 27:21; Lev. 6:20, 24:3; Num. 9:15, 21; Deut. 16:4, 28:67; 1 Sam. 17:16; 1 Kings 17:6; 2 Kings 16:15; 1 Chron. 16:40, 23:30; 2 Chron. 2:4, 13:11, 31:3; Ezra 3:3; Esther 2:14; Job 4:20; Ps. 55:17, 90:6; Eccles. 11:6; Isa. 5:11, 17:14; Ezek. 24:18, 33:22; Zeph. 3:3.

each occurrence a twenty-four day is signified."[8] Thus, he continues, "Any combination of the words 'morning,' 'evening,' and
yôm use their extra-linguistic referential value to its fullest extent;
pointing to the length of time which is normally associated with
these words." Consequently, here in Genesis 1 it seems most likely
that both terms ("evening"/"morning") stand *pars pro toto*: as a
part for the whole, i.e., the evening representing the whole period of darkness and the morning the whole time of light.

Analogical day advocate Collins (2005, 137) argues that
the evenings and the mornings in Genesis 1 "are the end-points
of the 'nighttime' (Hebrew *lylh*)." But even if the two words are
coupled together to mark the boundaries of the daylight hours,
we still must recognize a normal 24-hour period between each
successive evening or between each successive morning. So the
normal day-frame is secured.

Framework advocates, though, argue that the six evening/
morning qualifiers "cannot be used in their normal senses prior
to the fourth day in the one-week, chronological interpretation"
(M. Ross 1999, 128). This complaint is not well put, for they
can be used in their "normal senses"; though they cannot be used
of our normal *experience* — because we did not experience the
original creation week. In the first three days of the creation week
there is no "*sun*-rise" such as effects our morning today. But the
same phenomenon associated with our present-day sunrise (i.e.,
"morning") is caused by the direct, supernatural recurring pattern
of light (Gen. 1:4). The Hebrew word *bōqer* derives from a root
that means "to break, cleave, divide," and speaks of "the breaking through of the daylight" (TWOT, 1:125; compare TDOT,
2:219). Hence, even today we may call the morning "day-*break*."

---

8. Compare Stambaugh 2015, 3; Keathley and Rooker 2014, 157. "Day" is used with
"evening" in Exod. 12:18, 18:13; Lev. 6:20; Num. 9:15, 19; Deut. 16:4; Josh. 5:10,
8:29; Judg. 20:26; 1 Sam. 14:24, 30:17; 1 Kings 22:35; 2 Chron. 18:34; Jer. 6:4;
Ezek. 12:4, 7; Zech. 14:7. "Day" is used with "morning" in Exod. 10:13, 18:13,
19:16; Lev. 6:20, 7:15, 22:30; Num. 9:15; Deut. 16:4; Judg. 19:5, 8; 1 Sam. 11:11;
2 Kings 7:9; Ps. 59:16, 73:14; Isa. 17:11, 28:19, 38:13; Amos 5:8.

The "breaking" of night's dark veil, or the "scattering" of the darkness, occurs at each morning, or each new day of the creation week. This prevails even on the first three days *before* the creation of the sun. As the *Theological Dictionary of the Old Testament* (2:223) observes: "Light (*'ôr*) as such is not identical with the sun (cf. Gen. 1:3f.), though it emanates from the sun." The same sort of analysis holds true for the "evening" (*'ereb*), as well. The verbal form (*arab*) means "to grow dark" (TDOT, 2:694), and is related to the noun *'ōrēb,* which means "raven, crow" (because the verb origin means "be black," BDB, 788).

Dabney (1973, 255) argues that this evidence alone should compel adoption of a literal day view: "The sacred writer seems to shut us up to the literal interpretation, by describing the day as composed of its natural parts, 'morning and evening. . . .' It is hard to see what a writer can mean, by naming evening and morning as making a first, or a second 'day'; except that he meant us to understand that time which includes just one of each of these successive epochs: — one beginning of night, and one beginning of day. These gentlemen cannot construe the expression at all. The plain reader has no trouble with it. When we have had one evening and one morning, we know we have just one civic day; for the intervening hours have made just that time."[9]

With the evening ending each day of creative activity, the following morning serves as the border separating the previous day from the next, thus introducing a new day. This passing of literal days may also be expressed as "morning after morning" or "morning by morning" (Exod. 16:21; 2 Sam. 13:4; 1 Chron. 9:27; Isa. 28:19; Isa. 50:4; Ezek. 46:13–15). "Whenever clear reference is made to the relationship between a given day and the next, it is precisely sunrise that is accounted the beginning of the second day" (Cassuto 1998, 28).[10] In the New Testament, a

---

9. See also Cassuto 1998, 28; Keil and Delitzsch 2001, 32; Berkhof 1941, 154; Reymond 1998, 393; Hasel 1984, 28; and Shaw 1999, 206.
10. Compare Keil and Delitzsch 2001, 31; Shaw 1999, 206; TWOT 2:694.

related pattern of "night and day" shows a full 24-hour day (Acts 20:31, 26:7; 1 Thess. 2:9, 3:10; 2 Thess. 3:8; 1 Tim. 5:5; 2 Tim. 1:3). Even the framework advocates in their Majority Report (1999, 5) agree with this function of "morning."

Mornings and evenings are phenomena recurring in the temporal realm and have no correspondence to eternity where there is no night (Rev. 21:25), where time has no effect (Ps. 90:4; 2 Pet. 3:8). "God's eternity is no indefinitely extended time, but something essentially different, of which we can form no conception. His is a timeless existence, and eternal presence" (Berkhof 1941, 130).

If the "days" themselves are metaphorical devices, why does Moses relentlessly employ this additional verbiage ("evening and morning") that gives the clear and distinct impression he wants to emphasize their literal reality? The phrase "evening and morning" — which is, in fact, missing from one of the days (day 7) and from the references to the "six days" elsewhere in Scripture (Exod. 20:12, 31:17) — would not be necessary for any supposed metaphorical imagery. Interestingly, in another context Irons (1998, 4) argues that the Westminster Confession of Faith (at 4:2) does not teach a temporal period of six solar days because the divines did not qualify their "days" as "24-hour" days or "solar" days. Why does he not follow his own line of reasoning here, noting that Moses *does* qualify his days, thereby signifying their 24-hour duration?

After engaging a careful semantic analysis of the use of *yôm* in Genesis 1, Stambaugh (2015, 11) well notes on the recurring evening/morning refrain: "The point of discussing the semantic approach should be rather obvious. God, through the 'pen' of Moses, is being redundant for redundancy's sake. God is going out of His way to tell us that the 'days' of creation were literal solar days. He has used the word *yôm*, and combined this with a number and the words 'morning' and 'evening.' God has communicated the words of Genesis 1 in a specific manner, so that the interpreter could not miss His point. God could not have communicated the timing of creation more clearly than He did in Genesis 1."

3. Argument from Numerical Prefix

Genesis attaches a numeral to each of the days of creation week (Gen. 1:5, 8, 13, 19, 23, 31, 2:2-3): the cardinal prefix, "one" (Gen. 1:5; compare LXX *hēmera mia*) and ordinal prefixes on the remaining days, "second," "third," "fourth," "fifth," "sixth," and "seventh." Moses affixes numerical adjectives to *yôm* 119 times in his writings. And these always signify literal days, for as Mulzac in the *Eerdmans Dictionary of the Bible* (324) comments, "When 'day' is accompanied by a definite number (e.g., Gen. 1:5, 8, 7:11; Exod. 16:1; Lev 23:34), it points only to a 24-hour period." The same holds true for the 357 times numerical adjectives qualify *yôm* outside the Pentateuch.

Note the following samples from Moses' writings (emphasis added):

- Exodus 12:15: "Seven days you shall eat unleavened bread. On the *first day* you shall remove leaven from your houses; for whoever eats leavened bread from the *first day* until the *seventh day*, that person shall be cut off from Israel."
- Exodus 24:16: "The glory of the LORD rested on Mount Sinai, and the cloud covered it six days; and on the *seventh day* He called to Moses out of the midst of the cloud."
- Leviticus 12:3: "On the *eighth day* the flesh of his foreskin shall be circumcised."

See also: Exodus 12:16, 13:6, 16:26–27, 29–30, 20:10, 23:12, 31:15, 17, 34:21; Leviticus 13:5–6, 27, 32, 34, 51; Numbers 6:9, 7:48, 19:12, 28:25, etc.

In fact, according to Waltke and O'Connor, the anarthrous cardinal "one" (Heb., *'echād*), which begins the series of days, expresses "an emphatic, counting force."[11] Moses intends for the series of enumerated days to count off the passing of time during creation week. In fact, Steinmann (2002, 583) argues regarding the day designated "one":

> Gen. 1:5 begins the cycle of the day. With the creation of light it is now possible to have a cycle of light and darkness, which God labels "day" and "night." Evening is the transition from light/day to darkness/night. Morning is the transition from darkness/night to light/day. Having an evening and a morning amounts to having one full day. Hence the following equation is what Gen 1:5 expresses: Evening + morning = one day.
>
> Therefore, by using a most unusual grammatical construction, Genesis 1 is defining what a day is. . . .
>
> It would appear as if the text is very carefully crafted so that an alert reader *cannot* read it as "the first day." Instead, by omission of the article it must be read as "one day," thereby defining a day as something akin to a twenty-four hour solar period with light and darkness and transitions between day and night, even though there is no sun until the fourth day.[12]

Jewish commentator Cassuto (1998, 28) agrees that Genesis 1:5 is a statement which "completed the first calendar day (one day)."

As Hasel (1984, 26) observes, "This triple interlocking connection of singular usage, joined by a numeral, and the temporal definition of 'evening and morning,' keeps the creation 'day' the same throughout the creation account. It also reveals that time is conceived as linear and events occur within it successively. To depart from the numerical, consecutive linkage and the 'evening-morning' boundaries in such direct language would mean

---

11. Bruce K. Waltke and M.O'Connor, *An Introduction to Biblical Hebrew Syntax* (Winona Lake, IN: Eisenbrauns, 1990), p. 270.
12. Compare Keathley and Rooker, p. 157.

to take extreme liberty with the plain and direct meaning of the Hebrew language."

Some point to Hosea 6:2 as an example of a nonliteral use of *yôm* in the singular and with a numerical prefix: "He will revive us after two days; He will raise us up on the third day, that we may live before Him." For instance, Justin Taylor (2015, 4) writes that "Hosea 6:2 ('third day') seems to be used in an analogical way that does not refer to a precise 24-hour time period."

Despite nonliteralists, however, Hosea 6:2 is no counter example to the enumerated days being literal days in Genesis 1, for in this prophecy the "third day" does one of two things. (1) It functions idiomatically, indicating the certainty of Israel's national resurrection, by using the literal time period at which a body begins to decompose (John 11:39) to underscore their hope. On "the Jewish view this separation [of soul and body] did not take place for certain until the fourth day" (TDNT, 2:949). Or perhaps it is the literal expectation of the time of recovery from a sickness.[13] (2) Like many of the Church fathers supposed, it may allude to Christ's Resurrection on the third day as containing Israel's ultimate hope. Hosea 6:2 appears to be the only backdrop for Paul's statement in 1 Corinthians 15:4, where he declares that Christ was "raised on the third day according to the Scriptures."[14]

4. Argument from Numbered Series

A related, though slightly different observation regarding the numerical prefix serves to underscore the literalist view. That is, when *yôm* appears in *sequentially numbered, uninterrupted series,*

---

13. J. Andrew Dearman, *The Book of Hosea* (NICOT) (Grand Rapids, MI: Eerdmans, 2010), 194.

14. Commentators who think Paul may have used Hos. 6:2 as his Old Testament backdrop include G. Delling in TDNT 531; David E. Garland, *1 Corinthians* (BECNT) (Grand Rapids, MI: Baker, 2003), p. 687; Roy E. Ciampa and Brian S. Rosner, *The First Letter to the Corinthians* (PNTC) (Grand Rapids, MI: Eerdmans, 2010), p. 748.

it always specifies natural days (e.g., Exod. 12:15–16, 24:16; Lev. 23:39; Num. 7:12–36, 29:17ff). This is another means by which Moses indicates literal days are in view, not images like "the day of the Lord" or metaphorical time frames.

By all appearance, while being carried upon an ever deepening tide of evidence, Genesis 1 presents a series of consecutively numbered days for a reason: to indicate sequentially flowing, calendrical days, as is Moses' consistent writing practice.[15] If the days were simply structuring devices for presenting us with metaphorical pictures of an orderly creation, why are they numbered? Seriatim numbering not only gives the distinct appearance of sequential development (which the framework hypothesis denies for Genesis 1), but it also fits the numbering pattern of literal earthly day references elsewhere. It seems that Moses is going out of his way either to make it difficult for the reader to get his point (if he is interested only in literary effect, as per the framework hypothesis), or that he is locking in his meaning with various qualifying factors (if he is promoting historical accuracy, as per the traditional view).

This is all the more problematic in that the framework hypothesis denies temporal sequence by collapsing days 1 and 4 into one creative episode (a serious problem with other negative implications to which I will return later). Futato (1998, 16) argues, "The account of God's work on Days 1 and 4 are two different perspectives on the same creative work." He then cites Kline (1996, 7–8), who states, "These effects which are said to result from the production and positioning of the luminaries on day four are the same effects that are already attributed to the creative activity of day one (Gen. 1:3–5)." But if the week is anthropomorphically arranged, why this recapitulation? Men do not recapitulate work during the week.

---

15. In addition, Cassuto (1998, 27) makes an important grammatical observation based on the syntactical structure of at least one portion of the passage (on Day One): "It is a fundamental rule of Biblical narrative style that verbs describing acts that took place in sequence should head their respective clauses."

As Young (1964, 100) observes against the framework view, "If Moses had intended to teach a non-chronological view of the days, it is indeed strange that he went out of his way, as it were, to emphasize chronology and sequence. . . . It is questionable whether serious exegesis of Genesis 1 would in itself lead anyone to adopt a non-chronological view of the days for the simple reason that everything in the text militates against it." Kidner (1967, 54–55) agrees: "The march of the days is too majestic a progress to carry no implication of ordered sequence; it also seems over-subtle to adopt a view of the passage which discounts one of the primary impressions it makes on the ordinary reader." Grudem (1994, 303) concurs: "The implication of chronological sequence in the narrative is almost inescapable." As Bédard (2013, 95) expresses it, besides the temporal markers expressing the succession of days, "it is clear that the historical narrative account presents *successive acts* of creation. Each of the days *is built upon* what has been created during the preceding days."

In fact, this chronological sequencing is further demanded by the irregular appearance of the divine appreciation formula ("it was good"). In addition to marring the "artistry" of Genesis 1,[16] we must note that *after* God creates the light, but *before* He separates it from the darkness, we read: "God saw that the *light* was good" (Gen. 1:4). On other days (but *not* at all on day 2) the appreciation formula follows the *completed* divine activity. Why this difference? The answer points to the necessity of sequential divine activity. Note the following.

Although the creation of man as male and female is "good" — actually "very good" (Gen. 1:31) — this was not originally so. Genesis 2 informs us that at the moment when God first created Adam it was "*not good* for the man to be alone" (Gen. 2:18,

---

16. The appreciation formula appears in the middle of the creative activity on day 1; does not appear at all on days 2 or 7; appears after the creative activity on days 3–6; appears twice on day 3; and appears in two different styles of expression (compare day 1: "he saw that the light was good" and days 3–6: "saw that it was good").

emphasis added). How does He correct this deficiency so that He may indeed declare man's creation "good"? He *separates* woman out of the man (Gen. 2:21–22). *Then* once they *both* exist, He declares the final result "good" (Gen. 1:27, 31). The creation of man is not complete, it is not "good," i.e., it is not what God wants as a final result *until* Eve is separated out of Adam later on day 6. The Lord is then finished with His creation of mankind, establishing male and female as the categories to prevail throughout history. This leads to the next step in my argument.

When God separates the waters below from the waters above on day 2, absolutely *no* appreciation formula appears (see 1:6–8). This is no accident.[17] Nor is it insignificant. Robert Godfrey (2003, 81) is quite mistaken in declaring that we "cannot easily account for the absence of the statement 'And God saw that it was good' in day two.' " Though God divides the water by creating the "firmament," which separates the waters into lower and upper realms on day 2, He is not finished with the waters until day 3. On that day He separates the land and the water, forming what He only then calls "the seas" (1:9–10). Then, and only then, does He declare His work with the water "good" (1:10) — which declaration interrupts the activity of day 3 and causes the appreciation formula to appear twice on that day (1:12). Day 3 *must* follow sequentially from day 2. Thus, the Lord is not through with the waters until day 3, so His work cannot be declared "good" until that time.

So then, *why* does the appreciation formula appear seemingly "out of place"? Because, like the other separations (in man, among the waters) the separating of light and darkness does not reach its *final*, permanent, providential form until later — on day 4 when the Lord creates the heavenly bodies "to govern the day and the night, and to separate the light from the darkness" (Gen. 1:18). Then, and only then, is God's separating the day from the night

---

17. The much later Septuagint translation wrongly "fixes" this deficiency by placing the formula in v. 8.

declared "good": "and God saw that it was good" (1:18). Irons (1998, 25) stumbles when he writes, "Apparently the separation had already been accomplished on day one, and it must have been sufficient enough for God to declare it to be 'good.' " He totally misreads the passage.

Thus, the rationale for withholding the divine appreciation formula from the separating of light and darkness, day and night, on day 1 is because the *final, providential means of separating light and dark does not prevail until the creation and appointment of the sun, moon, and stars for that purpose.* And this does not occur until later on day 4. As Kline (1970, 82) states of the divine appreciation formula, "In so far as they furthered that purpose [i.e., 'to be man's habitation'] various developments were called *good*." I agree with his developmental observation; but this supports the six-day creationist's sequential approach.

Irons (1998, 7) admits "the divine author has not only numbered the days, *a fact which by itself would lead to a sequential reading*." The sequencing of the days in seriatim fashion fits perfectly with the chronological view of the days as proposed by the *prima facie* reading of the passage and the historically accepted exegesis — though it goes contrary to the innovative requirements of the framework hypothesis. The "disruption" of the artistic balance does not present us with an interesting symmetric "dissonance" (Van Gemeren 1988, 45), but with an indispensable sequential demand.

5. Argument from Coherent Usage

The word *yôm* in Genesis 1 also defines days 4, 5, and 6. This is significant in that these days occur *after* God creates the sun expressly for undertaking the ongoing, providential task of marking off days (Gen. 1:14, 18). Interestingly, Moses even *emphasizes* day 4 by allocating the second greatest number of words to describe the divine activity of that day (day 6, the climax of the creation process, generates the largest volume of words). Not only so, but this day also has a larger statement of purpose, as compared to the other days prior to day 6:

> Then God said, "Let there be lights in the expanse of the heavens [1] *to separate* the day from the night, and let them be [2] *for signs* and *for seasons* and *for days and years*; and let them be [3] *for lights* in the expanse of the heavens [4] *to give* light on the earth"; and it was so. God made the two great lights, the greater light [5] *to govern* the day, and the lesser light [6] *to govern* the night; He made the stars also. God placed them in the expanse of the heavens [7] *to give light* on the earth, and [8] *to govern* the day and the night, and [9] *to separate* the light from the darkness; and God saw that it was good" (Gen. 1:14–18, emphasis added).

Surely day 4 and the following two days of creative activity are normal days — even actual *sun*-governed days. How could Moses inform his audience of the sun's creation for the expressly stated purpose of governing the day/night pattern, call this a "day," and *not* expect that his readership would also assume days 4 through 6 are real, historical days?

In fact, nothing in the text suggests a change of temporal function for *yôm* at day 4. Moses employs a coherent usage of his expressions, maintaining his set pattern while allowing a smooth flow of temporal process from the first three days into the last three days of God's creative activity. Each of the first three days is measured by the very same common, temporal designator (*yôm*), along with the same qualifiers ("evening and morning" boundaries, numerical prefixes, and numbered series placement). Should not days 1–3, then, demarcate 24-hour days also? Though the sun itself does not exist on day 1, the supernaturally created, regularly sequenced light does. And it does so in such a way that God declares that the light/dark pattern create "one day." Then on day 4, the sun is specifically designed to take over that lighting activity. (For more on the "problem" of day 4, see later discussion.)

Once again, we see the coherence of Moses' revelation — a coherence that points to a pattern of six sequential, 24-hour days within earth history.

6. Argument from Divine Exemplar

The Scripture specifically patterns man's workweek after God's own original creation week. Our workweek follows the pattern God established at creation:

- "For in six days the LORD made the heavens and the earth, the sea and all that is in them, and rested the seventh day; therefore the LORD blessed the Sabbath day and made it holy" (Exod. 20:11).
- "For six days work is to be done, but the seventh day is a day of sabbath rest, holy to the LORD. . . . It will be a sign between me and the Israelites forever; for in six days the LORD made the heavens and the earth, and on the seventh day he rested and was refreshed" (Exod. 31:15–17).

As Collins (2006, 89) notes, these verses undoubtedly make "an explicit reference to the creation Sabbath" in Genesis 2:1–3. We see a clear reflection of this Genesis 2 passage in the use of "LORD," "heaven and earth," "work," "seventh day," "rest," "blessed," and "made holy." We should also note that the Ten Commandments were directly written in the tablets of stone by God himself (Exod. 31:18, 32:15– 16, 34:1; Deut. 9:10).

Dabney's (1973, 255) comments are helpful in this regard: "In Gen. ii:2,3; Exod. xx:11, God's creating the world and its creatures in six days, and resting the seventh, is given as the ground of His sanctifying the Sabbath day. The latter is the natural day; why not the former? The evasions from this seem peculiarly weak." Young (1976, 47) writes: "In Ex. 20:11 the activity of God is presented to man as a pattern, and this fact presupposes that there was a reality in the activity of God which man is to follow. How could man be held accountable for working six days if God Himself had not actually worked six days?" Biblical scholars such as Louis Berkhof, Douglas Kelly, Noel Weeks, Robert Reymond, and many others agree.[18] (We must recognize that for the Jew and the Christian, the seven-day structure of the week derives from the original creation work of God. But this was not the case for pagan culture, which explains why we have pagan names for the days of the week.[19])

As stated in these passages, such is not for purposes of analogy (as per the framework hypothesis), but *imitation*. The Fourth Commandment clearly provides the reason that man shall work for six days and rest one day: "*For* [*kiy*] in six days" the Lord created all things, then rested (Exod. 20:11). The first-century Jewish historian Josephus wrote, "Accordingly Moses says, That in just six days the world, and all that is therein, was made. And that the seventh day was a rest, and a release from the labor of such operations; whence it is that we celebrate a rest from our labors on that day, and call it the Sabbath, which word denotes rest in the Hebrew tongue" (*Antiquities,* 1:1:1 §33). Calvin agrees: "I have said above, that six days were employed in the formation of the world; not that God, to whom one moment is as a thousand years, had need of this succession of time, but that He might engage us in the consideration of His works. He had the same end in view in the appointment of His own *rest,* for He set apart a day selected out of the remainder for this special use."[20]

---

18. John Calvin, *Commentaries of the First Book of Moses Called Genesis,* trans. John King (Grand Rapids, MI: Eerdmans, 1948), 1:78; see also, Berkhof 1941, 155; Young 1964, 45–47; Weeks 1988, 115; Kelly 1997, 109; Reymond 1998, 395.

19. In ancient pagan culture, the structure of the seven-day week was based on the seven visible "planets." Each day of the week was named after these "planets." The word "planet" is from the Greek *planânô* ("I wander") and refers to the seven stellar objects in the sky that did not appear to be fixed against the backdrop of the more distant, seemingly set stars: the sun, the moon, Mercury, Venus, Mars, Jupiter, and Saturn. Our current weekday names come from the Germanic-Norse culture through Hellenistic astrology: Sunday is based on Sunni (the sun); Monday is based on Mani (the moon); Tuesday is Tyr (Mars); Wednesday is Mercury (Woden); Thursday is Jupiter (Thor); Friday is Venus (Frigg); Saturday is Saturn.

20. Calvin, *Commentaries of the First Book of Moses Called Genesis,* 1:78 (at Gen. 1:5), 107 (at Gen. 2:3).

The phrase "in the space of six days" employs an "adverbial accusative of extent of time" or an "accusative of duration" (Collins 2005, 141). Thus, it is accurately translated "in the space of six days," or even as Collins suggests: "over the course of six days." As Hebrew professor Shaw (1999, 215) notes of both Exodus 20:11 and 31:17, "In both places the expected preposition *b* seems to be missing. This is the use of the accusative of temporal determination, a usage that indicates *how long* an action took." And we should note that this is not exalted prose (as in Gen. 1), but legal prescription.

Interestingly, as God does here in writing the Ten Commandments, elsewhere we see the creation order used to establish a pattern in several moral-spiritual contexts. For instance, Paul limits the preaching ministry to males on the basis of the fact of the historical order of the Fall: "I do not allow a woman to teach or exercise authority over a man, but to remain quiet. *For* [Gk.: *gar*] it was Adam who was first created, and then Eve" (1 Tim. 2:12–13).[21] And however we interpret the culturally difficult text in 1 Corinthians 11, the fact is that Paul bases a spiritual argument for male headship and a woman's head covering on the historical order of the creation of Adam first, then Eve: "For man does not originate from woman, but woman from man" (1 Cor. 11:8).

Consequently, man's workweek is *subsequent* to God's original creative week and is patterned after it. To make Genesis 1 a mere literary framework (as per the framework hypothesis) inverts divine revelation and denies historical reality, for man's week then becomes a pattern for God's! It effectively takes up Voltaire's maxim: "If God created us in his own image, we have more than reciprocated." As Young (1964, 78–79), following Aalders, remarks, "Man is to 'remember' the Sabbath day, for God has instituted it. . . . The human week derives validity and significance from the creative week. The Fourth Commandment

---

21. The Greek word *gar* has its primary function as a "marker of cause or reason, for." BAGD, 189.

constitutes a decisive argument against any non-chronological scheme of the six days of Genesis one" (compare Weeks 1988, 112). Fretheim argues incisively that the Fourth Commandment is "stated in terms of the imitation of God or a divine precedent that is to be followed: God worked for six days and rested on the seventh, and therefore you should do the same," and that such a command is *not* for the purpose of analogy.[22] If God did not create "in the space of six days" followed by a day of rest establishing a seven-day week, we have no reason for Israel's workweek.

Gerard Hasel makes an important hermeneutical observation on Exodus 20:11 and its significance to the creation debate. This text provides "an internal Pentateuch and Old Testament guideline" as to how God intended us to understand the days of Genesis 1 (Hasel 1984, 19). Thus the historical action serves as the rationale for the moral injunction. Interestingly, framework proponent Wenham (1987, 36) comments, "Exod 16:22–30 suggests that Israel first learned about the Sabbath in the wilderness, though Exod 20:8, like this passage [Gen. 2:2–3], asserts that the Sabbath idea is as old as creation itself. In observing the seventh day as holy, man is imitating his creator's example."

Kline (1996, 7) notes that "earthly time is articulated in the astronomical phenomena that structure its flow." That is certainly true for days (based on the period of time required for one rotation of the earth between successive sunrises), months (based on the lunar phase cycle ["month" is a cognate of "moon"]), and years (the orbital period of the earth revolving around the sun which, due to its angle relative to the sun, generates the four seasons). But this is not true for the *week*. The calendrical week is rooted in an historical, not astronomical, reality; it is rooted in God's original creative activity, just as Exodus 20:11 and 31:15–17 inform us.

---

22. Terence E. Fretheim, "Were the Days of Creation Twenty-Four Hours Long?" in *The Genesis Debate: Persistent Questions About Creation and the Flood*, ed. Ronald R. Youngblood (Nashville: Nelson, 1986), 20.

God dwells in timeless eternity (Isa. 57:15) where there is no succession of moments or temporal constraints (2 Pet. 3:8). Consequently, to what could the creation days be analogous? Irons (1998, 66) states that "God has not chosen to reveal that information." But as Pipa (1999, 172) complains: "Then the analogy is useless." Nor may we suggest that the days are anthropomorphic days,[23] for anthropomorphic language "can be applied to God alone and cannot properly be used of the six days" (Young 1964, 58). Old Testament scholar Beall (2010, 159) agrees: "Anthropomorphisms usually take the form of a body part or organ or movement to describe God's actions, but they never take the form of a unit of time such as a day." Besides, as Zylstra (2000, 5) queries, "Would it be plausible to suggest that Moses uses 'days' in two different senses here?" That is, as both literal and metaphorical, temporal and eternal?

I will return to the Sabbath question again in the next chapter when I begin examining and critiquing the framework position more closely.

7. Argument from Plural Expression

Exodus 20:11 and 31:17 also teach that God created the heavens and the earth "in six *days*" (*yāmiym*). As Reymond (1998, 394) reminds us, "Ages are never expressed by the word *yammim*." In fact, the plural *yāmiym* occurs 858 times in the Old Testament and always refers to normal days.[24] And this begins in creation week on day 4 when God establishes the sun to mark off "days" (Gen. 1:14). Exodus 20:11 (like Gen. 1) lacks any kind of poetic structure; it presents a factual, historical accounting. By this shorthand statement, God sums up His creative activity in a way that not only comports with, but actually demands a six-day creative process.

---

23. As per Majority Report 1999, 8–9; Irons 1998, 67–68; Blocher 1984, 50–57.
24. For a discussion of Hos. 6:2 and the apparent contradiction of this fact, see discussion above.

Interestingly, Exodus 20:11 lacks the preposition b^e. Thus, God's working six days is expressed by means of the accusative of temporal determination, "a usage that indicates how long an action took. . . . That is, 'during six days God made the heavens and the earth.' This use implies both that the days were normal days, and that the days were contiguous" (Shaw 1999, 217).[25] In addition, analogical day advocate Collins (2005, 142) discounts the framework view in noting that Exodus 20:11 "helps to confirm what most see in the Genesis 1 account, namely, the existence of sequence and of extent of time."

8. Argument from Unusual Statement

Due to the common Jewish practice of reckoning days from evening to evening (e.g., Exod. 12:18; Lev. 23:5), the temporal pattern "evening and morning" may seem unusual (because it assumes the day began in the morning, passes into evening, and then closes at the next morning). But Cassuto (1998, 28) explains that "whenever clear reference is made to the relationship between a given day and the next, it is precisely sunrise that is accounted the beginning of the second day."[26] For example, Exodus 12:18 has the 14th evening at the conclusion of the 14th day (compare Lev. 23:32).

Therefore, Genesis 1 presents literal days reckoned according to the civil — non-ritual, i.e., typological, symbolic — pattern. We see evening closing the daylight time, followed by morning, which closes the darkness, thereby beginning a new day (e.g., Gen. 19:33–34; Exod. 10:13; 2 Sam. 2:32). As non-six-day creationist Walton well notes, "The coming of evening and then of morning marked the first series of transitions and completed the cycle. . . . In other words, on day one there was no morning as a transition, simply God's creative act of daylight." Again, this all

---

25. See Paul Joüon, *A Grammar of Biblical Hebrew*, T. Muraoka, tr. and rev. (Rome: Pontifical Biblical Institute, 1991), Par. 126i.
26. Compare Hamilton 1990, 121; Kidner 1967, 47.

dovetails nicely with the traditional interpretation of a creation "in six days" (Exod. 20:11, 31:17) against the literary view of an open-ended creation time frame consuming billions of years, as per Kline (1996, 1).

9. Argument from Alternative Idiom

Had Moses intended that the six days represent six eras, he could have chosen a less confusing and more fitting expression: *ôlām*. This word is often translated "forever," but it also means a long period of time. For instance, *ôlām* describes the temporal longevity (short of eternity) of the Passover (Exod. 12:24), a slave's commitment to his earthly master (Exod. 21:6), various levitical functions (Exod. 29:28, 30:21; Lev. 6:18, 22, 7:34, 36, 10:15, 16:29, 31, 17:7, 23:14, 21, 41, 24:3; Num. 18:8; etc.), and Joshua's memorial stones (Josh. 4:7). According to *The Interpreter's Bible,* "There can be no question but that by *Day* the author meant just what we mean — the time required for one revolution of the earth on its axis. Had he meant an aeon he would certainly, in view of his fondness for great numbers, have stated the number of millenniums each period embraced."[27]

Furthermore, Moses should not have qualified the days with "evening and morning." This, of course, is more relevant to the day age theory, but it serves to broaden the evidentiary basis of the traditional, literal six-day creationist view.

10. Argument from Scholarly Admissions

Remarkably, scholars who deny the reality of the historically accepted exegetical conclusion of a six-day creation process recognize Moses actually meant literal days:

- Herman Gunkel: "The 'days' are of course days and nothing else."[28]

---

27. George Arthur Buttrick, ed., *The Interpreter's Bible*, Vol. 1 Genesis-Exodus (Nashville, TN: Abingdon, 1952), p. 471.
28. Cited in Hasel (1984: 21).

- BDB (1972, 398) presents "*Day* as division of time" and refers to Genesis 1 then states: "day as defined by evening and morning."
- Gerhard von Rad: "The seven days are unquestionably to be understood as actual days and as a unique, unrepeatable lapse of time in the world."[29]
- John Skinner: "The interpretation of *yôm* as eon is opposed to the plain sense of the passage and has no warrant in Hebrew usage."[30]
- Walter Russell Bowie: "There can be no question that by Day the author meant just what we mean — the time required for one revolution of the earth on its axis."[31]
- Adolf Dillman: "The reasons advanced by ancient and modern writers for construing these days to be periods of time are inadequate."[32]
- James Barr: "If the word day in these chapters does not mean a period of twenty-four hours, the interpretation of Scripture is hopeless. So far as I know, there is no professor of Hebrew or Old Testament at any world-class university who does not believe that the writers of Genesis1–11 intended to convey to their readers that creation took place in a series of six days which were the same as the days of twenty-four hours we now experience."[33]
- *Theological Lexicon of the Old Testament* (2, 528) asserts that *yôm* in Genesis 1 means "in the sense of the astronomical or calendrical unit."
- Victor Hamilton (1990, 54): "Whoever wrote Gen. 1 believed he was talking about literal days."

29. G. von Rad, *Genesis*, rev. ed., trans. J.H. Markes (Philadelphia, PA: Westminster, 1972), p. 65.
30. John Skinner, *A Critical Commentary on Genesis*, 2 ed. (Edinburgh: T and T Clark, 1930), p. 21.
31. Walter Russell Bowie, "Genesis," in George Arthur Buttrick, ed, *The Interpreter's Bible* (Nashville, TN: Abingdon, 1952), 1:471.
32. Cited in Leupold (1942, 57).
33. Personal communication cited in Kelly (1997, 51).

- TDOTTE (2, 420): "Its primary meaning is the time of daylight as distinct from the period of darkness, the night. For example, in Gen 1:5 God called the light 'day. . . . (b) The term is also used for day in the sense of the complete cycle that includes both daytime and nighttime, e.g., Gen 1:5: 'And there was evening, and there was morning — the first day.' "
- Gordon Wenham (1987, 19): "There can be little doubt that here 'day' has its basic sense of a 24-hour period. The mention of morning and evening, the enumeration of the days, and the divine rest on the seventh show that a week of divine activity is being described here."
- Howard Van Till (1986, 91): Theistic evolutionist Christian scholar Howard Van Till admits that "the days of the Genesis 1 story are clearly ordinary days."

Thus, Gerhard Hasel (1984, 21) concludes: "The author of Genesis 1 could not have produced more comprehensive and all-inclusive ways to express the idea of a literal 'day' than the ones that were chosen. There is a complete lack of indicators from prepositions, qualifying expressions, construct phrases, semantic-syntactical connections, and so on, on the basis of which the designation 'day' in the creation week could be taken to be anything different than a regular 24-hour day. The combinations of the factors of articular usage, singular gender, semantic-syntactical constructions, time boundaries, and so on, corroborated by the divine promulgations in such Pentateuchal passages as Exodus 20:8-11 and Exodus 31:12–17, suggest uniquely and consistently that the creation 'day' is meant to be literal, sequential, and chronological in nature."

Stambaugh engages a rather thorough semantic analysis of *yôm* in the Old Testament, emphasizing not merely its semantic meaning but its syntagmatic relations.[34] He states that

---

34. Stambaugh (2015, 2) cites Anthony C. Thiselton in defining "syntagmatic": "A syntagmatic relation 'is a linear relationship with other words or units with which it is chained together.' "

"the syntagmatic relationships of *yôm* in Genesis 1 have been considered and it has been demonstrated that, when used with a number, the pattern is always a normal time period. If 'night' is combined with *yôm*, it always denotes a 24-hour day. If *yôm* is used with either 'morning' or 'evening,' they too refer to a literal day. When 'morning' and 'evening' are used together, with *yôm*, it always signifies a solar day. So the syntagmatic relationships that *yôm* has illustrate clearly that the meaning is to be; considered a normal time period, consisting of one axial rotation of the earth, called a 'day.' " He concludes, "If something other than a literal day was intended by the use of *yôm* in Genesis 1, then the words of the text and reality have nothing in common. It seems clear, from the syntagmatic evidence, that the word, designated as a 'day' by Genesis 1, is a reference to a literal day of twenty-four hours" (Stambaugh: 2015, 5).

Though the word *yôm* can be used in a nonliteral sense, Hasel (1984, 15) points out that "the extended, nonliteral meanings of the term *yom* are always found in connection with prepositions, prepositional phrases with a verb, compound constructions, formulas, technical expressions, genitive combinations, construct phrases, and the like." But he notes on the same page that in Genesis 1 *yôm* is not "combined with a preposition, genitive combination, construct state, compound construction, or the like. It always appears as a plain noun."

Consequently, under divine inspiration while writing historical narrative, Moses informs us that God created the whole universe in the span of six chronologically successive and contiguous periods of 24-hour durations each. The evidence is overwhelming and not in the least "subtle." Again, as noted above, Young (1964, 192) argues, "If Moses had intended to teach a nonchronological view of the days it is indeed strange that he went out of his way, as it were, to emphasize chronology and sequence." Bédard (2013, 171) agrees: "It is difficult to imagine a use of language in Genesis 1 that could more clearly communicate that the universe was made in the space of six days." Framework advocate Mark Ross (1999, 18) honestly confesses, "It is admitted by all that the first impression of Genesis 1:1–2:3 is of a sequential, chronological account of a six-day creation with a seventh day of rest."

Incredibly, though, Irons and Kline (2001, 221) can state: "The order of narration alone is not sufficient in itself to determine the historical sequence; other considerations, such as theological concerns and general revelation, must be factored in as well." They declare this *as if* a simple order of narration stands alone in Genesis 1.

Yet Blocher (1984, 50) attempts to stave off the traditional view of Genesis 1 by stating, "The rejection of all the theories accepted by the scientists requires considerable bravado." I would note that the same can be said of the affirmation of the fact that God created the world (by whatever means) and the belief in the special creation of Adam in God's image. Such bravado must have moved Copernicus and Galileo to reject the prevailing, centuries-old Aristotelian science paradigm in their day. I would turn the charge upon Blocher. I would complain that it "requires considerable bravado" to reject all the exegetical evidence from Scripture that I present above. I do not see how God could have made it *more* clear than He has.

Speaking of bravado, Bédard (2013, 101) well complains that the "proponents of the figurative views tend to say that they are sure that they know what the primary purpose of God was when He wrote Genesis. It usually indicates that they cannot accept the literal interpretation of the text." And their confidence is rooted in purposes that are *not* stated in the text (as are the exegetical evidences for the formative history of the world actually found in Genesis 1). Instead, they argue that the creation narrative is basically declaring God created the world, or is providing a sabbatic theology, or a polemic against idolatry, or whatever.

For instance, framework commentator Arnold (1998, 23) writes that "the important lesson from Genesis 1 is that he did in fact create it, and that he made it orderly and good in every respect."[35] (Of course, in any evolutionary-influenced view of origins, the creation process must include volcanism, earthquakes, tectonic upheaval, tsunamis, recurring animal death, the extinction of whole species, and more as "orderly and good in every respect.") Longman (2005, 107) agrees with Arnold: "So what is the creation account telling us? God created creation! Genesis 1–2 celebrates God's creation of the universe." Indeed, he holds that Genesis is "not concerned to tell us the process of creation. Rather it is intent on simply celebrating and asserting the fact that God is Creator" (Longman 2005, 104). Or consider Irons and Kline (2001, 226): "Deliberate schematic arrangements are a common feature of scriptural history. In this case we are particularly concerned with *sabbatical* symbolism used to structure biblical history." They even go so far as to argue that "the real theological message has been drowned out by its alleged sequential and chronological message. This fundamental misreading of the text is based on an unexamined assumption regarding the nature of biblical history" (2001, 218). "Alleged sequential and chronological message"? How is reading the text as it stands "alleged"? And how can such be deemed a "fundamental misreading"?

As Kulikovsky (2001, 237) complains, if Genesis 1 is only presenting us with a theology of the Sabbath, "why is there so much excess detail?" In fact, he echoes Davis when he muses, "If all Genesis 1–2 communicates is that God is creator of all, then the first verse would be enough" (Kulikovsky 2001, 242).[36] Dyer (1999, 234) points out that when all is said and done, "The literary framework hypothesis reduces the entire chapter to a general statement that God created everything in an orderly fashion.

---

35. Arnold (1998, 24) advocates a framework structure for Gen. 1. And though he holds to the necessity of God in the creation process and a special creation for man (p. 27), he states that young-earth creationism runs count to "current geological evidence [that] suggests the earth is around 4.5 billion years old." Then he states that "we should not be too concerned with the issue of how long it took God to create the universe" (p. 23).
36. Compare Davis 1975, 75.

How God actually did create is left unanswered. We end up with too much saying too little."

But even if these purposes lie behind the Genesis creation narrative, Duncan (2001, 25) notes, "The mere presence of an apologetic in the narrative does not compromise the cosmogony it contains." God can inspire factual history in support of theological truths and in opposition to religious error. In fact, true history under the sovereign creative and providential activity of God *is* a statement against all forms of unbelief. Indeed, "If the cosmogony or aspects of it are merely a literary framework or a didactic tool, then the theology loses its force in countering pagan opinion" (Duncan 2001, 25).

Remarkably, framework proponents can read Genesis 1 with all of these indicators and declare: "We should not be too concerned with the issue of how long it took God to create the universe. . . . If it were important to know how long it took God to create the world, the Bible would have made it clear" (Arnold 1998, 23)! And Longman (2005, 104) argues, "It appears that Genesis itself is not interested in giving us a clear and unambiguous understanding of the nature of the creation days. This ambiguity fits in with the overall impression we get of the passage, that it is not concerned to tell us the process of creation. Rather it is intent on simply celebrating and asserting the fact that God is Creator." He goes on to state, "As we read Genesis 1–2 closely, we note just how little the narrative is interested in telling us about the process of creation" (Longman: 2005, 106). Apparently, Moses did not take into account the ingenuity of Christian scholars in reinterpreting Scripture according to the latest scientific theories. Sadly, they seem to be asking, "Indeed, has God said?"

Despite all the evidence for Genesis 1 presenting 24-hour days, framework (and analogical day and day age) advocates see problems. I will now turn to briefly consider these.

Chapter 5

Response to Literalism Problems

The framework school absolutely rejects the traditional view of Genesis 1 and the creation narrative. Irons and Kline (2001, 89) declare, "The 24-hour interpretation is decisively refuted by several exegetical problems — especially the Day 1/Day 4 problem and the unending nature of Day 7." Several of these "problems" some scholars have with the six-day creation position are generated from within the day age camp, rather than the framework hypothesis school. Nevertheless, I desire to demonstrate the integrity of the traditional exegesis that results in a literal, six-day creation approach to Genesis 1, even as I respond to the framework hypothesis specifically. Later I will counter other alleged "problems" with the historically accepted view of Genesis 1 while critiquing the three-fold foundation of the framework hypothesis (see chapters 6ff).

The Fourth Day Problem (Gen. 1:14-19)

Objection

On day 4, God creates the sun to "give light on the earth" (1:15) and "to separate the day from the night" (1:14). But light was previously created on day 1 (1:3), and there "God separated the light from the darkness" (1:4). This shows that the creation days are not chronologically ordered, but thematically cross-linked. In this particular case, day 4 is recapitulating day 1; it is not making chronological progress over day 1. Thompson (1968, 20) emphasizes that this "presents serious difficulties on any chronological view." Irons (1998, 25) concurs, noting that "neither the day-age nor the literal reading of Gen. 1 can do justice to the close connection between day one and day four."[1] In fact, this argument holds a special "importance as an independent argument against the solar-day and day-age views" (Kline 1996, 7). In their joint chapter, Irons and Kline (2001, 220) forcefully state the problem as they see it: "an outstanding instance of the nonsequential ordering is found in the relation of Days 1 and 4, where the narrative order does not coincide with the historical sequence."

The Framework Hypothesis Argument

I will specify the nature of the alleged problem framework advocates have with the traditional exegesis. Irons provides a helpful explanation and defense of the entire framework hypothesis in which he provides a succinct statement of the day 4 "problem." I will cite Irons first, then critique the argument. Irons presents the following three-fold argument:

(1) Framework hypothesis advocates complain that the traditional exegesis promotes an unnecessary supernaturalism. "Those who wish to maintain a literal, sequential reading argue that the light of day one was maintained by supernatural power (or at least some non-ordinary means) for three days, until the creation of the luminaries on day four. . . . But this interpretation is inconsistent with the principle stated in Genesis 2:5: during the creation period, God maintained the created entities by ordinary providence rather than supernatural power" (Irons 1998, 25). Elsewhere he cites Kline's maxim "that there was an

---

1. See also M. Ross 1999, 119–20.

'avoidance of unnecessary supernaturalism in providence' during the creation week" (Irons 1998, 34).[2] Futato (1998, 17) adds that day 4 must recapitulate day 1 because "light without luminaries is not part of the real world in which the original audience lived."

(2) Framework hypothesis proponents argue that the traditional exposition suppresses the significance of the sun's creation. On their view, the literal interpretation:

> . . . does not explain why the luminaries were said to have been created "in order to give light on the earth . . . and to separate the light from the darkness' (1:17–18). It would be one thing if the text had said that the luminaries were created in order *to maintain* the previously created light and the previously established separation. But that is not what the text says. Rather, the luminaries were created in order *to give* light and *to separate* the light from the darkness. Exegetically there is no way around the stubborn fact that the divine purpose for the creation of light on day one and the purpose of the creation [*sic*] the luminaries on day four are one and the same" (Irons 1998, 25).

(3) Framework hypothesis adherents suggest that the long-accepted interpretation overlooks the integrity of the divine labor. "Furthermore, even if an exegetical case could be made for reading the two infinitives ('to separate' — 1:14, 18) as shorthand for 'to maintain the separation,' there would still be another problem. Apparently, the separation had already been accomplished on day one, and it must have been sufficient enough for God to declare it to be 'good.' Why, then, does God feel the need to discard that arrangement and replace it with a new one on day four?" (Irons 1998, 25).

---

2. Compare Kline 1958, 150.

Some would proffer other "problems,"[3] but Irons has nicely summarized these as the leading framework counter-evidences against the historic, traditional, and confessional exegesis.

The Traditional Interpretation Response

I will interact with Irons' presentation in reverse order. I would note, first, that Irons stumbles in his third argument by misreading the day 1 account. He mistakenly claims "the separation" was "sufficient enough for God to declare it to be 'good.' " His error is caused not only by a superficial reading of these verses, but by failing to note the pattern of their setting. Since this has already been noted above, I will only briefly rehearse the matter here.

We must understand that on day 1 God declares "good" the newly created *light* — but *not* His *separating* it from darkness to form the day/night pattern. "Then God said, 'Let there be light'; and there was light. God saw that the light was good; and God separated the light from the darkness" (Gen. 1:3–4). Note that *after* God declares the newly created light "good," *then* He separates the light from the darkness (Gen. 1:3-4). This unusual pattern (appreciation formula *before* completion of work) occurs for a reason: the final, providential mechanism for separating night and day (the sun, moon, and stars) will not be created until day 4.

Thus, when day 4 ends, and the permanent historical, providential means for separating light from darkness is in place, we finally read it "was good": "God placed them in the expanse of the heavens to give light on the earth, and to govern the day and the night, and to separate the light from the darkness; and God saw that it was good" (Gen. 1:17–18). This matter is widely noted by

---

3. For instance, we often hear the complaint that vegetation cannot grow without the sun. But this is no problem to the traditional view: First, actually plants require *light*, and God directly creates that on the First Day. Besides, even today plants can be grown indoors with artificial light, quite out of the reach of the sun. Surely if man can accomplish this, God can. Second, even apart from this consideration, on the traditional interpretation the plants would only be denied sunlight for a few hours — less than one day, for on day 4 God creates the sun.

commentators.[4] For instance, Hamilton (1990, 120) well argues, "The major difference between this work of separation and the other two in Genesis 1 is that here the pronouncement of God's benedictional statement — *God saw how beautiful the light was* — precedes the separation. In vv. 6–8 and 14–19 this sentence of evaluation follows the separation. Thus it is the light itself that is *beautiful* (or good, Heb., *tôb*), not the creation per se of time into units of light and darkness."

As observed previously, this is similar to the separation of the waters above and below on day 2, which is not declared "good" until the final separation from the land on day 3 (Gen. 1:9) (Waltke 1976, 29). Waltke notes, "The sky was separated from the water on the second day, but no pronouncement of good was given because spatial separation was not yet complete. Only with the separation of land, the third life supportive system, did God pronounce the spatial separation as good or complete" (Waltke 1976, 29).

Irons' mistake is no mere writer's gaffe; rather it exposes a fault line running through the framework foundation itself. The well-ordered revelation of Genesis 1 assumes chronological progress — even here where the sequential approach is thought doomed. Thus, *even the appreciation statements await the proper stage of progress and are not spoken too soon.*

Kline (1996, 9) complains that creating light on day 1 and the light-bearers on day 4 "would raise questions about the wisdom of the divine procedure." M. Ross (1999, 121) agrees: "God supplies an alternative means for producing these effects. That in itself raises questions about the divine procedure (why the need for an intermediate solution? What purpose was served by the day-and-night cycle, the light-and-darkness separation, prior to day four?)." Why would God create a light source on day 1, then create the sun for purposes of lighting on day 4?

---

4. See Keil and Delitzsch 1998, 54 (n1); Cassuto 1998, 34, 40; Wenham 1987, 19; Mathews 1996, 151. Waltke 1976, 29; Sailhammer 1990, 26; and Hamilton 1990, 124.

But the final establishment of the permanent arrangement on day 4 no more casts a shadow upon God's wisdom than does his employing separate and distinct fiats to separate the waters above and below (1:6), *then* on the next "day" the land from the waters (1:9). We might ask as well: Why would God create Adam alone, and even bring the animals to him, before creating woman to be his helper? Or why did God not create all things at once? Why did He allow sin to enter and corrupt his good creation? In the final analysis we must always remember: "'My thoughts are not your thoughts, nor are your ways My ways,' declares the Lord. 'For as the heavens are higher than the earth, so are My ways higher than your ways and My thoughts than your thoughts'" (Isa. 55:8–9).

Besides, this two-step procedure surely casts less doubt upon "the wisdom of the divine procedure" than does a creation over billions of years, for the evolutionary method of creating entails tremendous chaos and upheaval, the arising of sentient life forms, genetic mutations, the constant pain, suffering, and death of individual members over millions of generations, and the extinction of whole species — a "Nature, red in tooth and claw" (Tenneyson).

The historical, six-day creation understanding of Genesis 1 greatly emphasizes the wisdom, power, and majesty of God by creating rapidly and "very good" (Gen. 1:31), without the trial-and-error destruction of whole families of sentient life forms. As Hebrew scholar and analogical day advocate Collins (2006, 75) notes regarding the appreciation formula "it was good": "The effect of this, besides reinforcing the idea that creation is entirely good, is to drive home the divine pleasure in the material creation: its goodness means that it pleases him." But the non-survival of the least fit does not seem to match up to a good creation by God — especially since His prophets can envision an eschatology that surely reflects protology, where "the wolf will dwell with the lamb, and the leopard will lie down with the young goat, and the calf and the young lion and the fatling together; and a little boy will lead them. Also the cow and the bear will graze, their young will lie down together, and the lion will eat straw like the ox" (Isa 11:6–7). Or in which "the wolf and the lamb will graze together, and the lion will eat straw like the ox" so that "they will do no evil or harm in all My holy mountain" (Isa 65:25). This imagery surely reflects the original peaceful and herbivorous diet of man and beast alike (Gen. 1:29–30).

This is especially problematic for the wisdom of God due to its temporal implications, for we must realize that this demands that after such a multi-billion-year creation process, we have only just *very, very recently* exited that creation process — and now after a couple of hundred thousand years are expecting the return of Christ to *end* the temporal order! This is all the more remarkable in that "the framework advocates teach that the 'six days' of creation comprises a closed era within which God completed His work of creation" (Irons and Kline 2001, 235). Since they believe in evolution, and evolution continues, when did the creation era close?

What is more, Scripture teaches God's redemptive plan was planned prior to creation: "He chose us in Him before the foundation of the world, that we would be holy and blameless before Him" (Eph. 1:4; compare 2 Thess. 2:13; Rev. 13:8, 17:8). Dabney (1973, 263) aptly suggests that it is "reasonable to suppose that [God] would produce at once the world which He needed for His purpose" rather than waiting for an enormous period of time. Why would God have this pre-temporal redemptive plan, then take 13.8 billion years to create the universe in which man only arises about 200,000 years ago? This gives new meaning to "God is patient." As Dyer (1999, 230) muses, "It would be like having hours and hours of prelude for a five-minute program."

In fact, most of the material in Genesis 1 *demands* chronological order. Even framework advocates recognize this, though they write it off as "accidental" — despite the numbered-series

structure, the recurring evening and morning cycles, and all else
we have discussed.[5] Irons and Kline (2001, 220) admit that "we
cannot conclude that *nothing* in the text has been arranged sequentially. The Sabbath of the seventh day, for example, must
follow the previous six days of creation, and man is created last
due to his position of delegated dominion over creation." Such a
context and flow suggests that even the surprising order of light-
then-sun must also be chronological.

Not only is Genesis 1 structured by 55 *waw* consecutives
(see discussion below), indicating narrative sequence, but note:
separating the waters on day 2 requires their prior creation on
day 1 (Gen. 1:2). Creating the sea on day 3 must predate the sea
creatures of day 5. Day 3 logically has dry land appearing before
land vegetation later that day. Day 3 must also predate day 6, in
that land must precede land animals and man. In fact, days 1–4
establish the environment of man and animal. Day 6 must appear as the last stage of creation, in that man forms the obvious
climax to God's creation. Day 6 logically has man being created
after animal life (days 5 and 6) in that he is commanded to rule
over the animals. Day 7 must conclude the series in that it announces the cessation of creation (Gen. 2:2). And so on.

Collins (2006, 73) well notes that "Kline's version of the
framework view does not suit the data. To begin with, it would
make the workweek of creation into three days (told from two
perspectives) instead of six." Yet it is clear from God's own statement of the Fourth Commandment that His creative activity was
accomplished "in six days" (Exod. 20:11). Collins (2006, 74)
continues by noting that this commandment uses the "Hebrew
accusative of time, expressing the extent of time over which the
work is distributed."

Irons' second argument is widely deemed a serious
complication for the traditional view by those adopting an
artistic-literary approach to Genesis 1. Framework advocates

---

5. Futato 1998, 1; Irons 1998, 59 n128; Blocher 1984, 50.

argue that the luminaries are created *to give* light and *to separate* light and darkness, but that these functions are already taken care of on day 1. The luminaries, they argue, are not to *maintain* that which already exists — they *establish* it. In addition to that which is noted above from Irons' paper, we learn from the Majority Report (1999, 4) that God "named the light 'Day' and the darkness 'Night' (Gen. 1:5). In naming them, he established their essential character and significance. If the characters were to change; the names would need to change as well." Thus, it is felt, these cannot be distinct creative events from separate creational days; day 4 must be recapitulating day 1.

Consider the following response:

This does not seem a significant problem to many notable commentators. For one example, Hamilton (1990, 121) notes, "What the author states is that God caused the light to shine from a source other than the sun for the first three 'days.' " In his footnote (1990, 121 n7) he explains that "the Bible begins and ends by describing an untarnished world that is filled with light, but no sun (cf. Rev. 22:5). Should not the one who is himself called 'light' (1 John 1:5) have at his disposal many sources by which he dispatches light into his creation? Just as Gen. 1 says there can be a day and light without sun, so Matt. 2 says there can be a son without a father. Calvin comments, 'Therefore the Lord, by the very order of creation, bears witness that he holds in his hands the light, which he is able to impart to us without the sun and moon.' " Young (1964, 95) agrees "that the heavenly bodies are made on the fourth day and that the earth had received light from a source other than the sun is not a naive conception, but is a plain and sober statement of the truth."

Furthermore, Scripture elsewhere suggests that light existed apart from the sun. Job 38:19 challenges: "Where is the way to the dwelling of light?" If the answer is "the sun," the question is not all that much of a challenge. Second Corinthians 4:6 declares, "For God, who said, 'Light shall shine out of darkness.' "

Clearly, "The language of vv. 5–6 resonates with key vocabulary used of the creation in the opening chapter of Genesis ('image of God,' 'God . . . said,' 'Let there be light')."[6] In fact, the Bible begins (Gen. 1:3) and ends with light existing apart from the sun (Rev 22:5).

In addition, after surveying the evidence, Young (1964, 97) declares, "Day four, we may assert with all confidence, presupposes the existence of the light which was created in day one." The revelation of God's creating the astral bodies on day 4 *assumes* the chronological sequence outlined in Genesis 1. Day 4 presupposes that light/darkness and day/night already exist. On day 1 (1) God creates the light by direct fiat; (2) personally separates it from the darkness; then (3) calls the light "Day" and the darkness "Night" (1:5). On day 4, though, God creates the *luminaries* (*mā'ôr*, "place of light") themselves, "to separate the day from the night" (1:14) and "the light from the darkness" (1:18).

Notice the way the "Day" and the "Night" are mentioned: the *luminaries* are to separate that which *already* exists ("light" and "darkness"), and this light and darkness produce an effect already established ("day" and "night"). The luminaries do not *initiate* the light, nor do they begin the light/dark sequencing; that was established on day 1. The sun was created to fit the day, not vice versa. On day 1, God created the light *de novo* and named the "day" and the "night"; on day 4 he creates the "place of light," the *mā'ôr*, i.e., the "luminaries." The luminaries are "set" to take over the lighting function, to "govern" its coming and going (Cassuto 1998, 43). As Hamilton (1990, 121) puts it: "The creation of light anticipates the creation of sunlight." Furthermore, the luminaries are placed "in the expanse of the heavens" (1:14, 17), which was not created until day 2. And the luminaries formed on day 4 are to "give light on the earth" (1:15), which function assumes the prior extrusion of the earth's

---

6. Paul Barnett, *The Second Epistle to the Corinthians* (NICNT) (Grand Rapids, MI: Eerdmans, 1997), p. 225. Barnett should have begun with 2 Cor. 4:4, not at 4:5.

surface from beneath the waters and its naming ("earth") on day 3 (1:10).

The Majority Report (1999, 4) correctly observed that naming the "day" and the "night" establishes "their essential character and significance." This is *precisely* in keeping with my previous arguments, and this helps confirm my commitment to a literal 24-hour day. By God's creating light, then naming its earthly appearance "day," we learn the character of the day that God has ordained for temporal history: it is (1) a period of time, (2) for light to shine on the earth, that (3) continually returns (4) during every 24-hour cycle. What is the problem? We do not see the *sun* included in the definition of "day" here in Holy Writ, just the *light*. We know, of course, that *today* we think of the sun when we think of (day)light, but in Genesis 1 we are dealing with a unique period of time: the creation of the entire universe by the very command of God. From the very beginning, God established the time structure of the created order by ordaining the cycles of light and darkness — even before creating the sun.

What is more, Kline (1970, 82) even notes that the "heavens and earth" of Genesis 1:1 "are viewed in their earliest not perfected state, yet as a totality, this being the idiomatic force in Hebrew of such contrasted pairs."[7] As Wenham (1987, 15) expresses it, "Commentators often insist that the phrase 'heaven and earth' denotes the completely ordered cosmos. Though this is usually the case, totality rather than organization is its chief thrust here. It is therefore quite feasible for a mention of an initial act of creation of the whole universe (v 1) to be followed by an account of the ordering of different parts of the universe (vv 2–31)." Longman (2005, 103) explains in more detail: "Genesis 1 then seems to make a general statement in the first verse, 'God created the heavens and the earth,' and then proceeds to a more detailed telling of the story in which the first thing he created was matter, which was 'formless and empty mass,' covered by 'deep

---

7. Compare Kline 1977, 82; Young 1964, 95.

waters.' "[8] Consequently, the enormous change effected from the universe's "earliest not perfected state" to the final well-ordered condition does not require calling the *earliest* stage something other than "heavens and earth." Why may not the word "day" be used before and after the sun — especially since the four fundamental characteristics of the "day" still prevail?

The Majority Report (1999, 3) was quite mistaken when it alleged: "The 'Day' must be an ordinary day, governed and lighted by the sun. The 'Night' must be an ordinary night, governed and lighted by the moon and the stars. This is what those words mean. There is nothing in the text that suggests we are reading about an orderly alternation of light and darkness, supernaturally maintained in the absence of sun, moon, and stars."

In the first place, I have read and re-read the Mosaic revelation regarding day 1, and I have yet to find mention of "the sun." The word "day" (*yôm*) does not *mean* "an ordinary day, governed and lighted by the sun." The Hebrew word for the "sun" (*šemeš*) is not a constitute element of the word "day," which is *yôm*.[9] Secondly, despite the bold denial by our framework brothers, there

---

8. Compare Mathews 1996, 142; P. Taylor 2007, 2. McCabe (2010, 218) notes that "the mainline narrative does not begin until verse 3. This indicates that the first creative activity of verse 1 initiating the space and time continuum provides an informing background for the development of the narrative line in Genesis 1:3–2:3." Then he shows that the mainline employs 46 *waw* consecutives to progressively form and fill creation.

9. Apparently, the reason Moses does not mention the words "sun" or "moon" is because Israel had recently come from and is now on her way to regions that worshiped the sun and moon: Egypt and Canaan. Moses' creation account downplays the sun as something not to be worshiped. For instance, the word "place of light" is used ten times by Moses outside of Genesis 1. In every case it refers to a lamp (in the Tabernacle, Exod. 25:6, 27:20, 35:8, 14 [2x], 28, 39:37; Lev. 24:2; Num. 4:9, 16). The distinct impression left in Moses' slight to the sun and the moon is that they are not to be worshiped; they are but lamps. In fact, they are lamps to serve man by giving light and making seasons (1:14–15), so that the plants (Gen. 1:11-13) may grow for food (Gen 1:29, 2:9, 16). In Moses' other writings he warns against worship of the sun and moon (and stars) (Deut. 4:19, 17:3). This was a cultural temptation that eventually led Israel into such worship (2 Kings 17:16, 21:3, 23:5; Isa. 40:25–26). God even rebukes Babylon for just such actions (Isa. 47:13).

is, in fact, something "in the text that suggests we are reading about an orderly alternation of light and darkness, supernaturally maintained in the absence of sun, moon, and stars." Incredibly, *every element* of their denial is justified by reading the text of Genesis 1:3–5! Consider the text for yourself (with my interpretive comments in brackets): "Then God said, 'Let there be light' [this surely is a supernatural activity]; and there was light [this surely is a supernatural result — one that does *not* mention the sun at all]. God saw that the light [not "the sun"] was good; and God [Himself, supernaturally] separated the light from the darkness. God called the light [just mentioned] day, and the darkness He called night. And there was evening and there was morning, one day."

The Majority Report (1999, 4) was correct when it noted of "the man on the street" that "he would never guess from this language that what is being referred to is a sunless day." *But* the "man on the street" is not simply given a collection of terms — "day," "night," "morning," "evening" — to judge by. The man on the street should not be playing Scrabble, but reading Scripture. Neither is he left to "guess" about the meaning; rather, he is given a carefully structured passage revealing six successive days that states that the naked light was created on day 1, and *only later* on day 4 the sun, which becomes the bearer of that light. In *that* context, he would do what the "majority" (Blocher) of Christians have done from time immemorial: recognize that in this *unique* period, light existed three days *before* the sun. Thus, once again, we must recall that Ridderbos (1957, 29) confesses that "one who reads Genesis 1 without prepossession or suspicion is almost bound to receive the impression that the author's intent is to say that creation took place in six ordinary days." As noted earlier, framework advocate Mark Ross (1999, 118) agrees: "It is admitted by all that the first impression of Genesis 1:1–2:3 is of a sequential, chronological account of a six-day creation with a seventh day of rest."

Incredibly, the Majority Report (1999, 5) stated of the traditional view "that interpretation cannot possibly derive this impression from the text of the first three days." This is remarkable! For that is *precisely* the most immediate impression that is derived "from the text of the first three days." The framework hypothesis has to read material *back into* the text of the first three days, to make their view work. I stated that this assertion is "incredible" because after discounting the traditional interpretation that derives solely from what the text actually says, the Majority Report (1999, 8) reads into Genesis 1 the following anti-textual story: "The picture in Genesis 1 is clear. God wakes up. He works until evening. He lies down for the night and repeats the process in the morning." The literary approach of the framework hypothesis *denies* what is *expressly written* so that it may *declare* what is *absolutely omitted* from the text. To quote framework advocate Irons regarding his concerns in another context: "But that is not what the text says" (Irons 1998, 25).

Furthermore, the Majority Report (1999) argument is torn by dialectical tension in its own successive paragraphs on this point. On page 8 it states, "More subtle, but more to the point, God's manner of working is anthropomorphic. He works during the day. He stops when it gets dark. When the sun rises, He goes to work again." Notice the "more subtle" statement. The *American Heritage Dictionary* defines "subtle" as follows: "a. So slight as to be difficult to detect or analyze; elusive. b. Not immediately obvious; abstruse." But then in the very next paragraph in the Majority Report (1999) the original subtlety gives way to unmistakable clarity: "The picture in Genesis 1 is clear. God wakes up. He works until evening. He lies down for the night and repeats the process in the morning. The Spirit has gone out of His way to present the work of God on the analogy of the work of man."[10]

---

10. Framework writer Justin Taylor (2015: 5) agrees: "God is portrayed as a workman going through his workweek, working during the day and resting for the night. Then on his Sabbath he enjoys a full and refreshing rest. Our days are like God's workdays, but not identical to them." Collins' (2006, 77) presentation of the

Which is it? Is this picture "subtle," i.e., difficult to detect, elusive, as per paragraph five? Or is it so "clear" that it is evident "the Spirit has gone out of His way to present" the picture, as in paragraph six? Such exaggerations and contradictions constantly mar framework hypothesis presentations.

Now back to the matter of explaining the day 4 problem. According to Young (1964, 96), "The origin of heaven and earth, however, was simultaneous [cf. Gen. 1:1], but the present arrangement of the universe was not constituted until the fourth day. The establishment of this arrangement is expressed by the verb *wayitēn* but we are not told how God 'gave' or 'set' these light-bearers in the firmament." That is, apparently the material and rough order of the astral bodies was created on day 1 and in "their earliest, not perfected state" (Kline 1970, 82[11]) but were not finalized until later when they become the actual sun, moon, and stars that we know today. "Verse one is a narrative complete in itself. Verses 2–31 likewise constitute a narrative complete in itself." This is much like our hard-rock and cool-water planet being created to be our habitat (Isa. 45:18), though originally in its first stages it was an inundated and uninhabitable mass (Gen. 1:2). Later, it was properly organized by the various divine fiats effecting the two water separations that provide its atmosphere, seas, and dry land (days 2 and 3), clothing it with verdure (day 3), and populating it with all the sentient life forms, including man (days 5, 6). Wenham (1987, 22) notes of Genesis 1:14, "This verse, though, affirms the relationship between sun and daylight for all time from the creation of the sun on the fourth day. It must therefore be supposed that the first three days were seen as different: then light and darkness alternated at God's behest."

Now on day 4, the astral bodies are transformed from dark masses to be made into *māôr*, i.e., light-bearers, luminaries,

---

analogical day view also uses this image: "The structure of the account shows us that our author has presented God as if he were a craftsman going about his workweek."

11. Compare Kline 1977, 250; see also: Young 1964, 9, 14, 95.

localized places for light. They are not only to separate day and night and give light upon the earth (as the God-created light on day 1 did previously), but also to serve "for signs and for seasons and for days and years" (Gen. 1:14). God's directly sustaining the naked light during the first three days was not intended for an *ongoing* and *permanent* illuminatory mechanism; the original light directly ordained and briefly sustained by God set the *temporal pattern* by distinguishing the short-term night-and-day cycle during the first half of the original creation week. The final, providential mechanisms taking over that short-term cycle (the sun, moon, and stars) will also provide for measuring whole "seasons" and entire "years" for the long term, not just the original, limited seven-day week.

Third, Irons' first argument, derived from Kline, is perhaps the most surprising to the traditional interpreter — and it is only a problem in the minds of framework interpreters; it is no problem for a theology of absolute creation by an omnipotent God. Framework advocates speak of "unnecessary supernaturalism" during the very creation of the universe. But we must remember that the creation period was a unique, unrepeatable period wherein the entire universe was created *ex nihilo*. The very idea of *ex nihilo* creation presupposes its highly supernaturalistic character. McClintock and Strong (CBTEL 3, 780) state: "We must not too hastily build an argument upon our ignorance. We do not *know* that the existing laws of creation were in operation when the creative fiat was first put forth. The very act of creation must have been the introducing of laws; but when the work was finished, those laws must have suffered some modification. Men are not now created in the full stature of manhood, but are born and grow."

Supernaturalistic creation is also set against the "naturalistic providence" of evolution that teaches: "When the observable universe was a trillionth of a trillionth of a trillionth of a second old, it abruptly expanded from something billions of times smaller than a proton to about the size of a fist, thereby locking in its near-uniform properties."[12] The traditional exegesis is not in the least embarrassed by any charge of "unnecessary supernaturalism" — especially since nothing required is bizarre or illogical from within a Christian theistic worldview.

Though Klinean framework proponents prefer providence over "unnecessary supernaturalism," the fact is that all providence is at its very essence supernaturalism at work. God's actions define providence; and God's actions are necessarily supernatural. One famous definition of providence is found in the Westminster Confession of Faith, and in this definition the supernatural activity of God is inescapable: "God the great Creator of all things does uphold, direct, dispose, and govern all creatures, actions, and things, from the greatest even to the least, by His most wise and holy providence, according to His infallible foreknowledge, and the free and immutable counsel of His own will, to the praise of the glory of His wisdom, power, justice, goodness, and mercy" (WCF 5:1). We should expect a clear supernaturalism in the original creation week. Light apart from the sun "was a miracle in a week saturated with the miraculous" (Duncan 2001, 52).

In his commentary on Genesis 1:3, John Calvin noted long ago: "To nothing are we more prone than to tie down the power of God to those instruments the agency of which he employs." Besides "it is no accident that God is the subject of the first sentence of the Bible, for this word dominates the whole chapter and catches the eye at every point of the page: it is used some thirty-five times in as many verses of the story" (Kidner 1967, 43).

Rather than serving as a trampling foot that crushes the traditional exegesis, framework reliance on Genesis 2:5, to which

---

12. Francis Ready, "How the Universe Will End," *Astronomy* (Sept 2014): 39. See also: "By some calculations, inflation increased the size of the universe by a factor of around 1026 during that tiny fraction (far less than a trillionth) of a second, expanding it from smaller than the size of a proton to about the size of a grapefruit." Luke Mastin, "Cosmic Inflation," Web, "The Physics of the Universe."

Irons refers, is the system's Achilles' Heel. This is true both in this particular argument, as well as in the broader system-structuring. I will note a couple of quick debilitating problems here, while reserving my main response to the Genesis 2:5 argument for a more thorough critique in a later chapter.

Observe that *even if* this lone verse highlights deficiencies at a certain stage (day 3) in the temporal order of creation, Kline's providential argument is not the most likely solution. First, the two-fold deficit which supposedly dissuades us from an "unnecessary supernaturalism" is: no *rain* and no *man*, which together explain the problem of no vegetation. This supposedly demonstrates "that as far as the time frame is concerned, with respect to both the duration and sequence of events, the scientist is left free of biblical constraints in hypothesizing about cosmic origins" (Kline 1996, 1). But the context clearly provides water for plant life, for the next verse reads, "But a mist used to rise from the earth and water the whole surface of the ground" (Gen. 2:6). The word translated "mist" (*'ēdh*) is a difficult word, but likely means "stream" or "water flow" (NIV; NRSV; NAB; NJB; DOTTE 1:256), as per the Septuagint translation: *pēgē* (compare Gen. 7:11, 16:7, 24:13; Exod. 15:27; Lev. 11: 36; etc.).[13] Then four verses later we read, "Now a river flowed out of Eden to water the garden; and from there it divided and became four rivers" (Gen. 2:10).

Now then, what are we to make of this "unnecessary supernaturalism" principle, as claimed by framework advocates? Ironically, God rectifies the man-deficit by a direct, miraculous, and highly — "unnecessarily"? — supernaturalistic activity (Gen. 2:7), as even Kline admits (1970, 83). Why, then, must we require that the other problem (the rain-deficit) be handled by means of slow providence? The manner by which God creates man wrecks the "unnecessary supernaturalism" argument by importing a bold supernaturalism of the highest sort into

---

13. Cassuto 1998, p. 103–04.

the account. And remarkably, at the very point where slow providence is allegedly affirmed — *and* in a way that appears to the
liberal to suggest the most obvious evidence that "the conception
of Jehovah is extremely primitive," and that "the story, with all
its naive beauty, is intended for an audience intellectually and
spiritually immature."[14]

But also, *even if* rain is lacking after the land extrusion and
before its vegetational cloaking, the text specifically declares that
God's divine fiat causes the appearance of vegetation (1:11). This
fiat affirmation demonstrates that God's activity here is "necessarily supernatural," rather than merely providential. But how could
the lack of rain be a deficit that becomes a problem for plants?
After all, as noted above we read in the very verse in question: "a
mist [or "stream"] used to rise ["was going up," ESV] from the
earth and water the whole surface of the ground" (Gen. 2:6).
And just four verses later we read: "A river flowed out of Eden to
water the garden" (Gen. 2:10). As Cassuto (1998, 104) explains,
"The garden was watered by a river emanating from a spring, and
not by rain." Though Collins (2006, 104 n7) translates the verb
here as "was going up," he notes that Waltke and O'Connor's
textbook on Hebrew syntax state: "It is possible to infer from the
context that the particular nuance of the process aspect [of the
verb] is inceptive action: 'It was *beginning to* go up . . . it was *beginning to* water.' " Whichever reading we take, it does not imply
the passing of a long period of time.

Kline's "new" (Blocher 1984, 53) approach to creation theology based on the one verse in Genesis 2:5 is not sufficient to
overthrow the long-standing traditional approach rooted in the
whole chapter of Genesis 1:1–31. It cannot detour the majestic
"march of days" that becomes "one of the primary impressions
it makes on the ordinary reader" (Kidner 1967, 54–55), nor

---

14. Theodore H. Robinson, "Genesis," in Frederick Carle Eiselen, Edwin Lewis,
and David G. Downey, *The Abingdon Bible Commentary* (New York: Abingdon,
1929), p. 221.

may it disrupt the obvious "chronological succession of events" (Young 1964, 87). Scripture teaches that during the course of providence-dominated, post-creation history, God can impose "unnecessary supernaturalism" upon the world. For instance, we see this in Moses' turning a river into blood (Exod. 7:20), his dividing the sea (Exod. 14:21), the Jordan River divided (Josh. 3:14–17), Joshua's long day (Josh. 10:11–14), Hezekiah's sun reversal (2 Kings 20:9–11), Jesus' quieting the mighty tempest (Matt. 8:23–27), and so forth. Why then is it so remarkable that during this uniquely supernatural creation period, God would employ this unexpected and highly supernaturalistic means of providing light for three days without the sun? Especially in that he produces light apart from the sun frequently today (e.g., by lightning and through bioluminescent creatures).

And what of Mark Futato's statement that light existing apart from luminaries was "not part of the real world" in which Moses' audience lived? Again, neither is creation *ex nihilo*, nor is a world totally covered by water (Gen. 1:2; compare 2 Pet. 3:5), nor men being created from the dust (Gen. 2:7), nor man living in perfect, peaceful harmony with the animals (Gen. 2:20). This is the original creation week, not an ordinary week. Nevertheless, light without a luminary was in fact a part of Israel's *conceptual* world, as we can see from several passages of Scripture. Job knew the sun produced light for the earth (Job 9:7, 31:26), but he could ask, "Where is the way to the dwelling of light?" (Job 38:19).[15] Solomon keeps the sun, moon, and stars distinct from the light: ". . . before the sun and the light, the moon and the stars are darkened" (Eccles. 12:2). The Psalmist sees God as clothed in light (not with the sun): "Bless the LORD, O my soul! O LORD my God, You are very great; You are clothed with splendor and majesty, covering Yourself with light as with a cloak" (Ps. 104:1–2). After all, God is the one who creates

---

15. See Francis I. Andersen, *Job* (TOTC) (Downers Grove, Ill.: Inter-Varsity, 1976), 277.

light: "The One forming light and creating darkness, causing well-being and creating calamity; I am the LORD who does all these" (Isa. 45:7).

In Isaiah 60:19–20 we read, "No longer will you have the sun for light by day, nor for brightness will the moon give you light; but you will have the LORD for an everlasting light, and your God for your glory. Your sun will no longer set, nor will your moon wane; for you will have the LORD for an everlasting light, and the days of your mourning will be over." As Jon Levenson informs us regarding this passage, "We hear a prediction of the transformation of reality." So that here "in this oracle the alternation of night and day, which serves as a refrain throughout Genesis 1, is to be brought to an end, as YHWH will ceaselessly enlighten the world. The light of the first three days of the hexameron [i.e., the six days of creation], which derived from God without celestial mediation, will return."[16]

In fact, Israel *did* have a real-world experience of light without luminaries: "The LORD said to Moses, 'Stretch out your hand toward the sky, that there may be darkness over the land of Egypt, even a darkness which may be felt.' So Moses stretched out his hand toward the sky, and there was thick darkness in all the land of Egypt for three days. They did not see one another, nor did anyone rise from his place for three days, but all the sons of Israel had light in their dwellings" (Exod. 10:21–23). Similarly, while Israel was escaping Egypt, we read, "The angel of God, who had been going before the camp of Israel, moved and went behind them; and the pillar of cloud moved from before them and stood behind them. So it came between the camp of Egypt and the camp of Israel; and there was the cloud along with the darkness, yet it gave light at night" (Exod. 14:19–20). Apparently, God is not embarrassed with unnecessary supernaturalism — or light apart from the sun.

---

16. Jon D. Levenson, *Creation and the Persistence of Evil: The Jewish Drama of Divine Omnipotence* (Princeton, NJ: University Press, 1988).

The New Testament also alludes to the original creation of light apart from the sun: "For God, who said, 'Light shall shine out of darkness . . .' " (2 Cor. 4:6).[17] In Revelation, we have John famously speaking of the new Jerusalem: "The city has no need of the sun or of the moon to shine on it, for the glory of God has illumined it, and its lamp is the Lamb" (Rev. 21:23; compare 22:5).[18] In all of this we must always recognize "God's capacity to work with or without, above or against, secondary causes" (Duncan 2001, 35). In fact, even Irons and Kline (2001, 280) admit that "the sovereign, miracle-working God of Scripture could very well have sustained the light for the first three days in a supernatural manner."

Besides all this, not only should we not be surprised to find a remarkable (not "unnecessary") supernaturalism at the beginning of creation, but we also find abundant miracles in Genesis and the other Mosaic historical writings in the Pentateuch. For instance, in Genesis (which quickly leads to the historical call of Abraham and eventually the formation of the 12 tribes of Israel) we read of the creation of Adam from the dirt (Gen. 2:7), Eve's creation from Adam (Gen. 2:21–22), the talking serpent (Gen. 3:1), the Noahic Flood (Gen. 7–9), the confusion of tongues at Babel (Gen. 11:1–9), the destruction of Sodom and Gomorrah (Gen. 19:24), Lot's wife turning to a pillar of salt (Gen. 19:26), and Sarah's conception at an extremely advanced age (Gen. 21:1). In Exodus, which records the history of Israel's escaping bondage to Egypt to become a free nation, we see the burning bush (Exod. 3:3), Moses' staff turning to a serpent (Exod. 4:2–4), Moses' hand becoming suddenly leprous (Exod. 4:6), the staffs of Moses and Pharaoh's sorcerers' becoming serpents (Exod. 7:9–12), the ten

---

17. Balla notes that "at 2 Cor. 4:6, Paul makes use of some OT motifs in this verse. Paul probably refers primarily to the creation story (Gen. 1:3)." Peter Balla, "2 Corinthians," in G.K. Beale and D.A. Carson, *Commentary on the New Testament Use of the Old Testament* (Grand Rapids, MI: Baker, 2007), p. 763.

18. Though these Revelation verses are from a highly symbolic book, they show that Scripture writers can conceive of light without the sun. That God is called "light" shows his sovereignty over the light (compare 1 John 1:5).

plagues upon Egypt with Israel's exemption (Exod. 7:20–12:30; compare 9:14 with 8:22, 9:4, 6, 10:23, 11:7, 12:13), God's leading Israel by a pillar of cloud by day and smoke by night (Exod. 13:21–22, 14:19, 24), the parting of the sea allowing Israel to escape and causing Pharaoh's destruction (Exod. 14:5–31), water from a rock struck by Moses' staff (Exod. 17:6; compare Num. 20:11; Deut. 8:15; Neh. 9:15; Ps. 105:41), Israel's prevailing in battle when Moses holds up his staff (Exod. 17:8–13), and Moses' face glowing (Exod. 34:29–35). We know of many other acts of "unnecessary supernaturalism," in Israel's foundational history (e.g., Num. 12:10–15, 20:7–11, 21:8–9, 22:23–30; Deut. 8:4, 29:5).

In the final analysis, the literary approach to Genesis 1 from the framework hypothesis does not overthrow the "time honored" (Irons), "majority" (Blocher), "dominant" (Kline) exegesis of historic Christianity.

The Sabbath Day Problem (Gen. 2:2-3)

Objection

Genesis 2:2–3 establishes the seventh day of God's rest, which is ongoing and not a literal 24-hour day. The seventh day lacks the "evening/morning" qualifier, indicating that it continues today. Furthermore, the very fact that God has ceased and never resumed his creational work demands the seventh day continues. In fact, Hebrews 4:1–4 speaks of this Sabbath day as the abiding rest of God. Both day age and framework hypothesis advocates bring this objection to bear against the traditional view in demonstrating that the Genesis days are not literally 24-hour days.

According to the day age theorist, the ongoing nature of God's seventh day Sabbath (based on Ps. 95 and Heb. 4) shows that the preceding six days could also be long periods of time. This is especially significant in that Genesis 2:2–3 is the very context of the revelation of the six creative days and, in fact, is the concluding day of the original creation week. Harris (1990, 110) vigorously asserts, "I cannot see how it can be argued in the face of these verses [Ps. 95 and Heb. 4] that God's rest was only 24 hours." He continues: "Now if God's seventh day is an eternal day, as argued in the Psalms and Hebrews and yet it is paralleled to man's seventh day Sabbath, it follows that our weekdays cannot be duplicates of God's days of creation and rest, but are symbolic thereof. It seems to be an inescapable conclusion that our seventh day 24-hour Sabbath is symbolic of God's eternal Sabbath of rest from creation. If so, then there is no reason at all to deny that our particular six 24-hour days of labor are symbolic of, not equivalent to, God's six long days of creative labor."

Among framework scholars we read such comments as these by Mark Ross (1999, 121–122). Day 7 has "no concluding refrain, 'and there was evening and morning, day seven,' " which means "God's Sabbath, then, is not a 24-hour day." Irons and Kline (2001, 87) agree: day 7 "lacks the concluding evening-morning formula, thus suggesting that it is still ongoing." The Majority Report (1999, 104) also notes: "The day that ends the creation week is clearly not a literal 24-hour day. . . . It has neither evening or morning." Justin Taylor (2015, 3) adds, "The question we have to ask here is: was God's creation 'rest' limited to a 24-hour period?' On the contrary, Psalm 95 and Hebrews 4 teach that God's Sabbath rest 'remains' and that we can enter into it or be prevented from entering it." See also Blocher and Hughes.[19]

For Kline, Irons, and some other framework advocates, this day is crucial for establishing their Two Register Cosmogony (see chapter 9). Consequently, Kline (1996, 10) also believes this day was a long period of time (but for a different reason): "The seventh day has to do altogether with God, with the upper register." Irons (1998, 51) concurs: "God's rest 'on the seventh day' is interpreted

---

19. Blocher (1984, 56) and R. Kent Hughes, *Genesis: Beginning and Blessing* (Wheaton, IL: Crossway, 2004), p. 26–27.

in Hebrews as an upper register reality. . . . If the seventh day is an upper register day, then how can the previous six days be lower register days? In addition, the fact that the seventh day is *eternal* supports the notion that the entire seven-day scheme is a metaphor for the upper register time-frame of creation."

Response

Several distractions lead this battering ram off in the wrong direction, leaving the traditional exegesis standing.

The argument is an *argument from silence*. The claim that the Sabbath day of Genesis 2:2–3 is a long "day" — as argued by both day age scholar Harris *and* framework advocates — is an argument derived from outside the text, and basically imposed on the text. The revelation of God in Genesis 2:2 does not inform us that *that* original Sabbath day is eternal. As Keil and Delitzsch (2001, 43) well note, "We must not, without further ground, introduce this true and profound idea into the seventh creation-day." Indeed, as Kelly (1997, 111) notes, such an argument rests "a great deal of weight on a very narrow and thin exegetical bridge." The text here clearly presents the seventh day as another in the well-defined series of days within the original creation week. In fact, this "seventh day" is the *conclusion* to the creation week, not only in that it is the seventh of only seven days, all properly enumerated. But also, on that day we have the historical cessation of the divine creative activity.

Literally, Genesis 2 informs us that God *"ceased"* his labor. As Wenham (1987, 35) observes, " 'He rested,' *šābat,* has three closely related senses: 'to cease to be,' 'to desist from work,' and 'to observe the sabbath.' It is clear that the second sense is central here." Mathews (1996, 178) adds, "The verb translated 'rested' here means 'the *cessation* of creative activity'; it has this same sense in its only other occurrence in Genesis, where God promises the postdiluvian world that the times and seasons 'will never cease' (8:22). Elsewhere we find that God 'rested' (*nûah,* Exod. 20:11;

napaš, 31:17), but here the passage speaks of the absence of work — 'he abstained' from work" (compare Kidner 1967, 53). Even framework adherent Thompson (1968, 22) admits the word in Genesis 2 means "cease," or "stop" (compare Hyers 1984, 75). Another framework theologian, Niehaus (2014, 254), adds his challenge to Kline: a "challenge to a literal day interpretation of the seventh day, fitting though it may seem, misses the point that the seventh day was a day of rest from God's *creative* work. It does not necessarily imply God's rest from work of any kind, and it need not be one eternal day."

Keathley and Rooker (2014, 133) point out that the seventh day differs from the other six in several ways. It lacks not only the evening-morning refrain, but any reference to God making anything, or His naming, or His declaring, "Let there be," or His evaluating (declaring "it was good"). Nor do we hear any "and it was so" affirmation. They argue that "the point of these omissions was to emphasize that day seven was the end of God's creative activity, as the two uses of *shavath* 'to cease,' clearly demonstrate" (Keathley and Rooker 2014, 163). Thus, in Genesis 2:2 Moses simply declares that God ceased His creative work, bringing the creation process to a close. And since even framework advocates believe that creation has ceased, it must have ceased at a particular moment in time, i.e., on *that* particular day.[20] In fact, God does not "rest" from *all* labor, for He "made" (*'āśâ*) coats of skins for Adam and Eve (Gen. 3:21). He *does* permanently cease from *creating the world*, but not from *all* temporal creative activity. All the text is stating is that "God's work of creation is done," for "He continues His work of providence" (Duncan 2001, 33).

McCabe (2010, 242) presents two more reasons that day 7 is not eternal. His first one is, "The evening-morning conclusion is

---

20. Interestingly, just a few verses previous to the three-fold "rest" declaration (of Gen. 2:2–3), God creates man in His "image," so that he will reflect God. Here in Gen. 2:2–3 cessation from labor is emphasized after six days of work. Man is to imitate God in this: a six-day work week followed by a day of rest. This point is driven home in Exod. 20:9–11.

one part of a five-fold structure that Moses employed in shaping the literary fabric for each of the days of the creation week. None of the other parts of this five-fold arrangement are mentioned on the seventh day. . . . By excluding the five-fold pattern, Moses' theological emphasis was to demonstrate in literary form that day 7 was a day of cessation from divine creative activity. . . . But because day 7 is a historic literal day, it is numbered like the previous six days." His other reason is that " 'all the days that Adam lived were nine hundred and thirty years' (Gen. 5:5), but the first day of his life was before the seventh day. If it was not literal, then just how long did Adam live and how do we make sense of Genesis 5:5? Furthermore, Whitcomb astutely observed, 'We must assume that the seventh day was a literal day because Adam and Eve lived through it before God drove them out of the Garden. Surely, he would not have cursed the earth during the seventh day which he blessed and sanctified.' "[21]

Some 1,500 years after Moses wrote Genesis, the writer of Hebrews refers to the original, creational Sabbath in Hebrews 4:4b to *develop* the concept of an ongoing or eschatological Sabbath. But his *theological point* may not be imposed upon the *historical meaning* of Genesis 2:2. Certainly, Hebrews applies Genesis 2:2 to the argument for an ongoing and/or eschatological Sabbath; but he does so only *typologically*. His argument in Hebrews 4:4 no more proves the *original* day in Genesis 2:2 is ongoing, than his typological proof for Christ's eternity in Hebrews 7 proves Melchizedek actually lacked human genealogy. There he argues that Christ has an ongoing existence by alluding to Genesis' not providing a genealogy for Melchizedek (Heb. 7:3). This does not prove that the original revelation regarding historical Melchizedek actually indicates he had no earthly lineage. This is typological argument; it is not *expositing* the text's original meaning, but *extending* it. Framework proponent Niehaus (2014, 254) disputes the use of Hebrews 4 in the debate: "It is,

---

21. Cited by McCabe (2010, 244).

however, not clear that the 'Sabbath rest' of Hebrews 4:9 [and 4:4] is a one-day — even one eternal day — affair. . . . God may *on that seventh day* have entered an eternal *rest*, but that does not mean his eternal rest was *one day long*. An eternal Sabbath could be an eternal rest from the *work of creating* but rest that *lasts many heavenly days* — an infinite number, in fact. We note that the word *Sabbath* does not mean 'a day' but, rather, 'rest' (from the verb *sbt*, 'to rest,' not 'to rest for one day')."

This is all the more significant in that even some framework advocates admit Hebrews 4 is a "notoriously difficult passage" (Blocher 1984, 56). We must agree with Young (1964, 77 n73): "There is no Scriptural warrant whatever (certainly not Hebrews 4:3–5) for the idea that this seventh day is eternal."

The attempt to suggest John 5:17 into the debate only shows the desperation of non-traditional, literary views of Genesis. For instance, Irons (1998, 51 n113) writes, "John 5:17 also implies that God's Sabbath is eternal. . . . If the Father is working on the Sabbath 'until now,' then his Sabbath also must continue 'until now.' "[22]

Two immediate problems arise upon this exposition of John 5:17.

First, the problem of internal contradiction. The question naturally arises then: *Did God cease from labor on the Sabbath, or not?* On the literal construction resulting from the traditional exegesis, Genesis 2:2–3 informs us that He did in fact cease from labor *on that particular day*. Only the literal analysis, then, can avoid the contradiction inherent in the eternal Sabbath position supposedly rooted in Genesis 2. That is, in the eternal Sabbath view God *does* cease from labor on His Sabbath and He does *not* cease from labor. Actually, though, Jesus is here referring to the weekly recurring earthly Sabbath, noting that God Himself works on that particular recurring temporal day — through Jesus' healing on the Sabbath (John 5:8, 16).

---

22. Compare Kline 1996, 10; Blocher 1984, 57.

Second, the problem of eternal creation. Is the framework hypothesis willing to argue consistently from their understanding of John 5:17? That is, on Jesus' statement here, they argue God's original Sabbath mentioned in Genesis 2 continues. Therefore, by parity of reasoning Jesus' statement that "the Father is *working*" would seem to demand that He is *still* creating the universe.

The eternal Sabbath argument can be turned upon itself. As Harris (1999, 109) puts it, "The seventh day is presented as very special. Unlike the others, it has no conclusion mentioned. There was no evening to it and no morning leading to anything else. God rested from his creative activity." Kline (1996, 10) agrees: "In the Genesis prologue the unending nature of God's Sabbath is signalized by the absence of the evening-morning formula from the account of the seventh day." The Majority Report (1999, 7) concurs: "The day that ends the creation week is clearly not a literal 24-hour day, even though it also is referred to by the name 'day.' It has neither evening nor morning. It is eternal." Consequently, if we accept the implications of such an argument, then the seventh day *differs* from the preceding six in a way that *demands* the preceding days *were in fact* literal! For the first six days *are* most definitely limited by the "evening/morning" refrain.

Grammatical reasons, though, explain the lack of the "evening/morning" refrain on day 7. As Cassuto (1998, 28) notes, "Whenever clear reference is made to the relationship between a given day and the next, it is precisely sunrise that is accounted the beginning of the second day."[23] Since the week of God's creating is ended, that is, since God's original creative activity has "ceased" (this matter is emphasized by three-fold repetition in Gen. 2:2–3), no following creational day in the series is expected or prepared for. Hence, the dropping of the "evening/morning" marker on the seventh day shows that this series of creation-days has ended forever. The Sabbath is the *seventh* in the *sequence* of

---

23. See also, Ernest Kevan, "Genesis," in *New Bible Commentary*, Francis Davidson, ed. (Grand Rapids, MI: Eerdmans, 1954), p. 77.

creation days, even though no like days follow, in that creation is a unique period in earth history.[24]

Kline (1996, 10) asserts that "in the beginning" is a non-temporal, upper register matter and the Sabbath is also a timeless, upper level reality. Therefore, the six days of creation are upper level (divine, timeless) realities, since "the six days are part of the same strand as the seventh day, and the 'beginning.' " In that he is mistaken on the Sabbath question, his argument falls to the ground. But even if he were correct, the days in between would then be distinguished from the Sabbath day by the various calendrical limitations not associated with day 7. Besides, does not the *beginning*, which he mentions, initiate temporal reality where time *is* relevant? Is not the sun on day 4 designated as a temporal ruler to mark off the passing of time?

This view of an eternal Sabbath based on Genesis 2:2 contradicts Exodus 20:9–11. There, God commands us to observe a weekly Sabbath after six days of work for the express purpose of *imitating* Him in His original creative week. The *original* Sabbath *day* (Gen. 2:3) was a literal day following upon six prior literal days. Again, since the "Sabbath day" is the seventh in a series of six preceding literal days, how can we interpret it other than literally?

God does not bless *His eternal rest* but *the particular day* in the temporal realm when His creative work is finally concluded. That work was effectively declared as ended by the divine appreciation, "behold, it was very good" (Gen. 1:31). If the "Sabbath day" *of Genesis 2:2–3* is ongoing, it would imply no Fall and Curse. After all, God would then be continually hallowing and blessing that "ongoing day," that is, all of time from that moment to the present. Analogical day scholar Collins (2006, 75) agrees that this is a problem for the Framework argument: an

---

24. Pipa (1999, 169) suggests that the day may also be left open-ended intentionally, allowing it to serve (much like Melchizedek's lack of genealogy) as a *type* of the eternal Sabbath.

open-ended seventh day "would mean that the rest of human history takes place during God's Sabbath."

The Long Day Problem

Objection

Genesis 2:4 reads, "This is the account of the heavens and the earth when they were created, in the day that the LORD God made earth and heaven." Some argue that this speaks of the entire creation week as a "day," showing that "day" may not be a term applying to a literal 24-hour time frame. For instance, Hyers (1984, 40) writes, "The six-day account of Genesis 1–2:4a and the single-day account of Genesis 2:4b and following hardly agree in time-frame, sequence, or detail." Justin Taylor (2015, 4) agrees: "This use of *yom* presents a puzzle for those who insist that 'young-earth' exegesis is the only interpretation that takes the opening chapters of Genesis 'literally.' " This is especially significant in that it is found in the creation account itself.

Response

In this verse the word *yôm* appears in a prepositional phrase: *bᵉyôm*. This phrase involves a preposition in construct with an infinitive forming a temporal conjunction, and appears 60 times in the Old Testament (TLOT, 2:529).[25] This adverbial construction is an idiomatic expression meaning "when." This is widely recognized among Hebrew grammarians. For instance, the *Theological Lexicon of the Old Testament* (2, 529) states: "The construction *bᵉyôm* + inf. 'on the day when' = 'at the time when' = 'as/when' . . . (e.g., Gen. 2:4 'at the time when the Lord God made the earth and heaven')."[26]

---

25. See for example: Gen. 2:4, 17, 3:5, 5:1ff, 21:8ff; Exod. 10:28, 32:34; Lev. 6:13, 7:16; etc.

26. They note that this usage "occurs over 60x." See also: BDB 400; TWOT 1:851; TDOT 6:15; Cassuto (1998: 99).

Even day age advocates admit this idiomatic expression does not militate against the literal day view.[27] Several notable translations treat it thus: NIV, NRSV, NAB, NET, CEB, NLT, CSB. For instance, the NIV reads: "This is the account of the heavens and the earth when they were created. *When* the LORD God made the earth and the heavens." But even more significantly, even analogical day proponent John Collins (whose literary approach is perhaps the closest to the framework view) notes that Genesis 2:4 is "a bound form in an idiom *bym* + infinitive construct, which cannot give us semantic information about the meaning of *yom* outside this expression" (Collins 2005, 147).

Even if Genesis 2:4 did use "day" in a different sense, this would not undermine the meaning of the first chapter. Genesis 1 carefully qualifies its creative days in several clear ways (as noted above). And such qualifications are lacking in Genesis 2:4.

Objection

Many point to the apparently different order of creation in Genesis 2 and note the overly busy nature of Adam on the sixth day as evidence that the days are neither literal nor sequential. In Genesis 2:19–20 we read: "Out of the ground the LORD God formed every beast of the field and every bird of the sky, and brought them to the man to see what he would call them; and whatever the man called a living creature, that was its name. The man gave names to all the cattle, and to the birds of the sky, and to every beast of the field."

Framework scholar Futato (1998, 10) argues that "a straight-forward reading of Gen. 2:19, in other words, puts Gen. 2:4–25 in conflict with a chronological reading of Gen. 1:2–2:3, where the animals were formed before the man (Gen. 1:24–27)." Irons and Kline (2001, 283) agree: "If the *waw*-consecutive in Genesis 2:19 . . . denotes chronological sequence,

---

27. "I would rather argue that *b⁺yôm* of Gen. 2:4 is a prepositional phrase simply meaning an indefinite 'when.' " R. Laird Harris (1999: 109).

we have an apparent discrepancy with Genesis 1:24–28, which places the creation of the living creatures *before* that of man." But since they do not believe the days of Genesis are literal or the days chronological, this poses no problem for them.

M. Ross (1999, 123–124) concurs and adds:

> If Genesis 2:4–25 is chronological, then there are problems in reconciling this passage with a chronological view of Genesis One. . . . Then a comment is made on the fact that it is not good for the man to be alone, and the decision is made to make a helper suitable for him. We then read of the animals which God created, and how He brought them to the man to see what he would call them. The result of all this zoological taxonomy is that no helper suitable for Adam is found among all the animals which God created. . . .
>
> The narrative order of the Genesis Two account, if taken as a chronological sequence, stands in contradiction to the narrative order of Genesis One, if that too is taken as a chronological sequence. . . . The survey of the whole animal kingdom was principally motivated to draw out the fact that Adam was not a mere animal.

This "clash" between Genesis 1 and 2 has long been deemed by liberals to be a problem for the integrity of the biblical account, demonstrating it to be composite narrative that has been subjected to sloppy editing. For instance, Speiser (1964, liv, 8–9) notes that the two accounts are "fundamentally different" and that there is "a marked difference" because "we have two separate accounts of this theme." Regarding Genesis 2:19, Skinner writes, "The naïeveté of the conception is extraordinary" in its presenting "an unsuccessful experiment to find a mate for him."[28] Evangelical framework advocates, on the other hand, defend the

---

28. John Skinner, *Critical and Exegetical Commentary on Genesis* (ICC) (2d. ed.: Edinburgh: T & T Clark, 1930), 67.

narratives against charges of contradiction by proposing that "his creative work in a week of days is not to be taken literally. Instead it functions as a literary structure in which the creative works of God have been narrated in a topical order" (Irons and Kline 2001, 219).

Framework sympathizers Miller and Soden (2012, 54, 56) argue that "in chapter 2, the man is created from clay first, then the garden is planted, and then animals and birds are created from clay, as well as 'every bird of the heavens' (2:19). . . . Everyone who assumes the two accounts are not contradictory but complementary will also argue that the author intended to give a nonchronological order in chapter 2 in order to make a theological point." Consequently, "If chapter 2 is out of order for theological reasons, why must chapter 1 be in order chronologically?" And they point out, "The description of the day 6 in Genesis 2 has led some people to conclude that day 6 may not, in fact, be a literal twenty-four-hour day, but rather it represents a longer creation day."[29]

How does the six-day creationist explain the apparent conflict in the order of the creation of Adam and the animals, and the seemingly too-busy nature of Adam's activity in Genesis 2:19?

Response

The grammar of the text of Genesis 2:19 uses the *wayyiqtol* verb form that normally functions as the backbone of historical, sequential narrative (as in Gen. 1). Thus, the NASB translates it: "Out of the ground the LORD God formed every beast of the field and every bird of the sky." And it could even be translated "out of the ground the LORD God then formed." Nevertheless, a number of commentators and Bible translations see this as a special use of the verb form and understand it to function as what we would call the pluperfect tense: "had formed." See for example the NIV, ISV, GW, and ESV. Note also, Keil and Delitzsch,

---

29. Their presentation of the triad framework appears on p. 51.

Jamieson-Fausset-Brown, Green, Whitelaw, Leupold, Aalders, and Collins.[30]

Leupold (1942, 130) declares "that in reality they had been made prior to the creation of man is so entirely apparent from chapter one as not to require explanation." This would seem to be the conclusion of the majestic march of days in Genesis 1, which the context there so demands.

Even though Collins (1995, 140) is an analogical day scholar, he provides a careful exegetical argument demonstrating that "there is, therefore, good reason, both from Hebrew grammar and from the structure of the first two chapters of Genesis, to support the pluperfect interpretation in 2:19." I will be summarizing his argument (thus parenthetical page references refer to his article). He points out that the "literary environment ('co-text')" of a given text "can establish the 'logic of the referents,' " which inform us of the author's intended sequence of events (p. 139). Thus the pluperfect reading of 2:19 suggested by the "elaborate chiasmus" in Genesis 2:4 draws together the narratives of Genesis 1 and 2. Here is Collins' (1995, 138) presentation of chiasmic structure Moses presents:

These are the generations of

    a: the heavens

        b: and the earth

            c: when they were created

            c′: when[31] the Lord God made

        d′: earth

    a′: and heaven

Collins (1995, 139) explains the significance of this chiasm: "Note how the word order 'the heavens and the earth' (**a** and **b**), as well as the verb *bārā'*, 'create' (**c**), point us back to 1:1 (as well as 1:21, 27)

---

30. Keil and Delitzsch 2001, 54; Green 1910, 25–26; Leupold 1942, 130; Collins 1995, 126ff. See also Whitelaw 1950, 94.

31. Though the NASB has "in the day," this is the idiomatic expression *bᵉyôm* which means "when." See discussion above.

for the verb; whereas the change in the divine name from *'ĕlōhîm*, 'God' (ch. 1) to *yhwh 'ĕlōhîm*, 'the Lord God' (chs. 2–3) are reflected in the **c'** element." He aptly concludes, "If we take Genesis 1:3–2:3 as conveying the broad-stroke story line, which seems to be the simplest way to read it, we are entitled . . . to read *wayyiṣer* in 2:19 as a pluperfect." Thus, "had formed" functions as a "flashback" (p. 117) in the narrative. It is referring back to day 6, the day on which Adam was created (note that in Gen. 2:18 God says that "it is not good for the man to be alone"). This could not be said after the end of day 6 because by then we read, "God saw all that He had made, and behold, it was very good" (Gen. 1:31).

Consequently, the seeming dischronology presented in Genesis 2:19 is actually an intentional flashback. As McCabe (2010, 232) puts it, "The temporal recapitulation in verse 19 transcends the immediate pericope of 2:4–25 and looks back to the previous pericope in 1:1–2:3. Therefore, it is better to view this as an example of a pluperfect." Framework advocates even recognize this possibility (M. Ross 1999, 124; Blocher 1984, 46).

Next let's analyze the point of the text. The text appears to present us with too much to be accomplished on one day. After all, he must survey "every beast of the field and every bird of the sky" (Gen. 2:19), then name them (Gen. 2:20a), and finally to discover after the process that "for Adam there was not found a helper suitable for him" (Gen. 2:20b). We must, however, take a closer look at what is actually happening.

We see very clearly that Genesis 1 focuses on the entire world (and even includes the stellar bodies — though only in their relationship to the earth, Gen. 1:15). But when we enter Genesis 2, the setting narrows down from the whole earth to some particular region of the earth where God makes man, then escorts him to "the garden of Eden" (Gen. 2:15). The context strongly suggests that Adam is only engaging the animals of Eden. Leupold (1942, 30–31) provides three reasons for this surmise: (1) The reference to the "beasts of the field [*śādeh*]" does not include the whole "earth ['eres]" of Genesis 1:24, and so "may refer to the garden only." (2) We should notice that the "fish of the sea" (Gen. 1:26, 28) are not mentioned "as being less near to man" and wholly out of his habitat (whereas birds "multiply on the earth," Gen. 1:22). (3) "The garden could hardly have been a garden if all creatures could have overrun it unimpeded."

Furthermore, it would seem that Adam was naming only a representation, a sampling of the creatures, and not literally "every" one of them. Scripture commonly uses "all" and "every" in non-universal contexts. It is simply a popular way of speaking of a great number. Also we must understand that not all species of particular "kinds" of animals existed from the very beginning, thereby limiting the potential number of animals in this project. In addition, we must recognize that Adam was unfallen at that time and surely had a greater intellectual capacity, enjoying a mind unencumbered by sin and distortion (e.g., Eph. 4:17).[32]

Genesis 2:19 is not a naive record of a long, drawn out effort by God to find a mate for Adam in the animal kingdom. God did not continually bring a sampling of the Edenic animals to Adam in a failed attempt to *find* him a companion, but in order to show him that he *needed* a companion.[33] The animals had their mates by which they could reproduce, but Adam was alone. Keathley and Rooker (2014, 86) point out the recurring demonstrative pronoun *zō't* ("this") in Genesis 2:23 emphasizes that only the woman corresponds to the man: "Then the man said, 'This [*zō't*] at last is bone of my bones and flesh of my flesh; this [*zō't*] one shall be called Woman, for out of Man this [*zō't*] one was taken" (NRSV). Thus, Cassuto (1998, 128) suggests that "the Lord God wished to engender in the heart of man a desire for a helper who

---

32. This is called the noetic effect of sin, i.e,, the effect on the "mind" (Gk. *nous*). See: Stephen K. Moroney, *The Noetic Effects of Sin: A Historical and Contemporary Exploration of How Sin Affects Our Thinking* (Lanham, MD: Lexington, 2000).

33. As per Leupold 1942, 130; Aalders 1981, 94; Mathews 215–16; Whitelaw 51; Robert Jamieson, A.R. Fausset, and David Brown, *Commentary Critical and Explanatory on the Whole Bible* (Englewood Cliffs, N.J: PrenticeHall, n.d.), p. 19.

should correspond to him exactly" so that "he would be ready to appreciate and cherish the gift that the Lord God was to give him." And for the reader, this shows once again that man is distinct from the animals — as seen earlier in his bearing the image of God (compare Gen. 1:26) and God's special forming of him distinct from the animals (Gen. 2:7).

Conclusion

Six-day creationism is committed to a literal interpretation of Genesis 1. It sees Moses using historical genre to present his original audience (and us) with a basic statement of where the world and man came from. We argue that the narrative presents us with a sequential series of six 24-hour days, followed by a seventh day wherein God ceases from His creation labor.

Framework advocates argue for Moses' engagement in a sophisticated literary project. They reject the notion that his use of six days governed by evening/morning time-coordinates is meant to be taken literally. One means whereby they argue thus is by attempting to expose weaknesses in any literal approach to the text. In this chapter I surveyed their three leading objections in this regard: (1) The problem of the fourth day, which they take as a recapitulation of day 1 and therefore not intended to be read sequentially. (2) The Sabbath day problem that seems to them to be eternal day, which overthrows any argument that the preceding days must be taken literally. (3) The long-day problem that they surmise from Moses' use of *yôm* as summarizing the entire "week" of creation.

We have weighed these arguments in the balance and found them wanting. The relentless majestic march of days cannot be so easily overthrown, for not only do we have ample exegetical evidence that Moses intended these as literal days, but the objections to this reading are easy to answer.

Now I will turn my focus particularly on the framework hypothesis errors in their positive presentation of their view.

Part III

The Framework
Hypothesis Errors

Chapter 6

Introduction to Rebuttal

Numerous arguments have been offered in attempting to substantiate the framework hypothesis. Many of these are basically disputes *against* the traditional, historical view of Genesis 1, rather than arguments *for* the hypothesis itself. Space constraints forbid a response to each and every argument. They even preclude a *thorough* analysis of the basic arguments. Nevertheless, an *adequate* response can be presented in summary fashion against the *foundational* principles of the hypothesis.

Foundational Issues

Once again, I appreciate the yeoman's work of Lee Irons in conveniently organizing, summarizing, presenting, and defending what surely are the three key arguments for the framework hypothesis.[1] Consequently, Irons' presentation will provide the structure for my critique.

Irons declares that "there are three exegetical arguments for the framework interpretation." Summarily stated and employing abbreviated descriptions of Irons' presentation (1998, 27), these are: (1) The triad argument. "The intentional literary design of the text, as reflected in the symmetry of the two triads." (2)

---

1. Irons 1998: Section titled "Three Exegetical Arguments."

The providential argument. That which "Gen. 2:5–6 establishes regarding the mode of divine providence during the creation week" shows that the "creative acts are not narrated sequentially." (3) The cosmogony argument. "The specifically metaphorical nature of these nonliteral days is given a coherent explanation within the broader context of the Bible's two-register cosmological teaching."

Certainly Irons' three arguments serve as a set of "keys to the kingdom," as it were. They grant access to any who would enter into the framework world of "kingdoms and kings" in Genesis 1. He forthrightly declares that the triad structure is "the primary exegetical basis of the framework interpretation" (Irons 1998, 27). He and Kline state that "the first exegetical argument for the framework interpretations begins with the observation that the days form a framework consisting of two parallel triads" (Irons and Kline 2001, 224). Kline (1958, 156) suggests that "the literary character" involving "parallelism" serves to "compel the conclusion" of a "figurative chronological framework for the account." Indeed, this feature provides "confirmation" of the framework approach (p. 157).

And certainly, framework advocates deem crucial the evidence drawn from Genesis 2:5–6. When Kline (1958, 148) first developed and presented his new exegetical insight, he noted that he had formulated the "decisive word against the traditional interpretation." He insists it is the "conclusive exegetical evidence . . . that prevents anyone who follows the analogy of Scripture from supposing that Genesis 1 teaches a creation in the space of six solar days."[2] Futato (1998, 1) speaks of features of his exegesis of Genesis 2 as "foundational," playing a "major role," and serving as a "key to understanding" the framework approach to creation. Irons (1998, 27) proclaims it as an "exegetical conviction" for the view.

---

2. Meredith G. Kline, "Review of *The Christian View of Science and Scripture*," *Westminster Theological Journal* 18:1 (November, 1955): 54.

Regarding the less familiar and more complex esoteric foundation stone, Kline (1996, 1) insists of his two-register cosmogony argument that "this idea developed into the main point and has become the umbrella under which the other, restated arguments are accorded an ancillary place here and there." Irons (1998, 36) deems Kline's two-register paper to be "the most comprehensive and convincing exegetical defense of the framework interpretation available."

Before we actually engage the arguments, we should note some surprising matters regarding these "three exegetical arguments" as we consider the following.

Foundational Concerns

Despite these summary elements of the framework hypothesis being confidently presented, complications arise in establishing the innovative theological system on these foundation stones.

Foundational erosion. As noted above, framework advocates frequently point to these foundation stones as securing their theological house. Nevertheless, these stones appear to be made of damp sand rather than solid rock. Indeed, not one stone here shall be left upon another that shall not be torn down.

Although the *triad framework* gives the hermeneutical system "its name," *immediately* upon mentioning this as the "first" point in the "positive exegetical basis," Irons (1998, 27) admits, "By itself, this does not prove beyond a reasonable doubt that the days are non-literal, or that the narrative is topical." Rather, we discover, it leaves "that impression." In fact, this results from a problem he admits later: "Certainly it is possible to acknowledge the presence of a schematic element in Gen. 1 and yet to argue that a non-literal, non-sequential interpretation is an additional logical step that does not necessarily follow" (1998, 29). Kline (1958, 157) confesses that the matter of proper chronology in Genesis 1 must "be an open exegetical question," which, in his opinion, is "actually closed by the exegetical evidence of Gen. 2:5."

Framework disciples point to the most ornate stone of the house that Kline built — the *two-register cosmogony* stone — and proclaim, as it were, "Behold what a wonderful stone and what a wonderful building." But when we turn to consider this stone, we are surprised to learn from Irons (1998, 3) that "one may or may not be persuaded of this particular aspect of Kline's argument and still be able to hold the framework interpretation itself." In fact, this feature of the system is seldom mentioned outside of a tight circle of Kline disciples (e.g., Thompson, M. Ross, and Blocher do not employ it). Interestingly, this "umbrella" argument (Kline 1996, 1) was (wisely, I believe) not mentioned in the Majority Report (1999).

Consequently, after stripping away the non-essentials, we are really left with their exegesis of Genesis 2:5. But this presents us with a new frustration.

Foundational novelty. Admittedly, a deep suspicion runs among traditional exegetes that the framework hypothesis arose among evangelicals as a new option in the creation debate only *after* the challenge of evolution presented itself. (Framework advocates would dismiss this as a *post hoc phenomenon*.) Waltke (2012, 6, 9) admits the framework view "in fact aims to support the theory of creation by evolution" and has been "promoted to reconcile the Genesis account of creation with evolution." Not only so, but the framework hypothesis presents us with an evolving target, with various new features arising from time to time.

As Blocher (1984, 50) points out, the original promoter of the framework view among evangelicals was Arie Noordtzij (1924). Thirty years after Noordtzij's work, and despite the deep, broad, and long-standing interest in and debate over Genesis 1–3, Kline (1958) published an innovative exegetical analysis of Genesis 2:5, which Blocher (1984, 53) calls "a new argument" created by one "who is not afraid to leave the beaten track." More recently, Futato published a further development on Kline's research on Genesis 2:5. Futato (1998, 1–2) promotes his "new insights" on the text "which have not yet been set forth." Thus, the last framework hypothesis foundation stone remaining after discarding the non-essential ones is a novelty. Forty years later, Kline molded for us a new theological construct, the two-register cosmogony (1996). Kline (1996, 1) presents his latest research as "adding something somewhat fresh to the old debate." A foundational portion of this new theological argument is his innovative view of the theophanic presence of God in Genesis 1:2–3, which allows him to "start fresh" and that encourages his discovery of "a key new element" in the creation record (Kline 1977, 250).

Foundational difficulty. What is more, the absolutely essential providential argument is derived from Genesis 2:5–6. This passage, according to Kidner (1966, 109, 111), contains several "words of debatable meaning" and inheres with a "difficulty" that is "reflected in the variety of interpretations that have been put forward." The framework hypothesis, then, is dependent upon a new and innovative exposition of a passage that is noted for its difficulty and that contains ambiguous terms. As I will show below, a more plausible and widely held view is readily available, making the unique framework conclusions wholly unnecessary — and it does so while preserving the majestic "march of days" in Genesis 1 and shamelessly affirming "unnecessary supernaturalism" on at least one occasion during the creation week.

Chapter 7

The Triad Structure

Having established the basics of the framework argument, I will now analyze and critique it. The surface appearance of the triad is appealing and can initially seem persuasive, but it ultimately fails of its purpose, as I will show.

Triad Symmetry Introduction

We must remember that it is "primarily" because of this triadic structure "that the term 'framework' has been attached to the position" (Irons 1998, 28). It is argued that the triadic parallelism between the first three days and the last three indicates a *topical* rather than chronological arrangement, as represented in the following table published in the Majority Report (1999, 6).

DOMAINS	RULERS
Day 1 Light	Day 4 Luminaries
Day 2 Sky Seas	Day 5 Sea creatures Winged creatures
Day 3 Dry land Day 3b Vegetation	Day 6 Land animals Day 6b Man
THE RULER OF ALL Day 7 Sabbath	

This is all very nice and neat.[1] And it certainly is quite an interesting alignment. But as noted above, this does not prove the non-chronological nature of Genesis 1, for "not all" who recognize the symmetric arrangement of the divine creative activity "espouse the framework interpretation" (1998, 29).[2] This is because "there is no theoretical reason why literary and historical interests cannot coincide" (Osborne 2005, 683). In fact, not only do some chronological-sequence adherents affirm the symmetry, but framework advocates admit that "a non-literal, non-sequential interpretation is an additional logical step that does not necessarily follow" (Irons 1998, 29).

However, other triad problems weaken the framework hypothesis. The framework system reminds us of the duck that appears to be gliding effortlessly across the pond, but underneath the water's surface, a whole lot of fancy footwork is going on. Let me show how this is the case.

Triad Symmetry Confusion

Even among advocates of a literary framework approach to Genesis 1, we find confusion over the model. This sort of problem should not surprise us, for literary framework advocate Wenham (1987, 6) notes, "The arrangement of 1:1–2:3 is itself highly problematic. Briefly, the eight works of creation are prompted by ten divine commands and executed on six different days. Many attempts have been made to discover a simpler, more symmetrical arrangement underlying the present scheme. None of these suggestions has proved persuasive." This leads McEvenue to speak of the "dissymetric symmetry" of Genesis 1.[3]

Framework theologian Van Gemeren (1988, 45) speaks of the "dissonance" within the creation account where "on the one

---

1. We must note the chiastic relationship between the events of day 2 and day 5 does not contradict the arrangement.
2. See also Cassuto 1998, 28, 42; Young 1964, 69; Kelly 1997, 201.
3. S.E. McEvenue, *The Narrative Style of the Priestly Writer* (Rome: Pontifical Institute, 1971), 113-15. Cited in Wenham 1987, 6.

hand, the fourth day belongs to the formative aspect of God's creation (days 1–3) and, on the other hand, it is part of the filling of the created world (days 4–6)." Thus, from one perspective, day 4 is attached to the formative part of creation along with days 1–3, thereby seeing days 1–4 as related. From another angle, day 4 is attached to the latter days of creation, forming a set of days 4–6.

Illustrating the disagreement among framework advocates, VanGemeren accurately presents a slightly different scheme. But though he is *more* accurate, he fails to be *totally* accurate, and both precision problems expose a stain on the alleged artistic tapestry. Notice that he (correctly) has the "seas" created on day 3 (compare Gen. 1:10), which contradicts the schema of the Majority Report (1999, 6). It also throws off the balance with day 5 because the aquatic creatures are then placed in "the seas" (1:22). Notice also that the water that will eventually form the seas is not *created* on day 2, it already exists on day 1 (Gen. 1:2); even Kline admits that Genesis 1:2 is a part of day 1.[4] VanGemeren's diagram is presented thus:[5]

Formation of the World	Filling of the World
Day 1 darkness, light	Day 4 heavenly light-bearers
Day 2 heavens, water	Day 5 birds of the air; water animals
Day 3 seas, land, vegetation	Day 6 land animals; man; provision of food

Wenham's analysis even suggests the waters are insignificant, for he neither portrays them in his table nor mentions them in his explanation:

---

4. Kline's heading shows that day 1 is contained in Gen. 1:1–5; and the text specifically declares it, when he comments that we must understand "the beginning as the commencement of the seven-day history." Kline 1970, 82; see also, Young 1964: 87, 104.

5. It also is the scheme presented in Mathews 1996, p. 115–116.

Day 1 Light	Day 4 Luminaries
Day 2 Sky	Day 5 Birds and Fish
Day 3 Land (Plants)	Day 6 Animals and Man (Plants for food)
Day 7 Sabbath	

The triad structure appears to be malleable according to need: it attempts to be all things to all people. Thus, it seems to be a Transformer action figure used for fighting battles against traditionalist academic findings. Embarrassing features may be overlooked (Wenham), re-arranged (Majority Report (1999), or presented warts and all (VanGemeren). The framework position in the Majority Report (1999) absolutely misconstrues what Moses actually says. Here the tabular error is openly declared as fact in the text: "God creates the sky and seas on Day 2" (p. 6). That is wholly mistaken; and serves as evidence of the error of the triadic structure. We expressly read of the *third day* that God separated the land and the water, gathering the water "into one place" and *only then* naming this body of water "the seas" (Gen. 1:10). Remember — two pages previous in the Majority Report (1999) the authors emphasize the significance of "naming" (p. 4) — apparently unless it undercuts their position.

Triad Symmetry Imbalance. The framework hypothesis works on the assumption that the Genesis 1 material presents a topical arrangement rather than temporal advancement. It suggests that the "obvious" balance and parallel between days 1–3 and days 4–6 is clear evidence of the overriding *topical* nature of Moses' concern. Unfortunately, the proposed hypothetical, nonchronological framework for Genesis 1 fails structurally and logically, as has been noted since the days of Keil and Delitzsch (2001, 38): "The work of creation does not fall, as *Herder* and others maintain, into two triads of days, with the work of the second answering to that of the first." Thus, it possesses only an apparent and superficial parallelism, a parallelism that can be equally accounted for, if need be, by the providential action of God in creation.

What is worse, this interpretive procedure overthrows the very obvious chronological development revealed in Genesis 1, the majestic "march of days." This is a serious methodological flaw in the framework hermeneutic in that Genesis 1 provides both the revelational explanation of the origin of the universe and the world. It also provides us with the historical revelation of the development of the human race and of redemption in Genesis, which in turn is foundational to the theology and redemptive history of all of Scripture. And as Collins (2005, 142) points out, "parallelism is not the same as identity." Or we might say, "similarity does not entail identity."

The "dissonance" in Genesis 1 leads to problems of severe imbalance in the proposed triad — which may help explain why framework advocates admit the parallelism does not prove their point (see previous discussion). The dissonance is deafening. Numerous discordant features disrupt the supposed harmony of the framework. Indeed, the arrangement not only fails symmetrically, but it also neglects to account for and organize all features of the six-day revelation. For instance, as Kline, Young, and others note, "the waters" are created on day 1 (Gen. 1:2), not day 2.[6] Consequently, day 4 lacks an appropriate parallel inhabitant for the waters.

In addition, Genesis informs us that the water creatures produced on day 5 are to swim in the "seas" (*yāmiym*), which were formed *not* on the parallel day 2 but established (even *named!*) on day 3. Regarding the divine activity on day 3 we read, "Then God said, 'Let the waters below the heavens be gathered into one place, and let the dry land appear'; and it was so. God called the dry land earth, and the gathering of the waters He called seas" (Gen. 1:9–10). The living creatures of day 5 are to "fill the waters in the *seas*" (1:22) and are called "fish of the *sea*" (1:26, 28). In addition to the problem mentioned above, this results in the

---

6. Gen. 1:1 stands "as the commencement of the seven-day history," Kline 1970, 82; see also Young 1964, 104; Kelly 1997, 79.

"seas" separated out on day 3 having no corresponding inhabitant created on its supposed "parallel" day, day 6. No wonder
Ridderbos (1957, 34–35) urges that the problem of the fish in
the seas "must not be given much weight." Too much weight
would wreck the fragile framework. Thus, the whole scheme is
exposed as erroneous by such discoveries.

Furthermore, the birds created on day 5 require the prior up-
thrusting of the continental land masses on day 3, thereby failing
to parallel day 2: the birds are commanded to "multiply on the
earth" (1:22). Besides, this also leaves the creation of the "waters
above the expanse" on day 2 without an inhabitant on its parallel
day 5. The original waters of day 1 and the waters above the expanse are being lost in the shuffle.

Still further, the birds are called the "birds of the *sky*" (Gen.
1:26, 28). That is, their unique sphere of operation is the "expanse"
or "firmament," which was *named* "heaven" or "sky" (*šāmāyim*) on
day 2. Thus, the creation of the birds assumes in the literary process
the prior existence of the "heaven" of day 2 as well as the "earth"
of day 3. That is, they assume the sequential progress of Genesis 1.
We should also wonder why man is not formed out of the vegetation of day 3 since the animals are formed out of the earth of day
3: "Then God said, 'Let the earth bring forth living creatures after
their kind' " (Gen 1:24). Even framework scholar Futato (1998,
14) admits, "It may seem that the parallelism breaks down at the
end, because vegetation and mankind may not seem like much of
a parallel." Where is the symmetry?

We must wonder why framework advocates deem the "problem" of the sun's creation on a literal, chronological day 4 to be
a stumbling block for the reader. Why should this be a concern,
since the fish and birds are left without their proper habitats in
terms of the literary arrangement of the material? Of course,
none of these problems affect the common sense, historically
promoted, traditionally held, exegetically established, chronological approach.

Other dissonant features of the alleged artistry of Genesis 1 include days 3 and 6 being emphasized by each possessing two acts of creation (as opposed to one act on each of the other days), two announcements of "and God said" (Gen. 1:9, 11, 24, 26), and two benedictions (Gen. 1:10, 12, 25, 31). Yet days 4 and 6 are emphasized by their wordiness — these two days receiving more discussion by Moses than the other days. And we must remember that according to Van Gemeren, day 4 is a member of the first set of days (days 1-4) *and* the second set (days 4-6). And day 4 also allegedly "recapitulates" day 1. This all becomes very confusing.

An interesting feature that has frustrated modern commentators (as well as the Jewish translators of the Septuagint) is the disharmony of numerical features: "The eight works of creation are prompted by ten divine commands and executed on six different days" (Wenham 1987, 6). Also, we find God uttering blessings on days 5–7, but not on days 1–4. We note that the fulfillment formula of the first day differs from that of the other five days: "And there was *x*" (one time) versus "and it was so" (six times). The formula of execution usually precedes the formula of appreciation, but in verse 4 it follows it. The fourth day differs from the other creative days in that it "is the only day on which no divine word subsequent to the fulfillment is added" (Wenham 1987, 23). Rather than representing the picturesque smile of Mona Lisa, they cause the perplexed frowns of Many Literalists. I will present this in tabular fashion in my "Table of Discordant Features" (see following pages).

Furthermore, the lack of linguistic symmetry in the creation account can be presented in tabular format, as well (adapted from Van Gemeren 1988, 44). Some of these have been presented before, but this format allows a quick glance to reveal disruptions of patterns that undercut any literary artistry in the order of the framework hypothesis (see following pages).

Table of Discordant Features

Kingdoms / Realm		Kings / Rulers	
Day 1	1) Absolute creation (Gen. 1:1–2; compare Exod. 20:11) 2) Waters exist (Gen. 1:2) 3) Light 4) Light 5) Light *fills* space 6) Creation by fiat alone	Day 4	1) No corresponding element 2) No corresponding inhabitant-king 3) Lightbearers (but placed *in "firmament"* [3x] created on day 2 [5x]) 4) Lightbearers assigned "rule" (Gen. 1:16, 18; differs from day 5) 5) Lightbearers *exist* (fill/exist order differs day 2/5; day 3/6) 6) Creation by fiat *and* making. 7) Wordy emphasis of day 4 (not day 3 to correspond with lengthy day 6) 8) Strong palistrophic chiasm pattern (lacking on D1)
Day 2	1) Firmament 2) Waters of day 1 separated to above firmament 3) Waters of day 1 separated to below firmament 4) Waters 5) Waters *exist* 6) Firmament 7) Firmament *exists*	Day 5	1) Birds fly in firmament (but "multiply" "on the earth," Gen. 1:22) 2) No corresponding inhabitant-king 3) Water creatures (but in "seas" [1:22, 26, 28] of day 3) ("waters" already exist on day 1 [1:2]) 4) Water creatures not assigned rule 5) Water creatures "fill" the seas 6) Birds not assigned "rule" 7) Birds fill ("multiply") — but "on the earth" (1:22)

Day 3	1) Seas 2) Dry land 3) Vegetation 4) Seas exist 5) Dry land exists 6) No wordy emphasis corresponding to day 6 (day 4 instead)	Day 6	1) No corresponding inhabitant-king 2) Beasts and man inhabit; but only man rules. 3) No corresponding element 4) Sea creatures fill ("teem") the seas 5) Man "fills" the earth 6) Wordy emphasis of day 6 (like on day 4)

Inconsistent Linguistic Symmetry in Genesis 1–2:3

	Day 1	Day 2	Day 3	Day 4	Day 5	Day 6	Day 7
"And God said"	1	1	2	1	1	4	—
"Let there be"	1	2	3	1	2	2	—
"And it was so"	—	1	2	1	—	2	—
Description of divine act	—	1	1	2	1	2	—
Divine naming	1	1	2	—	—	—	—
Divine blessing	—	—	—	—	1	1	1
Declaration "good"	1	—	2	1	1	1	—
"Evening & morning"	1	1	1	1	1	1	—

Triad Symmetry Chronology

The (general) symmetry and (slight) parallelism in Genesis 1 do not necessarily overthrow the text's chronological progress. Indeed, framework advocates even recognize this. For instance, Sloane (2003, 5) notes that "the framework has a clear literary function, and tells us important things about God and his creation. Of course this does not mean that it cannot also serve to assert that the cosmos was made in six 24-hour periods." What is more, traditionalist interpreters frequently recognize divine design in the parallelism, which comports with the historical fact of the creation process.

As Young (1964, 65–66) observed long ago, despite "the fact that some of the material in Genesis one is given in schematic form, it does not necessarily follow that what is stated is to be dismissed as figurative or as not describing what actually occurred. . . . Nor does it even suggest, that the days are to be taken in a non-chronological sense." Thus, six-day advocate Beall (2010, 157) rightly replies to the framework argument: "Just because something is presented according to a pattern does not mean that the pattern is non-literal." After all, theologian Jean-Marc Berthoud well states, "What difficulty would it be for [the Author of the Universe] to cause the most complex, refined literary form to coincide with the very way in which He Himself created all things in six days. Artistic form is in no sense opposed to an actual relation of facts, especially since the Author of the account is none less than the actual Creator of the facts which are described in that account."[7] Symmetry no more undermines literal history than mathematically predictable planetary orbits undermine the reality of astronomical motion or than the aesthetic beauty of a sunset destroys its actual occurrence. This is why many traditionalist interpreters of Genesis allow for the triad scheme or literary patterns in Genesis 1 without it requiring them to dismiss the literal chronology.[8] God is a God of order in His revelation of creation just as He is in execution of creation.

Weeks (1978, 17) responds to the framework assertion that the triad parallelism militates against historical chronology: "Short of some sort of metaphysical presupposition that regards history as totally random and all order in historiography as being a result of arbitrary human imposition, I cannot see how one would ever prove such a proposition." He continues by noting that an orderly creation may even be expected in that "a theologically structured history presupposes a God who actively shapes

---

7. Cited in Kelly 1997, 115; see also Weeks 1988, 107.
8. Kuliovsky 2001, 240ff; Keathley and Rooker 2014, 130; Pipa 2005, 170; Kay 2007b, 97; Duncan 2001, 262.

history so that it conforms to a plan" (Weeks 1978, 18). This would certainly comport with God's statement to Isaiah: "Remember the former things long past, for I am God, and there is no other; I am God, and there is no one like Me, declaring the end from the beginning, and from ancient times things which have not been done, saying, 'My purpose will be established, and I will accomplish all My good pleasure' " (Isa. 46:9–10).

Weeks (1978, 17) also points out that the patriarchal narrative history is presented with various parallels:

> The patriarchal narratives are structured history in the same way as the earlier chapters of Genesis. They fit within a framework created by the heading "These are the generations of . . . (2:4; 5:1; 6:9; 10:1; 11:10; 11:27; 25:12, 19, *etc.*). There are clear instances of parallel structure. Thus the experiences of Isaac parallel those of Abraham. Both have barren wives (15:2; 16:1; 25:21). Both lie concerning their wives (20:2; 26:7). Both face famine in the promised land (12:10; 26:1). Both make a covenant with the Philistines (21:22–34; 26:26–33). If parallelism of structure proves that a passage is not historical then the patriarchal narratives are not historical. This of course is the conclusion of many liberal exegetes, but evangelicals once more maintain an inconsistency, being willing to apply a higher-critical principle in one area of Scripture but not in another.

The God of creation is a God of beauty, order, and design. He can create in a literal chronological manner that also displays symmetric design. For instance, just as the dry land arose from beneath the primal waters and bore life (vegetation) on the third day, so Christ the Lord arose from the tomb to newness of life on the third day. Garland cites Christensen to this end: "Christ's rising on the third day is connected with the third day of creation (Gen. 1:11–13) and the new creation in Christ (2 Cor.

5:17; Gal. 6:15)."[9] Both are historically true, though an interesting parallel exists between them. As Jordan (1999) notes, in John 20:15, Mary Magdalene sees Jesus, the Second Adam, in a garden (John 19:41) and supposes that He is the gardener. This suggests to the student of Scripture a new Eve, restored from her sins, encountering the New Adam in the new garden of the new covenant. This theological imagery paralleling the original creation structure may very well be true here. But she really did see the resurrected Jesus in a literal garden.

When reading the revelation of divine creation, we must not allow its *stylistic harmony* to override its *emphatic progress*. The chronological succession leaves too deep an impression upon the narrative to be mere ornamentation. Besides, as I note above, most of the events of creation week demand the particular chronological order presented. This logical progress establishes a pattern of temporal development. Those one or two features that do not seem to be required in their particular order, nevertheless appear within the flow of carefully structured chronological progress and do not logically contradict it. The revealed pattern shows a clear preparation of earth for man: man's habitat is set in place, then man appears.

Framework advocates frequently argue — as does the Majority Report (1999, 44) — that "dischronology" is a frequent element employed by biblical writers (Irons 1998, 13–15). They even cite examples from Genesis 2, in the very context of our debate. What seems to escape them — due to their strong commitment to their hypothesis — is that dischronology does *not* occur in texts that expressly affirm historical sequence, as we see in the very samples they present. That is, Genesis 1 is so carefully sequenced that Kidner (1957, 54–55) reminds us, "The march of the days is too majestic a progress to carry no implication of

---

9. David E. Garland, *1 Corinthians* (BECNT) (Grand Rapids, MI: Baker, 2003), 687. Citing: Jens Christensen, "And That He Rose on the Third Day according to the Scriptures," *Scandinavian Journal of the Old Testament* 2: 101–13.

ordered sequence." Admitting dischronology as a literary device in general does not prove it is the literary point of Genesis 1 in particular. Such an argument commits the informal logical fallacy of sweeping generalization.

One illustration of Kline's literary approach to Genesis, for instance, dovetails perfectly with the sequential view of the traditional interpretation. Kline (1958, 114) writes, "Another literary interest at work within this parallelism is that of achieving climax, as is done, for example, in introducing men after all other creatures as their king." This "literary interest" happens also to present Adam as *God's* climax in His literal creation, not just *Moses'* climax in his literary production.

The fundamental problem for the traditional exegesis, according to the framework hypothesis, is the relationship of days 1 and 4. As Futato (1998, 16) argues, "Days 1 and 4 are two different perspective on the same creative work." Irons agrees: "Days 1 and 4 do not describe separate activities of God, separated by three days, but contemporaneous activities described from different perspectives."[10] This creates a problem by compounding two fiats into one: the creation of light and the creation of the luminaries; or else it makes two fiats result in only one effect.

Triad Symmetry Error

In many of the writings of framework proponents, the two triads of days are sorted out into two classes, either Realm and Ruler, Kingdoms and Kings, or, as the Majority Report (1999, 16) presents it (less aesthetically!): Domains and Rulers. Irons (1998, 28), following his mentor Kline, prefers "Creation Kingdoms" and "Creature Kings" in that "the concepts of dominion and kingship are prominent in Gen. 1:1–2:3. In each of the days of the second triad, the created entities are assigned a ruling task."[11]

---

10. Majority Report 1999: 6; compare Irons 1998, 58.
11. See Kline 1996, 5, 9.

This alleged structure of Genesis 1 promotes a false view of both the creation record and the creation result. This creates a problem for two reasons, one linguistic and one theological.

Linguistically, we must observe that the animals are not appointed "rule." Nowhere does the text mention that they are to rule. Niehaus (2014, 41) attempts to get around this problem by arguing, "The veracity of the proposed form is affirmed by the contents, because we read that God created the greater and lesser lights to 'rule over' the day and the night, and that he created the man and woman with the command to 'subdue [the earth] and rule over [the animals]' (Gen. 1:28). Bracketed by such institutions of authority, the principle may reasonably be inferred for day 5, in which the sea creatures rule the seas and the birds rule the air."

But as Kulikovsky (2001, 240) complains, there is "no philological or contextual evidence to indicate that God intended them [the aquatic and aerial creatures] to rule anything." Their command to "be fruitful and multiply" in the earth is not tantamount to a command to rule. After all, the plants of day 3 are designed also to "bear fruit" and "seed" and thereby multiply, *but they do not rule.* Yet Irons (1998, 28–29) writes, "The fish and birds of day five are blessed with a dominion mandate that implies rule over the spheres established by day two: 'Be fruitful and multiply, and fill the waters in the seas, and let birds multiply on the earth' (1:23). This 'be fruitful and multiply' mandate closely parallels the mandate given to man (1:26, 28) and is therefore to be understood in similar terms, as a dominion mandate." This fallacious reasoning also succumbs to a *reductio ad absurdum*: by parity of reasoning we could likewise infer that the luminaries are to be fruitful and multiply because they are, like man, given a dominion mandate![12]

The framework assertion here is another example of the serious methodological problem we have with the hypothesis: it

---

12. Interestingly, regarding the heavenly lights, the word "govern" (1:16) is *memšâlâ.* Whereas the "rule" that man is to engage uses the word *râdâ.*

constantly reads things into the text that are not there. We can see this in the incredible description of God "going to work" in the Majority Report (1999, 8) as cited above. Notice also my further response below. The notion of animal rule is simply alien to the text; it must be imposed in the narrative.

Theologically, only *man* is to rule. In fact, he is to rule *over the sea, air, and land creatures* (Gen. 1:26, 28). God *expressly* declares this. He could easily have employed similar language had He intended a ruling function for the animals — but He does not. The Psalmist is absorbed in praise when he recognizes *man's* rule over the animal kingdom (Ps. 8:5–8). Nowhere is man to share rule with the animals; man names the animals as he begins exercising *his* rule over *them* (Gen. 2:20). In fact, an important feature in the historical Fall of Adam is Adam's allowing the animal realm (the serpent) to exercise rule over him (Gen. 3:1–6; compare 2 Cor. 11:3)! Rather than Genesis 1 suggesting Realm-Ruler relations, the text actually reinforces man's uniqueness on the earth as the Ruler of all else (Gen. 1:26–28). In fact, this appears to be the very point of Genesis 1 — as well as Psalm 8.

Triad Symmetry Failure

Even if there is as much literary structure as framework advocates contend, what does that prove? Blocher (1984, 53) suggests that it at least proves that Genesis 1 should not be taken chronologically: "But could this extremely careful construction of the narrative not coincide with the chronological reality of the divine work, as certain literalists attempt to plead? Of course, you can always imagine anything. But, in the face of what the author shows of his method, there is no reason to suppose it."

His reason for this is somewhat obscure: "The hypothesis of the literary procedure gives sufficient explanation of the form of the text; anything further would be superfluous. Occam's razor, the principle of economy that argued against the multiplication of hypotheses, removes ideas of this kind. The suggestion betrays the a priori desire to find literal language" (Blocher 1984, 53). His argument seems to be that because the dischronology hypothesis is the simplest hypothesis for explaining the literary structure, we have no reason to think the text is chronological. But there are several problems with such reasoning.

First, he does not correctly apply Occam's Razor. Occam's Razor suggests that when two explanations are equally good (they both explicate the explanandum), the simpler one is to be preferred. For example, if your car will not start, two explanations may account for the problem. Explanation 1 proposes a dead battery; explanation 2, both a dead battery and gremlins. Occam's Razor would choose the simpler explanation, explanation 1.

Now back to our problem. It is difficult to determine which of the two views in question is the simplest explanation of the structure of Genesis 1. The framework hypothesis argues the explanation that this text has literary structure, which therefore dismisses chronology. The traditional interpreters counter by arguing the explanation that this text has a structure that emphasizes how God prepared the world for man to inhabit. But which is the simplest explanation? The issue does not lend itself to this type of analysis.

Even if the framework hypothesis could be shown to be the simpler view, it would only be preferred if all things were equal — in other words, if there were no other considerations involved. But as noted above, this is clearly not the case. Framework opponent Weeks' (1978, 18) comments are insightful: "A theologically structured history presupposes a God who actively shapes history so that it conforms to his plan. A liberal exegete who denies the existence of such a God must dismiss as true history all biblical accounts which see theological patterns in history. The evangelical has no basis for such an a priori dismissal of structured history. The fact that Genesis 1 displays a structure in no way prejudices its claim to historicity." Once again, I would note

Kidner's (1967, 54) observation that "the march of the days is too majestic a progress to carry no implication of ordered sequence."

Furthermore, appeals to economy of explanation prove too much. One could argue (as some do) that the best explanation for the literary structure is that the whole of Genesis 1 is to be taken figuratively — the chronology, as well as the events described. The events presented as if historical are simply parables to teach moral lessons. This obviously is a bridge too far.

In addition, to argue that literary structure (i.e., parallelism) implies dischronology is fallacious. For example, Exodus 7–13:17 contains parallelism and yet reports chronological progress. It contains three cycles of plagues with three plagues each and then a tenth plague. As Jordan reminds us, "The first plague of each cycle begins with a command to go to Pharaoh in the morning. The second in each cycle begins with a simple command to go to Pharaoh. The third in each cycle is not announced to Pharaoh at all."[13]

Young (1964, 65–66) is surely correct when he observes:

> In the first place, from the fact that some of the material in Genesis one is given in schematic form, it does not necessarily follow that what is stated is to be dismissed as figurative or as not describing what actually occurred. Sometimes a schematic arrangement may serve the purpose of emphasis. Whether the language is figurative or symbolical, however, must be determined upon exegetical grounds. Secondly, a schematic disposition of the material in Genesis one does not prove, nor does it even suggest, that the days are to be taken in a non-chronological sense. There appears to be a certain schematization, for example, in the genealogies of Matthew one, but it does not follow that the names of the genealogies are to be understood in a non-chronological sense, or that Matthew teaches that

---

13. James B. Jordan, "The Framework Hypothesis: A Gnostic Heresy," *Biblical Horizons* (July, 1998), 3. Web: BiblicalHorizons.com.

the generations from Abraham to David parallel, or were contemporary with, those from David to the Babylonian captivity and that these in turn are paralleled to the generations from the Babylonian captivity to Christ . . . . Why, then, must we conclude that, merely because of a schematic arrangement, Moses has disposed of Chronology?

As noted previously, even the leading framework scholar Kline (1958, 157) admits that the literary structure of Genesis 1 does not prove a non-chronological intent by Moses: "Whether the events narrated occurred in the order of their narration would, as far as the chronological framework of Genesis 1 is concerned, be an open exegetical question."

Conclusion

Despite its surface appearance, the triad argument for the framework hypothesis cannot withstand close scrutiny. This is significant in that a strong, textually derived and historically affirmed case exists for God's acting "in the beginning, to create, or make of nothing, the world, and all things therein whether visible or invisible, *in the space of six days*; and all very good" (Westminster Confession of Faith 4:1). I believe the traditional, literal interpretation of Genesis 1 is superior to the literary interpretation of the framework hypothesis at every point of conflict.

Besides this, Keathley and Rooker (2014, 134) well note:

There is not a single theological truth from the creation account that depends upon a framework reading of the text. Moreover, no particular insight has been discovered in the framework analysis that is also not apparent in other approaches to the study of creation in Genesis 1. In this regard the framework hypothesis has failed to deliver. It is virtually impossible to escape the drumbeat of the ongoing march of the creation days and the sequence of time in Genesis 1.

Chapter 8

The Genesis 2 Message

Genesis 2 Introduction

I come now to what Kline (1958, 148) deems the "decisive word against the traditional interpretation": Genesis 2:5. That text reads, "Now no shrub of the field was yet in the earth, and no plant of the field had yet sprouted, for the LORD God had not sent rain upon the earth, and there was no man to cultivate the ground."

But what does this lone verse teach that leads the Majority Report (1999, 9) so confidently to declare that it "introduces a principle" that "must affect how we understand everything that has gone before"? Excerpts from Kline (1958, 151–52) will inform us of the utility of this verse for the framework hypothesis:

> Embedded in Gen. 2:5 ff. is the principle that the *modus operandi* of the divine providence was the same during the creation period as that of ordinary providence at the present time. . . . In contradiction to Gen. 2:5, the twenty-four-hour day theory must presuppose that God employed other than the ordinary secondary means in executing his works of providence. To take just one example, it was the work of the "third day" that the waters should be

187

gathered together into seas and that the dry land should appear and be covered with vegetation (Gen. 1:9–13). All this according to the theory in question transpired within twenty-four hours. But continents just emerged from under the sea do not become thirsty land as fast as that by the ordinary process of evaporation. And yet according to the principle revealed in Gen. 2:5 the process of evaporation in operation at that time was the ordinary one.

Elsewhere, Irons and Kline (2001, 86) comment, "Our argument is that Genesis 2:5–6 informs us that the mode of divine providence during the creation period was *ordinary* rather than *extraordinary*. This rules out the possibility that the daylight was caused by a supernatural or nonsolar light source for the first three days." Framework scholar White (1974, 163) agrees: "The '*modus operandi* of the divine providence' was the same during the period of creation as that which characterizes the ordinary providence of the present and all other historic ages." Justin Taylor (2015, 4) follows Kline, noting that the lack of rain is "the *explanation* for this lack of vegetation which is attributed to *ordinary providence*." He continues, "The very wording of the text presupposes seasons and rain cycles and a lengthier passage of time during this 'day' [*yôm*] that God formed man."

To put it succinctly, Genesis 2:5 demands that the third day[1] had to be *much* longer than 24 because the waters removed early on day 3 leave the land so parched that it desperately needs rain before the landscape could be clothed with vegetation. Yet a full array of plant life appears at the end of that very day, day 3 (Gen. 1:11). Irons and Kline (2001, 233) conclude therefore: "We find that a literal, sequential interpretation results in a head-on collision with the principle that, during creation week, God used

---

1. Note Kline's quotations marks around "third day." And observe the Majority Report (1999: 5) and its wholly inaccurate statement that advocates of the traditional exegesis tend to put quotation marks around references to the biblical days!

ordinary means in His providential maintenance of the created order." Blocher (1984, 56) is confident that "this proof has not been refuted." Currid (2007, 54) notes against the six-day creationist view: "The major problem with the literal interpretation is it presupposes extraordinary providential care. That is, natural process must be discounted in the creation of the universe." This surely is the *locus classicus* for the framework hypothesis.

Before I begin, I must note several observations that should give one pause before too quickly adopting Kline's innovative exegesis.

Genesis 2 Caution

First, Genesis 2:5–6 is declared by many commentators to be "difficult" (Wenham 1876, 57), "most difficult" (Cassuto 1998, 103), and a "perplexing passage" with a significant "ambiguity" of focus (Mathews 1995, 193). Indeed, Kidner (1966, 111) observes that "the difficulty is reflected in the variety of interpretations that have been put forward." This passage is "widely misunderstood" (Kidner 1966, 113). Erroneous systems often flow from difficult passages (consider the Mormon baptismal theology that derives from 1 Cor. 15:29).

Second, by all accounts, Kline's exposition is "new" (Blocher 1984, 53). This novel exposition does not appear to flow from a dispassionate study of Genesis over the years. Rather, judging from Kline's own writings, it seems to be related to his seeking peace with the assured claims of naturalistic science. His first article introducing his new exegesis shows the heat of controversy in its first sentence, when he refers to "the debate over the chronological data of Genesis 1" (Kline 1958, 146). His second to last paragraph concludes, "And surely natural revelation concerning the sequence of developments in the universe as a whole and the sequence of the appearance of the various orders of life on our planet . . . would require the exegete to incline to a not exclusively chronological interpretation of the creation week."

His last sentence harkens back to "the primeval ages of creation" (Kline 1958, 157).

Kline's (1996, 2) later article opens with these words, "To rebut the literalist interpretation of the Genesis creation week propounded by the young-earth theorists is a central concern of this article. At the same time, the exegetical evidence adduced also refutes the harmonistic day-age view." The conclusion is that "as far as the time frame is concerned, with respect to both the duration and sequence of events, the scientist is left free of biblical constraints in hypothesizing about cosmic origins" (Kline 1996, 2). This concept is suggested also in Blocher's (1984, 22, 48, 222, 227, etc.) frequently referring to traditional exegetes as engaging in "anti-scientism." Erroneous systems often flow from difficult passages — when needed to prove a point.

Third, Kline's exegesis develops a *difficult* passage in a *unique* direction for dealing with a *contemporary* debate. Not only so, but his exposition is set against superior options — options that are compatible with the traditional exegesis and that do not dismantle the most obvious structuring device of Genesis 1. This may explain why Kline's exegesis is not adopted in most major commentaries. Rather than applying Genesis 2:5–6 to the global scene of day 3, Keil and Delitzsch, Allis, Young, Collins, and others apply the passage to what Keil and Delitzsch call "the place which God prepared for their abode" on day 6.[2] Kidner (1966) sees the passage as reflecting Genesis 1:2, stripping the present world of the important vegetation that man will need, while in verse 6, noting the flooding waters over the whole earth.[3] Cassuto, Hamilton, Mathews, Sailhammer, and others see the Fall of Adam anticipated here when these particular plants are introduced (see explanation below).[4]

---

2. Keil and Delitzsch 2001, 47–49; Allis 1951, 14; Young 1964, 61; Collins 2006, 111.
3. Compare Sailhammer 1990, 40.
4. Cassuto 1998, 102; Hamilton 1990, 154; Mathews 1996, 193; Sailhammer 1990, 40.

Fourth, in the final analysis there appears to be some confusion in the framework camp — which should not surprise us, given its inherent complexity. A few brief samples of random problems should suffice in getting the point across.

M. Ross (1999, 126) admits, "The language of the text suggests ordinary providence. Admittedly, the language of the text does not definitively settle the matter, for if Genesis One does teach that creation took place within one week, this language can be reconciled with that view." Futato expends fully half of his entire article in promoting a minority explanation of the *'ēd* ("mist," "cloud," "stream"?) in Genesis 2:6 as "the crux" of his argument, which he declares plays a "major role" and is a "key to understanding" his framework exposition. He adopts "rain cloud" over the more widely held "streams, river, flood" (NRSV, NIV, CEB, GW, GNT, CSB, NAB, NLT; compare NJB) — as originally held by Kline (1948, 151; 1970, 83) and currently by Blocher (1984, 113).[5]

Irons (1998, 3, 6) declares that "one who holds to the framework interpretation, then, is not bound to any particular view regarding the age of the earth." But then based on his and Kline's comments about the thirsty earth and moving continents, how could they be young earth advocates? The framework hypothesis' slow providence view will not allow continents to shift so enormously in a one-day period. Thus, Kline (1958, 115) speaks of the "aeons of creation history."

Genesis 2 Interpretation

A view far superior to Kline's is that of Cassuto, Hamilton, Mathews, Sailhammer, Waltke, and others. It avoids the novel approach to a single verse requiring a re-interpretation of the historical exegesis of the entire first chapter of Genesis for the

---

5. The great majority of commentaries (e.g., NIV, NRSV, NJPS, NJV, NAB) and scholars agree against Futato. For example, Hamilton (1990, 155). Young (1964, 62n) says "the translation 'mist' must be abandoned." See also Cassuto 1998; Kidner 1966, 193; Wenham 1987, 58.

purposes of engaging in a contemporary debate. It argues that this verse appears to anticipate the Fall of Adam and the consequent development of the story of redemption. As Young (1964, 74) puts it, "In chapter two events are narrated from the standpoint of emphasis, in preparation for the account of the fall." Let me explain.

The first chapter of Genesis provides an account of the creation of "the heavens and the earth" (Gen. 1:1). Both the traditional interpretation of creation and the framework hypothesis agree that the account of the creation of the universe actually is drawn to an emphatic conclusion with the first three verses of Genesis 2. Note the emphasis on the cessation of creation: "Thus the heavens and the earth were *completed*, and all their hosts. By the seventh day God *completed* His work which He had done, and He *rested on the seventh day from all His work which He had done.* Then God blessed the seventh day and sanctified it, because in it *He rested from all His work* which God had created and made" (Gen. 2:1–3, emphasis added).

Both the traditional interpretation of creation and the framework hypothesis agree that Genesis 2:4 serves as a *heading* to what follows: "This is the account of the heavens and the earth when they were created, in the day that the LORD God made earth and heaven."[6] The word "account" (NASB, NIV, CEB, NET) or "generations" (KJV, NRSV, ESV) is a translation of the Hebrew term *tôlēdôt*. As Kline (1996, 11) admits, "In keeping with the uniform meaning of this formula, Gen. 2:4 signifies that what follows recounts not the origins but the subsequent history of the heavens and the earth."

Both the traditional view[7] and the framework hypothesis agree that Genesis 2 "fixes attention . . . on Eden as it sets the stage for the covenant crisis of Genesis 3" (Kline 1996, 11). Allis (1951, 15) even declares of Genesis 2: "The whole second

---

6. For a careful explanation of verse 4, see Young 1964, 59–60.
7. E.g., Young 1964, 63; Keil and Delitzsch 2001, 76.

account is, broadly speaking, an expansion or elaboration of Genesis 1.27. The planting of the garden has nothing to do with i. 11, 12."

Where the conflict between the historic interpretation and the framework innovation arises is, of course, at Genesis 2:5. The framework hypothesis demands that the brief statement here establishes the principle of ordinary providence, which then must reach back and govern the entire, lengthy preceding creation account of Genesis 1. This requires that during creation "week" the various geological activities and biological entities are generated by God's fiats, but over an enormous period of time by means of slow providence and gradual evolution.

The traditional interpretation holds that the fiats of God were supernaturally miraculous in effect, producing their full-blown results immediately. The refrain of fiat-followed-by-result shows "the precision and celerity with which the injunction was carried out: as He commanded, and as soon as He commanded" (Cassuto 1998, 26). Of Genesis 1:11, Cassuto (1998, 40) states, "On the selfsame day, as soon as the inanimate matter, which serves as a foundation for plant-life, had been set in order, there were created, without delay, the various kinds of vegetation." When we read in Genesis 1 the declaration "and it was so," we must understand that "it was so instantly, in accordance with God's fiat" (Cassuot 1998, 41). Wenham (1987, 38) also notes the "immediate fulfillment of each command." And Jordan (1997, 4) points out that Genesis 1 says certain events occurred, but the framework hypothesis says they did not. As Duncan (2001, 98) puts it, "When Genesis 1 declares the formula 'God said . . . and it was so,' the text does not indicate that it means, 'God said . . . and it took awhile.'" Rather, Duncan continues, this "magnifies the miraculous creative work of God."

This of course comports with a literal, six-day creative process. It also is reflected in Psalm 33:9: "For He spoke, and it

was done; He commanded, and it stood fast." Thus, for instance,
the geological extrusion of the land surface from beneath the
ubiquitous waters transpired immediately rather than gradually.
Such action during creation would be similar to the supernatural
(non-providential) cosmic miracles of Scripture; for example, the
rapid drying up of the Red Sea for the Israelites (Josh. 2:10; compare Exod. 14:21), the incredible halting of the sun on Joshua's
"long day" (Josh. 10:12), the reversal of the sun for Hezekiah
(Isa. 38:7ff), and the stilling of the tempest and waves by the
Lord (Matt. 8:26–27).

Besides, God is not limited to ordinary providence in His
actions in history as we see from the record of miracles in the
Bible. And by the very nature of the case, "Creation begins *atyp-
ically* as compared to our experience" (Duncan 2001, 53). Why
would the absolutely unique period of creation constrain God to
act solely by means of ordinary (slow) providence? What is more,
Grossman well notes that "the presence of ordinary providence
does not disprove the possibility of extraordinary providence."[8]
Of course, God used ordinary providence during creation. He
established, then employed scientific laws in the beginning (e.g.,
gravitation, inertia, electromagnetism). What is not true, however, is that he used *only* providence. In fact, as Batten (2015, 3–4)
notes, "There is no miracle in the Bible that does *not* operate in
the midst of normal providence." For instance, the wine Jesus
made from water still remained in the water pots by gravity, it
still reflected light from its surface, it still created taste sensations,
and so forth. Batten continues on the next page by noting that
Peter anticipates this sort of objection from the scoffers: "Know
this first of all, that in the last days mockers will come with their
mocking, following after their own lusts, and saying, 'Where is
the promise of His coming? For ever since the fathers fell asleep,
all continues just as it was from the beginning of creation' " (2
Pet. 3:3–4). God created a world covered with water (2 Pet. 3:5),

---

8. Cited in Pipa 2005, 161.

but scoffers say everything has continued as they are now from the very beginning.

How then shall we interpret Genesis 2:5 if it does not establish a providential principle that causes us to alter "how we understand everything that has gone before" (Majority Report 1999, 9)?

We must begin by observing that in Genesis 2, Moses expressly narrows his focus from "the heavens and the earth . . . and all their hosts" (2:1) all the way down to Eden and its special host, Adam. Of course, as noted above, the framework hypothesis agrees with us in this general analysis. But the consequences of this re-orientation and the purpose of 2:5 escape the framework proponents.

In Genesis 2:4ff, Moses begins informing us of what becomes of God's beautiful creation. He opens by pointing out that the problem that his audience experiences in creation arises as the result of the actions of his highest created being: man. In Genesis 2:4, God's covenant name Jehovah (*yhwh*) appears for the first time in Genesis, which, along with the unusual word order of 2:4b ("earth and heaven" drawing attention to the earth) and the *tôlēdôt* heading, strongly suggests a change of emphasis.

In Genesis 1 *'elōhîm* ("God") appears throughout the creation account: *'Elōhîm* acting as "the mighty one" who accomplishes the creation of the entire universe ("the heaven and the earth," 1:1, 2:1, 4) effortlessly by His mere word: eight quick fiats spread over six brief days. But in Genesis 2, rather than emphasizing the powerful creation, Moses emphasizes the covenantal relation: God and man are in covenant, as indicated by Moses' importing the covenant name (*yhwh*) into the context of the intimate creative formation of man (Gen. 2:7; whereas animals were "mass produced," 1:20, 24) and the joyful preparation of a tranquil environment (2:8) with abundant provisions of water (2:6, 10, 13–14), food (2:9, 16), peaceful animals (2:19–20) — and a bride for Adam (2:21–24). In all of this beautiful environment there was no shame (2:25) — indeed, all was "very good" (1:31).

Now Genesis 2:5 is placed at the beginning of the *tôlēdôt* of creation, at the head of the account designed to inform us of what becomes of creation. Genesis 2:5 appears in such a way as to anticipate the Fall that soon comes (3:1–24). It informs the reader that he will now learn about the glorious, generous, and gracious provision of God for man — conditions that prevailed *before* the reader's well-known circumstances of discord, disappointment, and death. Thus it gives "a summary of certain aspects of creation in order to lay the foundation for subsequent events" so that it becomes then the foundation for the "inauguration of the covenant in the garden" (Pipa 1999:,157–158). Let me explain.

In Genesis 2:5, Moses speaks to the reader who has just learned that all was "very good" at the end of the creative process on day 6 (Gen. 1:31), and who still has ringing in his ears the sanctifying and blessing of God (2:2–3) on the work he himself accomplished (note the three-fold emphasis on "the work which he had done," 2:2–3). But Moses' audience lives in a wholly different moral and environmental context in the post-Fall world of sin, struggle, and death. Genesis 2:5 informs the readers that *originally,* when God readied himself to create man (on day 6) "no shrub of the field was yet in the earth, and no plant of the field had yet sprouted, for the Lord God had not sent rain upon the earth; and there was no man to cultivate the ground." This is not speaking of conditions that prevail throughout the earth. Actually, the ESV better renders Genesis 2:5–6, showing that it is focusing on a particular "land" or region, rather than the whole "earth": "When no bush of the field was yet in the land and no small plant of the field had yet sprung up — for the Lord God had not caused it to rain on the land, and there was no man to work the ground, and a mist was going up from the land and was watering the whole face of the ground."

As Collins (1999, 275) notes, "The semantic range of Hebrew *'eres* in verse 5" shows that "the word often means simply
'land' (cf. NIV margin), either as dry land (its sense in 1:10–31)
or as a specific region (its sense in 2:11–13)." He argues that this
probably refers to a local region from which God moved Adam in
order to get him into nearby Eden (Gen. 2:8) and to which God
removes Adam when He bans him from Eden (3:23). Scholars
such as Leupold, Cassuto, Young, and Kidner see it as referring
specifically to Eden itself.[9]

The "shrub of the field" here is the Hebrew phrase *siah-haśśā-
deh*; the "plant of the field" is expressed as *'eseb-haśśādeh*. As
Futato (1998, 3) himself ably demonstrates, "The phrase *si-
ah-haśśādeh*, refers to the wild vegetation that grows sponta-
neously after the onset of the rainy season, and *'eseb-haśśādeh*
refers to cultivated grains." This is a rather widely held interpretation found in Cassuto, Hamilton, Mathews, Sailhammer,
Waltke, and others.[10] But what does it *mean*? What is its *point*?
Its revelational *purpose*?

These two types of vegetation are emphasized from within a
creation process that highlights vegetation. Day 3 (Gen. 1:9–13),
on which vegetation is created (1:11–12), is emphasized with two
fiats (thereby differing from the single fiats of days 1, 2, 4, and
5). Even the framework hypothesis views day 3 as a climax along
these lines, holding that the day on which God creates vegetation
(day 3) corresponds to the day of man's creation (day 6).[11] In fact,
when man is created he is specifically given the earth's vegetation
for food (1:29).

Now when we come to Genesis 2:5, we discover that it also
emphasizes vegetation and its relation to man and his food supply. To properly grasp its significance we should note that the

---

9. Leupold 1942, 111–14; Cassuto 1998, 71ff; Young 1976, 61; Kidner 1967, 58–
   60.
10. Cassuto 1998,102; Hamilton 1990, 154; Mathews 1996, 193; Sailhammer
    1990, 40. Waltke 1976, 35.
11. Irons 1998, 30.

covenant-making Lord God places Adam in a garden with many fruit trees from which he is to eat (Gen. 2:8–9, 16). Adam, however, is forbidden access to one particular tree of testing in the midst of all of this lush, abundant, and accessible vegetation (2:9, 17). And as we well know, Adam fails the test by eating from the divinely prohibited vegetation (3:6). Because of this moral-spiritual rebellion, God curses man in a contextually appropriate and instructive way: God hampers Adam's harvesting of his vegetational food supply, which is necessary to sustaining his life (3:17–19, 23), and He cuts him off from the luxurious garden and its "tree of life" (3:22–24). But *still*: What is my point? Where is the framework hypothesis error?

Genesis 2:5 focuses on two general classes of plants: the wild scrub brush and the cultivated food grain. Again, as Futato (1998, 3, 6, 9) rightly points out, the thorny brush now flourishes in response to rain; and the grains, such as barley, corn, and wheat, require the cultivating labor of man. *And both of these types of plants are subjects of the divine curse in Genesis 3:17–19.*

Genesis 3:17–19 reads: "Cursed is the ground because of you; in toil you shall eat of it all the days of your life. Both *thorns and thistles* it shall grow for you; and you shall eat *the plants of the field*; by the sweat of your face you shall eat bread, till you return to the ground, because from it you were taken; for you are dust, and to dust you shall return" (emphasis added). Thus, here we learn that the divine Curse causes the field to produce the troublesome "thorns and thistles" and the ground to resist man's production of "plants of the field." The "plants of the field" in 3:18 is the exact phrase found in 2:5 (*'eseb-haśśādeh*). The "thorns and thistles" of 3:18 are *synonymous with* and are *specific classes of* the scrub brush (*śiah-haśśādeh*) of 2:5. Many commentaries recognize this relationship between 2:5 and 3:17–19, such as Cassuto, Hamilton, Mathews, Sailhammer, Waltke, and others.[12]

---

12. Cassuto 1998, 102; Hamilton 1990, 154; Mathews 1996, 193; Sailhammer 1990, 40; Waltke 1976, 35.

Thus, in Genesis 2:5, Moses is setting up his account of the moral testing of Adam in Eden. So here he informs his readers *in advance* of the story of the Fall, by taking them back to day 6 just before it occurs. Though his readers are familiar with labor-intensive fields of cultivated grains (Exod. 34:21; 1 Sam. 8:12; Ps. 141:7; Isa. 28:24) and the troublesome scrub brush (Job 5:5; Prov. 24:31; Isa. 5:6, 34:13; Hos. 10:8), it was not always so in God's creation. The grains were not organized into cultivated fields before Adam was created; the bothersome thorns did not infest the ground before Adam's Fall and God's Curse. In fact, God's glorious provision for man had him in the garden cultivating it by simply picking the fruit from the trees (Gen. 2:15–16) rather than hoeing the resistant ground by backbreaking effort (2:5b). After the Fall, man would have to labor by the sweat of his brow against soil hardened "like iron" (Deut. 28:23) and as tough as "bronze" (Lev. 26:19). He must do so in order that he may grow the grain that will be necessary to sustain his enfeebled and troubled life. No longer will he eat from the trees in the Garden of Eden (2:9, 16), but he "shall eat the plants of the field" (3:18b) by the "sweat of his face" (3:19a).

Consequently, in Genesis 2:5, as Moses *opens* his story of man's covenantal testing, he does not look back to the creation process on day 3, but to the creative result (Adam's Edenic environment) on day 6.[13] Keathley and Rooker (2014, 89) point out that Genesis 2 has no statement corresponding to Genesis 1:1 and its absolute creation, and that chapter 2 assumes the work of chapter 1. Moses thus "fills out events of the sixth day" and is therefore describing conditions on day 6 "and not of the creation week" (Collins 2006, 75, 110). He is especially anticipating the following story-line that presents the fateful consequences of the

---

13. Note that before God creates Eve we hear that it was "not good" that Adam should be alone (Gen. 2:18). But we know that at the end of day 6 "all that He had made" was declared by God as "very good" (Gen 1:31).

Fall. In fact, the whole paragraph of Genesis 2:5–9 anticipates the Fall. God's creating Adam from the "dust of the ground" (Gen. 2:7) anticipates that he will one day "return to the dust of the ground" (Gen. 3:19), which is the universal experience of Moses' post-Fall readers: "All came from the dust and all return to the dust" (Eccles. 3:20[14]). The presence of the "tree of the knowledge of good and evil" among the other trees in the garden (Gen. 2:6, 17) anticipates Adam's eating from it (Gen. 2:17, 3:3), which results in man's return to the dust (Gen. 3:19) — and also the serpent's curse to "eat the dust" (Gen. 3:14).

Conclusion

Thus, Genesis 2 is explaining the covenantal test of the well-provided-for man, and it is anticipating his dismal and tragic failure. *This* is the point of Genesis 2:5: God lovingly fashions man and gloriously provides for him prior to the scrub brush entangling his land and before it was necessary that he laboriously break the hard dirt clods to produce cultivated grains. *After* the Fall, futility overwhelms man's environment (Rom. 8:20–23). But according to Genesis 2:5, it was not always so. Consequently, as McCabe (2010, 231) notes, verses 5 and 6 "provide a setting for verse 7 and not a statement about God's mode of operation in the creation week." He lists the following scholars as concurring: Claus Westermann, Victor Hamilton, John Collins, Kenneth Mathews, William Reyburn, Euan Fry, and Allen P. Ross.[15] Framework scholar M. Ross (1999, 126) tellingly comments, "Admittedly, the language of the text does not definitively settle the matter, for if Genesis One does teach that creation took place within one week, this language can be reconciled with that view."

---

14. Compare Job 4:19, 10:9, 20:11, 21:26, 34:15; Ps. 22:15, 44:25, 90:3, 103:14, Eccles. 12:7

15. See Westermann 1984, 197; Hamilton 1990, 156; Collins 2006, 133; Mathews 1996, 193; A. Ross 1996, 119. See also William D. Reyburn and Euan McG. Fry, *A Handbook on Genesis* (New York: United Bible Societies, 1997), p. 60.

The strained interpretation of the framework hypothesis is clearly mistaken. Genesis 2:5–6 does not overturn the historic exegesis of Genesis 1, nor does it undermine creation "in six days" (Exod. 20:11, 31:17). Batten (2015, 3) cites Kline's bold statement regarding the passage: "The unargued presupposition of Gen. 2:5 is clearly that the divine providence was operating during the creation period." Then he replies, "Note that Kline admits that this alleged presupposition is not argued in the text. This would explain why no biblical scholar saw this for thousands of years." The new and unique exposition of one verse cannot sustain the enormous weight placed upon it by framework theologians.

Chapter 9

The Two-Register Cosmogony

We come now to what Irons and Kline (2001, 236) deem "the third exegetical argument in support of the framework interpretation: the two-register cosmology and Scripture, consisting of the upper (invisible) and lower (visible) register." In that the Majority Report (1999) does not deal directly with the two-register cosmogony (though elsewhere Irons declares it as one of three primary exegetical foundations; Irons 1998, 36–52) and because not all framework advocates hold to this difficult and peculiar argument, I will not deal with it in as much detail as with the other evidences.

The Two-Register Definition

As Irons and Kline (2001, 237) put it, "The upper register is the invisible dwelling place of God and His holy angels, that is, heaven. The lower register is called 'earth,' but includes the whole visible cosmos from the planet Earth to the star-studded sky (Col. 1:16)." Thus, the "upper register" is the realm of God's special presence, His throne, and His angelic court (it is not the eternal God himself), whereas the "lower register" is the earthly realm of man, matter, and time. These are two dimensions of the universe. This basic distinction is valid for evangelicals, for we believe in a two-level reality — God and all else, the Creator and the creature — which forms the necessary backdrop of the two registers: "The heavens are the heavens of the LORD, but the earth He has given to the sons of men" (Ps. 115:16). We are not idolaters who have "exchanged the glory of the incorruptible God for an image in the form of corruptible man" (Rom. 1:23a). We are not pantheists who believe all is God and God is all.

As a consequence of this two-register approach, framework advocates hold that "the days of Genesis 1 belong to the upper register" rather than the lower, temporal realm. This is because of "fundamentally analogical" relationship of the upper and lower registers: "the upper register is an archetype, and the lower register is an analogical replica of the upper register," which allows "lower-register features" to "describe upper-register realities" (Irons and Kline 2001, 239). Thus, "our argument, then, is that the language of the *days* and the 'evenings and mornings' is not literal but an instance of lower-register terms being used metaphorically to describe the upper register. . . . Because of the analogical relationship between the two registers, Scripture employs the language of earthly time to speak of the progress of heavenly time" (Irons and Kline 2001, 240).

As we are becoming accustomed to expect, we are not surprised to learn that Kline requires an unusual interpretation of Genesis 1:1 to establish his two-register cosmogony approach. The "heavens" mentioned in the phrase "the heavens and the earth" is not the astronomical universe, but God's home and the angelic realm (Kline 1996, 4; Kline 1977, 250). Nevertheless, not all framework advocates hold this interpretation. Thompson (1968, 19), for instance, promotes the traditional interpretation that "the heavens and the earth" simply means the universe.

Of course, extravagant exegesis is endemic in Kline, who is "not afraid to leave the beaten track" (Blocher 1984, 53). Nowhere do we discover angels or the angelic realm mentioned in the text. Satan's appearing in the guise of a serpent shortly after creation does not require the assumption that the "heavens and the earth" (Gen. 1:1, 2:1) also expressly speaks of the angelic upper register. For neither do we have an explanation of the fall of Satan, which is also assumed in Genesis 3 without prior textual comment.

From this suppressed premise (the two-register cosmogony) various interpretive problems flow. I will focus on the anthropomorphic error that is necessary to this framework concept. The assumed (but inappropriate) anthropomorphisms cause a re-interpreting of the creation week in light of the hidden upper register theology.

The Anthropomorphic Angle

The framework hypothesis employs anthropomorphisms in an unusual way. A generally received definition of anthropomorphism is built upon the word's etymology: "'attribution of human form or character' (OED) (Greek *anthrōpos*, man, *morphē*, form)" (DBI 28). Or as the *Evangelical Dictionary of Theology* (53) puts it, "The term . . . designates the view which conceives of God as having human form (Exod. 15:3; Num. 12:8) with feet (Gen. 3:8; Exod. 24:10), hands (Exod. 24:11; Josh. 4:24), mouth (Num. 12:8; Jer. 7:13), and heart (Hos. 11:8)." See also *Interpreter's Dictionary of the Bible, Baker Encyclopedia of the Bible, International Standard Bible Encyclopedia*, and *Zondervan Encyclopedia of the Bible*, and other standard reference works.[1] The writers of the Majority Report (1999, 8) begin with proper assertions, such as noting that anthropomorphism "describes [God] himself" and "God's actions" and "manner of working." But in the framework argument, Kline (1996, 9), Irons (1998, 46–52), and the Majority Report (1999, 8) do not apply anthropomorphism to God, His actions, and His manner of working, but to the *days* structuring creation week. Not only

---

1. IDB 1:140; BEB 1:117–18; ISBE[2] 1:202–04.

is this hermeneutically inappropriate (Young 1964, 57–58), but as I have asked previously, how can earth days be analogies of eternal reality, the "upper register," where there is no corresponding succession of moments? There is no "heavenly day"; the concept of "day" is a temporal, creational phenomenon.

Besides, the days of Genesis 1 appear in an appropriate context where time itself begins (Gen. 1:1, 5) and in a week wherein the sun was made for the express purpose of marking off days (Gen. 1:14, 18). In fact, "It is extremely difficult to conclude that anything other than a twenty-four-hour day was intended. . . . For now, on day one God created time" (Walton 2001, 81).[2] And, once again I must note, if the days represent the upper register, the "evening and morning" delimiters only confound the problem by having no point of contact with the eternal order, where there is no evening and morning. As Wenham (1987, 14) explains it, "Gen. 1 suggest[s] *rēʾšît* ["beginning"] refers to the beginning of time itself, not to a particular period within eternity."

What is worse, the Majority Report stands Scripture on its head with this attempt. The Report (1999, 7) states, "So we conclude that the creation narrative — specifically the picture of God's completing His creative work in a week of *days* — have [*sic*] been presented in terms of an analogy to a human week of work." But the Fourth Commandment expressly and unambiguously declares the very opposite: "Six days you shall labor and do all your work. . . . *For* in six days the LORD made the heavens and the earth, the sea and all that is in them, and rested on the seventh day" (Exod. 20:9, 11, emphasis added). The "for" statement gives the reason why man must work six days and rest one: because God set the pattern in His original creative activity (see discussion elsewhere in this book).

---

2. Walton is not a six-day creationist. Later in his commentary he will employ a functional approach to Genesis 1 with the result that, in his view, "the twenty-four-hour day will not be seen as posing the problem it has in the past."

Allegations of Anthropomorphisms

The framework hypothesis views Genesis 1 as an anthropomorphic revelation of divine creation. The Majority Report (1999, 8) vigorously asserts this in its section titled "The Clues That the Passage Must Be Taken Anthropomorphically." On the same page, the report notes that "there are many indications in Gen. 1:1–2:3 that God's actions are being described by analogy rather than directly."

Certainly, many commentators point to various divine activities recorded in the *second* and *third* chapters of Genesis and suggest that these are "highly anthropomorphic" images (Mathews 1996, 196; compare Hamilton 1990, 161). For instance, they note that the Lord's fashioning of Adam's body from the "dust from the ground" portrays His labor of love in terms expressive of a skillful potter (2:7).[3] If this is true, then perhaps framework advocate Ridderbos is a little closer to the truth than the Majority Report. Ridderbos (1957, 27) comments on the differences between Genesis 1 and the next two chapters: "In Genesis 2 and 3 the references to God are much more strongly anthropomorphic." But even this much-improved observation overstates the matter.

It is true that the more detailed and intimate nature of the revelation in Genesis 2 and 3 is more open to anthropomorphic interpretation. Nevertheless, when analyzed more carefully, true anthropomorphisms are actually absent even here. For instance, though the present participle of the verb "formed" (*wayîyser*, Gen. 2:7) means "potter" (e.g., Jer. 18:2), God's activity in Genesis 2:7 is, nevertheless, *realistic history* rather than *anthropomorphic condescension*. In fact, neither perspective (traditional or framework) proposes that Adam's formation here is really a revelational metaphor signifying only that God is ultimately his Creator, and

---

3. William Dyrness, *Themes in Old Testament Theology* (Downers Grove, IL: InterVarsity Press, 1979), p. 66–67.

nothing more. That is, *both* the novel framework hypothesis *and* the traditional interpretation agree that Adam's material body was actually fashioned from the dust of the ground by direct, immediate divine action.[4] The more conventional interpretation of creation would argue that Genesis 2:7 records a theophanic[5] activity — just as Kline (1970, 85) proposes of Genesis 3:8: "Theophany in human form was evidently a mode of special revelation from the beginning."

In fact, Moses does *not* mention anything such as God using His "arms" and "back" in digging up the soil for this special project — though he can speak of God's redemptive activity by using "arm" imagery elsewhere (Exod. 6:6, 15:16; Deut. 4:34, 5:15). Nor do we discover a reference to the Lord's "hands" and "fingers" carefully sculpting Adam's body, as in the metaphorical potter imagery found in the prophets (Isa. 45:9, 64:8; Jer. 18:4–6; Lam. 4:2). Genesis 2 presents a bold, supernatural event in unadorned, factual form: God formed Adam's body from the ground — without detailing *how* He did it. Thus, anthropomorphism is actually avoided in this revelation of the historical fact of God's creative activity. Furthermore, against any alleged anthropomorphic imagery in Genesis 2:7, we learn that Adam's body was formed from the dry "*dust* from the ground" — not "clay" as employed in the familiar potter's art in Israel (cf. Isa. 29:16, 41:25, 45:9; Jer. 18:4, 6). Even Hamilton (1990, 156) observes of the verb Moses employs: " 'Potter,' however, is a suitable translation only when the context clearly points to the fact that the work of formation being described is that of a potter."

In addition, Irons (1998, 55) misinforms his readers when he writes of the framework hypothesis that "only the chronological scheme of arranging the creative works of God within six day-frames is figurative." This simply is not true regarding what

---

4. Kline 1996, 15 n47; Irons 1998, 72; Majority Report 1999, 36.
5. "Theophany" is a compound of two Greek words: *theos* ("God") and *phainō* ("appear"). It is "a theological term used to refer to either a visible or auditory manifestation of God." EDT 1087.

the framework position asserts. And the Majority Report (1999, 8–9) he helped compose directly contradicts this with numerous (alleged) samples of anthropomorphic figures from Genesis 1. In fact, the Majority Report (1999, 6) vigorously declares: "There are many indications in Gen. 1:1–2:3 that God's actions are being described by analogy rather than directly." Note that Irons' "only" becomes "many" in the Majority Report. I will quickly refer seriatim to the various *supposed* anthropomorphic expressions drawn from the *first* chapter of Genesis, then rebut them.

The Majority Report (1999, 9) informs us that: "In the beginning, the Spirit of God is pictured as 'hovering' like a bird over the surface of the waters (Gen. 1:2). But no one supposes that the Spirit actually reined in His omnipresence and developed a locality for the purpose of creating." Yet Genesis 1:2 does not declare at all that God "reined in His omnipresence." This statement indicates a very important truth of God's relationship to the world: it highlights the *immanence* of God. Though Genesis 1 stresses God's lofty transcendence, whereas Genesis 2 highlights His loving immanence, this statement in 1:2 already prepares us for His immanence in creation. Genesis 1:2 simply points out for the reader that God's Spirit was present in creation — *without localizing Him*. After all, is not the Spirit *everywhere* (Ps. 139:7)? And if so, then He was *right there*, just as the text states. The Spirit is locally present because He is everywhere present. As the Puritan writer Thomas Watson put it, "God's center is everywhere; his circumference nowhere." Genesis 1:2 informs us that the Spirit is actively operating on the scene. This text is *not* like one that speaks of the "arm" of the Lord, which does not really exist. This is *not* figurative or anthropomorphic imagery, for the Spirit really *does* exist, and He *really was* present over the waters of Genesis 1:2.

As an illustration of this problem, the Majority Report (1999, 8) states, "God 'said' things many times during the Creation week. Yet no one supposes He exerted pressure on a diaphragm,

vibrated His larynx, and moved air out His mouth while manip-
ulating His tongue and lips." But nowhere does the text state *anything* about God's diaphragm, larynx, tongues, or lips. A problem
I have with the framework advocates is that "their eyes see strange
things," as it were. They see things in the text that simply are not
there; their *system* requires these things, not the *text*. Certainly
Scripture *often* refers anthropomorphically to the "mouth" of the
Lord (Deut. 8:3; Ps. 138:4), his "lips" (Job 11:5; Isa. 30:27), his
"breath" (2 Sam. 22:16; Ps. 33:6), and so forth. *But it does not do
so in Genesis 1.*

And just as surely, God *does* literally speak in Genesis 1. After all, in Genesis 2 and 3 we read of His literally speaking with
Adam alone (Gen. 2:16–17) and to Adam and Eve together (Gen.
1:28–30, 3:9–19). Do *these* actual conversations imply God has
a larynx and lips? *And* Genesis 1 *actually tells us He spoke* (Gen.
1:3, 6, 9, 11, 14, etc.) — contrary to the framework advocates
who tell us *He most certainly did not speak*. It is not absurd to
assume God speaks to the inanimate world, for we even read of
Christ literally speaking to quiet the tempest (Mark 4:39). Furthermore, one glorious difference (among many!) between God
and the idols is that the God of Israel speaks, whereas the idols
do not (Ps. 115:5, 135:16; Dan. 5:23; Hab. 2:18). Thus, I agree
with Young (1964, 56) against the framework hypothesis: "The
statement, 'and God said,' to take one example, represents a gen-
uine activity upon the part of God, a true and effectual speaking
which accomplishes his will."

The Majority Report (1999, 8) also states, "The same logic
must be applied when we hear that God 'saw' what He had made
and declared it to be good." But why is this deemed an anthropomorphism? Is not one of God's names *El Roi*, the "God who
sees" (Gen. 16:13)? Is not God capable of visualizing the material world He created? And His seeing that "it was good" simply
affirms that His creative power brought about precisely what He
intended.

The text of Genesis *could have* portrayed God as a worker "stretching out His arm" to perform some work (Exod. 6:6), extending a "mighty hand" (Deut. 4:34), rolling up His sleeves to get to work (Isa. 52:10), stirring up the "dust beneath His feet" (Nah. 1:3), and so forth. In fact, such anthropomorphic creation-related imagery does appear elsewhere in Scripture. For instance, Isaiah 40:12 asks, "Who has measured the waters in the hollow of His hand, and marked off the heavens by the span, and calculated the dust of the earth by the measure, and weighed the mountains in a balance and the hills in a pair of scales?" Such imagery also appears in Job 38–40, various Psalms,[6] and elsewhere[7] — and elsewhere in Moses' Pentateuch.[8] But again: *not in Genesis 1.*

Then the Majority Report (1999, 8) really stretches the facts: "The picture in Genesis 1 is clear. God wakes up. He works until evening. He lies down for the night and repeats the process in the morning. The Spirit has gone out of His way to present the work of God on the analogy of the work of man." Whatever else one might say, no one can assert that this picture presented by the framework hypothesis regarding Genesis 1 "is clear." Why has the church of Jesus Christ missed this "clear" revelation for so long? Nor may we even surmise that "the Spirit has gone out of His way to present the work of God on the analogy of the work of man." *Where* in Genesis 1 do we read anything remotely resembling God waking up, working all day, lying down for the night, and getting up the next day?

The Spirit has *not* "gone out of his way" to present Genesis 1 in these images, the Majority Report (1999) has. And that is a big and worrisome difference. Employing Blocher's delicious phrase, we believe that, like Kline, the Majority Report (1999) has "left the beaten path" — this time the Scriptures themselves,

---

6. E.g., Ps. 8:6, 10:12, 11:4, 17:14, 33:18, 34:15, 75:8, 89:10, 13, 98:1, 136:12.
7. E.g., Isa. 5:12, 25, 9:17, 30:30; Jer. 1:9, 6:12, 32:17; Ezek. 1:3, 6:14, 20:33; Hab. 2:16; Zech. 2:9, 13:7
8. E.g., Gen. 6:8, 49:23; Exdo. 3:20, 6:1, 9:3, 14:22, 15:6, 12, 16; Deut. 2:15.

which ought to be "a lamp to my feet and a light to my path" (Ps. 119:105). It has strayed either to the left hand or to the right. This is clear evidence that the framework system requirements are controlling the text, rather than the text controlling the system. And this greatly alarms those defending the historic, traditional view of creation.

The Majority Report (1999: 9) does not fare any better with its allegations of God "resting" on day 7 — as if that were anthropomorphic,[9] and bringing Exodus 31:17 to bear upon the topic does not help them whatsoever (Majority Report 1999, 9; Irons 1998, 68). Two reasons absolutely destroy the framework hypothesis argument at this point.

First, the text of Genesis 2:2–3 does not speak anthropomorphically of God "resting," as if relaxing. As I noted previously regarding the "Sabbath Day Problem," Genesis 2 actually informs us that God "*ceased*" His labor (Hamilton, 1990, 141–42). As Mathews (1996, 178) observes regarding Genesis 2:2–3: "The verb translated 'rested' here means 'the *cessation* of creative activity'; it has this same sense in its only other occurrence in Genesis, where God promises the postdiluvian world that the times and seasons 'will never cease' (8:22). Elsewhere we find that God 'rested' (*nûah*, Exod. 20:11; *napaš*, 31:17), but here the passage speaks of the absence of work — 'he abstained' from work." That is, God did *not* relax as if from weariness; He simply *ceased* from His creating. Actually the text is even stronger, for as Cassuto (1998, 63) puts it, "This verb has been translated or interpreted by many as if it signified 'to rest' or 'to cease work'; but this is incorrect. It has a negative connotation: 'not to do work.' " And most certainly it is literally true that God ceased His creative working. Though it was not a laborious chore for Him, it was most definitely "work" that effected something — the universe.

Second, importing the imagery of Exodus 31:17 into the debate will not help. The term "refreshed" (NASB), "rested" (NIV)

---

9. Compare Ridderbos 1957, 30; Irons 1998, 67–68.

(*nāpaš*) in that verse does not appear at all in Genesis 2:2–3. Again, the framework hypothesis tends to read into texts things that simply are not there. That God "rested" in the upper register (Irons 1998, 51) simply does not register with the point of Genesis 2:2–3: He "rested" — or better "ceased" — His creative work *in the "Lower Register"* — in time and on earth where His work occurred.

Besides, as McCabe (2010, 243–44) argues, "To say that the anthropomorphism of divine refreshment precludes a literal interpretation of the days of creation is a comparison of apples and oranges. Since there is no inherent connection between God's nature and the duration of His creative activity, the real issue focuses on whether Scripture affirms that God created on heavenly or earthly time." He adds that both Exodus 20:11 and 31:17 "use an adverbial accusative of time ('in six days'). This grammatical construction indicates the duration of God's creative activity by stating how long it occurred."

Absence of the Upper Register

Certainly all evangelicals believe in an "upper register" where God exists in His eternal glory and a "lower register" where we exist in our temporal limitation. But the Genesis 1 narrative does not emphasize the two registers in creation week. When we read the text as it actually stands, we discover that the focus is almost wholly upon the "lower register."

The creation narrative opens in the upper register: "In the beginning God" (Gen. 1:1), and it presents the upper register's Holy Spirit "moving over the surface of the waters" (Gen. 1:2). But both of these important introductory observations have God at work "in the beginning," as He creates "the heavens and the earth," and moves over the "surface of the waters." Clearly, the eternal Lord is at work creating and fashioning the temporal world, yet the emphasis is almost wholly upon the lower register temporal order, for we see God creating, separating, naming, gathering, placing, and making things in the lower register. Even the astronomical bodies created on day 4 (Gen. 1:16) are to function in behalf of the earth by being the providential mechanisms for providing its light (Gen. 1:17), governing its day and night (Gen. 1:18), marking its days and years (Gen. 1:14), and creating its seasons (Gen. 1:14).

Conclusion

These are a few of the problems encumbering the framework hypothesis and its two-register cosmology argument. The framework view of creation is more of a theological deduction than an exegetical conclusion. Its beauty is in the eye of the beholder. It is a strained concept created by an unrestrained imagination. Indeed, it seems to be an exercise in *creation ex nihilo*. Though the framework hypothesis is certainly not "without form," it surely is "void."

Part IV

Conclusion

Chapter 10

Final Observations

The framework hypothesis is an influential and potent approach to the creation account in Genesis. It possesses a remarkable air of sophistication that attempts to hold forth the authority of Scripture while allowing for "natural revelation," which suggests many features of evolutionary theory. Its literary approach to the interpreting of Genesis 1 presents us with an impressive and highly refined revelation from God to Moses some 3,500 years ago. Nevertheless, appearances can be deceiving. The massive re-interpretation of the biblical record required by this literary hypothesis should give pause to any who would initially be impressed with it.

Christians committed to the traditional interpretation of Genesis will need to prepare themselves if they desire intelligently and cogently to answer the framework objections to the historic position on creation. Though the framework approach has been around evangelical circles for over 75 years, it has within the past 10 years begun making remarkable inroads into evangelical theology. Just as the day age theory gained a certain influence among evangelicals in the early part of the 20th century, it appears that the framework hypothesis may be doing the same in the early part of the 21st century. We cannot ignore it and hope it goes away.

I have offered this work as a modest critique of the framework hypothesis, endeavoring to reach a wider audience. I hope to encourage others — minister and layman alike — to more vigorously engage the debate. Initial confrontation with this sophisticated approach to the creation account can seem overwhelming. One can easily be intimidated by the erudition so evident in the ornate structure of the system. Oftentimes Christians are cowered by the fear that they are acting as mere Bible thumpers, mindlessly promoting an outdated party line that actually embarrasses the integrity of our holy faith. Indeed, Christian astrophysicist Hugh Ross begins his introduction to one of his books, "Nearly half the adults in the United States believe that God created the universe within the last 10,000 years. What reason do they give? 'The Bible says so.' "[1] Yet a simple survey of the list of intelligent proponents of the traditional approach to the creation narrative should dispel such concerns. Furthermore, a careful analysis of the framework hypothesis itself — such as I have offered herein — should hearten those committed to the view that God created the world in the space of six, sequential, 24-hour days.

May our study of the creation account lead us to respond as David of old: "When I consider Your heavens, the work of Your fingers, the moon and the stars, which You have ordained; what is man that You take thought of him, and the son of man that You care for him?" (Ps. 8:3–4).

---

1. Hugh Ross, *Creation and Time: Biblical and Scientific Perspective on the Creation-Date Controversy* (Colorado Springs, CO: NavPress, 1994), p. 7.

Abbreviations

ABD   *The Anchor Bible Dictionary*. David Noel Freedman, ed. 6 vols. New York: Doubleday, 1992.

AHD   *The American Heritage Dictionary of the English Language*. 3d. ed. New York: Houghton and Mifflin, 1992.

BAGD   *A Greek-English Lexicon of the New Testament and Other Early Christian Literature*. Walter Bauer, William F. Arndt, F. Wilbur Gingrich, and Frederick W. Danker, eds. 3d. Ed. Chicago, IL: University of Chicago Press, 2000.

BDB   *Hebrew and English Lexicon of the Old Testament*. Francis Brown, S.R. Driver, C.A. Briggs, eds. Oxford: Clarendon, 1972.

BEB   *Baker Encyclopedia of the Bible*. Walter A. Elwell, ed. 4 vols. Grand Rapids, MI: Baker, 1988.

CBTEL   *Cyclopedia of Biblical, Theological, and Ecclesiastical Literature*. John McClintock and James Strong. 12 vols. New York: Harper and Bros, 1867–87; rep. Grand Rapids, MI: Baker, 1981.

DBI   *Dictionary of Biblical Interpretation*. R.J. Coggins and J.L. Houlden, eds. London: SCM, 1990.

DOTH   *Dictionary of the Old Testament: Historical Books*. Bill T. Arnold and H.G.M. Williamson, eds. Downers Grove, IL: InterVarsity, 2005.

DOTP   *Dictionary of the Old Testament: Pentateuch*. T. Desmond Alexander and David W. Baker, eds. Downers Grove, IL: InterVarsity, 2003.

DOTW   *Dictionary of the Old Testament: Wisdom, Poetry and Writings*. Tremper Longman III and Peter Enns, eds. Downers Grove, IL: IVP Academic, 2008.

DPL   *Dictionary of Paul and His Letters*. Gerald F. Hawthorne and Ralph P. Martin, eds. Downers Grove, IL: InterVarsity, 1993.

EBC   *The Eerdmans Bible Commentary*. Donald Guthrie and J.A. Motyer, eds. 3d. ed. Grand Rapids, MI: Eerdmans, 1970.

EDB   *Eerdmans Dictionary of the Bible*. David Noel Freedman, ed. Grand Rapids, MI: Eerdmans, 2000.

EDBT   *Evangelical Dictionary of Biblical Theology*. Walter A. Elwell, ed. Grand Rapids, MI: Baker, 1996.

EDT   *Evangelical Dictionary of Theology*. Walter A. Elwell, ed. Grand Rapids, MI: Baker, 1984.

IBD   *Interpreter's Dictionary of the Bible*. George Arthur Buttrick, ed. 5 vols. Nashville, TN: Abingdon, 1962.

ISBE²   *The International Standard Bible Encyclopedia*. Geoffrey W. Bromiley, ed. 4 vols. 2d ed. Grand Rapids, MI: Eerdmans, 1982.

NDB   *New Bible Dictionary*, J.D. Douglas, F.F. Bruce, et al, eds. Downers Grove, IL: InterVarsity, 1982.

SHERK   *Schaff-Herzog Encyclopedia of Religious Knowledge*. Philip Schaff, ed. 3 vols. Chicago, IL: Funk & Wagnalls, 1887.

TDOT   *Theological Dictionary of the Old Testament*. G. Johannes Botterweck and Helmer Ringgren, eds. 15 vols. Grand Rapids, MI: Eerdmans, 1990.

TDOTTE   *New International Dictionary of Old Testament Theology & Exegesis*. Willem VanGemeren, ed. 5 vols. Grand Rapids, MI: Zondervan, 1997.

TLOT   *Theological Lexicon of the Old Testament*, Ernst Jenni and Claus Westermann, trans. by Mark E. Biddle. 3 vols. Peabody, MA: Hendrickson, 1997.

TWOT   *Theological Wordbook of the Old Testament*, R. Laird Harris, Gleason L. Archer, Jr., and Bruce K. Waltke, eds., 2 vols. Chicago, IL: Moody, 1980.

ZEB   *The Zondervan Encyclopedia of the Bible*. Moises Silva, ed. 5 vols. Rev. ed. Grand Rapids, MI: Zondervan, 2009.

Select Bibliography

Aalders, G. Charles. 1981. Vol 1: *Genesis*. Grand Rapids, MI: Zondervan.

Alexander, T.D. 2002. *From Paradise to the Promised Land: An Introduction to the Pentateuch*. 2d. ed. Grand Rapids, MI: Baker.

Allis, O.T. 1951. *God Spake by Moses*. Nutley, NJ: Presbyterian and Reformed.

Arnold, Bill T. 1998. *Encountering the Book of Genesis*. Grand Rapids, MI: Baker.

Barker, Will S., and W. Robert Godfrey. 1990. *Theonomy: An Informed Critique*. Grand Rapids, MI: Zondervan.

Batten, Don, et al. 2015. "Is Genesis Poetry/Figurative, A Theological Argument (Polemic) and Thus Not Historical?: Critique of the Framework Hypothesis." *Creation.com*. Web. March 30, 2015.

Beall, Todd S. 2010. "Contemporary Hermeneutical Approaches to Genesis 1–11" in Mortenson and Ury 2010.

Bédard, Paulin. 2013. *In Six Days God Created: Refuting the Framework and Figurative Views of the Days of Creation*. n.p.: Xulon.

Berkhof, Louis. 1941. *Systematic Theology*. Grand Rapids, MI: Eerdmans.

Bibza, James, and John D. Currid. 1986. "A Cosmology of History: From Creation to Consummation" in Hoffecker 1986.

Blocher, Henri. 1984. *In the Beginning: The Opening Chapters of Genesis*. Downers Grove, IL: InterVarsity.

Boyd, Steven W. 2010. "The Genre of Genesis 1:1–2:3: What Means This Text?" in Mortenson and Ury 2010.

Bruce, F.F. 1984. "Interpretation of the Bible" in EDT.

Cassuto, Umberto. 1998. *A Commentary on the Book of Genesis: Part I: From Adam to Noah*. Trans. by Israel Abrahams. Jerusalem: Magnes, [rep. 1961].

Collins, C. John. 1995. "The *WAYYIQTOL* AS 'Pluperfect': When and Why." *Tyndale Bulletin* 46:1: 117–40.

———. 1996. "Response to Kline." *Perspectives on Science and Christian Faith*, 48:2.

———. 1999. "Discourse Analysis and the Interpretation of Gen. 2:4–7." *WTJ* 61, 269–76.

———. 2005. "Reading Genesis 1:1–2:3 as an Act of Communication: Discourse Analysis and Literal Interpretation." In Pipa and Hall 2005.

———. 2006. *Genesis 1–4: A Linguistic, Literary, and Theological Commentary*. Phillipsburg, NJ: P&R

Currid, John D. 2003. *Genesis*. EPSC. Holywell, UK: Evangelical.

———. 2007. "The Hebrew World-and-Life View" in Hoffecker 2007.

Dabney, Robert L. 1973. *Lectures in Systematic Theology*. Grand Rapids, MI: Zondervan, rep. 1973.

Davies, Margaret. 1990. "Genre" in DBI.

Davis, John J. 1975. *Paradise to Prison: Studies in Genesis*. Grand Rapids, MI: Baker.

DeVries, Carl E. 1988. "Genesis, Book of" in BEB 2.

Duncan, J. Ligon. 2001. "The 24-Hour View" in Hagopian 2001.

Dyer, Sid. 2005. "The New Testament Doctrine of Creation" in Pipa and Hall 2005.

Futato, Mark. 1998. "Because It Had Rained: A Study of Gen 2:5–7 with Implications for Gen 2:4–25 and Gen 1:1–2:3." *Westminster Theological Journal* 60:1 (Spring): 1–21.

Garland, David E. 2003. *1 Corinthians*. BECNT. Grand Rapids, MI: Baker.

Godfrey, W. Robert. 2003. *God's Pattern for Creation*. Phillipsburg, NJ. P&R.

Green, William Henry. 1910. *The Unity of the Book of Genesis*. New York: Charles Scribner's.

Grudem, Wayne. 1994. *Systematic Theology: An Introduction to Biblical Doctrine*. Grand Rapids, MI: Zondervan.

Gunn, Grover E. 1998. *Six Day Creation*. Greenville, SC: Southern Presbyterian.

Hall, David W. 1999. "What Was the View of the Westminster Divines on Creation Days?" in Pipa and Hall 1999.

Hamilton, Victor R. 1990. *The Book of Genesis: Chapters 1–17*. NICOT. Grand Rapids, MI: Eerdmans.

Harris, R. Laird. 1999. "The Length of Creative Days in Genesis 1" in Pipa and Hall 1999.

Harrison, Roland Kenneth. 1969. *Introduction to the Old Testament*. Grand Rapids, MI: Eerdmans.

Hasel, Gerhard F. 1984. "The 'Days' of Creation in Genesis 1." *Origins* 21:1: 5–38.

Hodge, Charles. 1973. *Systematic Theology*. 3 vols. Grand Rapids, MI: Eerdmans.

Hoffecker, W. Andrew, ed. 2007. *Revolutions in Worldview: Understanding the Flow of Western Thought*. Phillipsburg, NJ: P & R.

———, ed. 2006. *Universe, Society, and Ethics*. Vol. 2: *Building a Christian Worldview*. Phillipsburg, NJ: P&R.

Hyers, Conrad. 1984. *The Meaning of Creation: Genesis and Modern Science*. Richmond, VA: John Knox.

Irons, Charles Lee. 1998. "The Framework Interpretation: Explained and Defended." Personal paper (February).

———. 1999. "In the Space of Six Days: What Did the Divines Mean?" Internal Committee discussion paper: "The Report of the Committee to Study the Framework Hypothesis," "Majority Report." Presbytery of Southern California (OPC) (October 15–16).

Irons, Charles Lee, and Meredith G. Kline. 2001. "The Framework View" in Hagopian 2001.

Jordan, James B. 1997. "Meredith Kline Strikes Back (Part 1)." *Biblical Chronology* 11:2 (Feb.): 1–7.

———. 1999. *Creation in Six Days: A Defense of the Traditional Reading of Genesis One.* Moscow, ID: Canon Press.

Kaiser Jr., Walter C. 1970. "The Literary Form of Genesis 1–11" in Payne 1970.

Kay, Marc. 2007a. "On Literary Theorists' Approach to Genesis 1: Part 1." *Journal of Creation* 21:2: 71–76.

———. 2007b. "On Literary Theorists' Approach to Genesis 1: Part 2." *Journal of Creation* 21:3: 93–101.

Keathley, Kenneth D., and Mark F. Rooker. 2014. *40 Questions about Creation and Evolution.* Grand Rapids, MI: Kregel.

Keil, C.F., and F. Delitzsch. 2001. *Commentary on the Old Testament.* Vol. 1: *The Pentateuch.* Trans. by James Martin. Peabody, MA: Henderson.

Kelly, D.F. 1997. *Creation and Change.* Ross-shire, Great Britain: Mentor.

Kidner, Derek. 1966. "Genesis 2:5–6: Wet Or Dry?" *Tyndale Bulletin* 17: 109–14.

———. 1967. *Genesis: An Introduction and Commentary.* Downers Grove, IL: InterVarsity Press.

Kline, Meredith G. 1958. "Because It Had Not Rained." *Westminster Theological Journal* 20 (May): 156–57.

———. 1970. "Genesis" in EBC.

———. 1977. "Creation in the Image of the Glory-Spirit." *Westminster Theological Journal* 39: 259–72.

———. 1996. "Space and Time in the Genesis Cosmogony." *Perspectives on Science and Christian Faith* 48:1 (March): 2–15.

Kuliovsky, Andrew S. 2001. "A Critique of the Literary Framework View of the Days of Creation." *Creation Research Quarterly* 37: 237–44.

———. 2004. "The Keys to Interpreting Genesis: History and Genre. Review of *Yea, Hath God Said?* by Kenneth L. Gentry Jr. and Michael R. Butler." *Technical Journal* 18:3: 61–66.

Leupold, H.C. 1942. *Exposition of Genesis*. Vol 1. Grand Rapids, MI: Baker.

————. 2009. "Genesis, Book of" in ZEP vol. 2

Levenson, Jon D. 1988. *Creation and the Persistence of Evil: The Jewish Drama of Divine Omnipotence*. Princeton, NJ: University Press.

Longman III, Tremper. 2005. *How to Read Genesis*. Downers Grove, IL: InterVarsity.

MacRae, Allan A. 1959. "The Principles of Interpreting Genesis 1 and 2." Philadelphia, PA: Faith Theological Seminary: 1–9.

Majority Report. 1999. "The Report of the Committee to Study the Framework Hypothesis: Majority Report." Presbytery of Southern California (OPC) (October 15–16).

Mathews, Kenneth A. 1996. *Genesis 1–11:26*. NAC. Nashville, TN: Broadman.

McCabe, Robert V. 2010. "A Critique of the Framework Interpretation of the Creation Week" in Mortenson and Ury 2010.

Miller, Johnny V., and J.M. Soden. 2012. *In the Beginning . . . We Misunderstood: Interpreting Genesis 1 in Its Original Context*. Grand Rapids, MI: Kregel.

Moreland, J.P., and John Mark Reynolds, eds. 1999. *Three Views on Creation and Evolution*. Grand Rapids, MI: Zondervan.

Mortenson, Terry, and Thane H. Ury, eds. 2010. *Coming to Grips with Genesis: Biblical Authority and the Age of the Earth*. Green Forest, AR: Master Books.

Muether, John R. 1990. "The Theonomic Attraction" in Barker and Godfrey 1990.

Newling, Scott. 2011. "Genesis 1:1–2:3 Is Not Poetry and It Is Historical." Web: MatthiasMedia.com 5/2/2011.

Niehaus, Jeffrey J. 2014. *Biblical Theology: The Common Grace Covenants*. Wooster, OH: Weaver Book Co.

Osborne, Grant R. 2005. "Historical Narrative and Truth in the Bible." *Journal of the Evangelical Theological Society* 48:4 (December): 673–88.

Pipa Jr., Joseph A. 2005. "From Chaos to Cosmos: A Critique of the Non-Literal Interpretations of Genesis 1:1–2:3" in Pipa and Hall 2005.

Pipa Jr., Joseph A., and David W. Hall, eds. 1999. *Did God Create in Six Days?* Taylors, SC: Southern Presbyterian.

Poythress, Vern S. 2013. *Christian Interpretations of Genesis 1*. Phillipsburg, NJ: P & R.

Ramm, Bernard . 1955. *The Christian View of Science and Scripture*. Grand Rapids, MI: Eerdmans.

Reymond, Robert L. 1998. *A New Systematic Theology of the Christian Faith*. Nashville, TN: Thomas Nelson.

Ridderbos, N.H. 1957. *Is There A Conflict Between Genesis 1 and Natural Science?* Trans. by John Vriend. Grand Rapids, MI: Eerdmans.

Ross, Allen P. 1996. *Creation & Blessing: A Guide to the Study and Exposition of Genesis.* 2d. Ed. Grand Rapids, MI: BakerAcademic.

Ross, Mark. 1999. "The Framework Hypothesis" in Pipa and Hall 1999.

Ross, Hugh, and Gleason L. Archer. 2001. "The Day-Age View" in Hagopian 2001.

Robinson, B.A. 2014. "Creation Science: One of Three Models." Web. *Religious Tolerance.* July 11.

Sailhammer, John H. 1990. "Genesis," in Frank E. Gaebelein, ed. *The Expositor's Bible Commentary.* Grand Rapids, MI: Zondervan.

Scullion, John J. 1992. "Genesis, Narrative of" in *ABD* vol. 2.

Shaw, Benjamin. 1999. "The Literal Day Interpretation" in Pipa and Hall 1999.

Sloane, Andrew. 2003. "Theological Boundaries on Theistic Evolution." Collected Papers: God, Science and Divine Action." Morling College, Australia. Web: www.Iscast.org

Speiser, E.A. 1964. *Genesis.* AB. New York: Doubleday.

Stambaugh, James. 2015. "The Days of Creation: A Semantic Approach." Web. *Creation Ministries.* March 30.

Steinmann, Andrew E. 2002. "*Ehad* as an Ordinal Number and the Meaning of Genesis 1:5." *Journal of the Evangelical Theological Society* 45:4 (Dec.): 577–84.

Taylor, Justin. 2015. "Biblical Reasons to Doubt the Creation Days Were 24-hour Periods." *The Gospel Coalition.* Web. January 28.

Taylor, Paul F. 2007. *The Six Days of Genesis: A Scientific Appreciation of Chapters 1–11.* Green Forest, AR: Master Books.

Thompson, J.A. 1968. "Genesis 1: Science? History? Theology?" *TSF Bulletin* 50 (Spring): 12–23.

———. 1982. "Creation" in NBD.

Turner, L.A. 2003. "Genesis, Book of" in DOTP.

Van Gemeren, Willem. 1988. *The Progress of Redemption: The Story of Salvation from Creation to the New Jerusalem.* Grand Rapids, MI: Zondervan.

Van Till, Howard J. 1986. *The Fourth Day: What the Bible and the Heavens Are Telling Us about Creation.* Grand Rapids, MI: Eerdmans.

———. 2006. "From Calvinism to Freethought: The Road Less Traveled." Freethought Association of West Michigan. May 24. Web: Freethought Association.

Waltke, Bruce K. 1975a. "The Creation Account in Genesis 1:1–3.*Bibliotheca Sacra.* Part I: January.

———. 1975b. "The Creation Account in Genesis 1:1–3. *Bibliotheca Sacra.* Part II: April.

———. 1975c. "The Creation Account in Genesis 1:1–3. *Bibliotheca Sacra.* Part III: July.

———. 1975d. "The Creation Account in Genesis 1:1–3. *Bibliotheca Sacra.* Part IV: October.

———. 1976. "The Creation Account in Genesis 1:1–3. *Bibliotheca Sacra.* Part V: January.

———. 2001. *Genesis: A Commentary.* Grand Rapids, MI: Zondervan.

———. 2012. "Barriers to Accepting the Possibility of Creation by Means of an Evolutionary Process." Web, *Biologos* (March 27): 1–13.

Walton, John. 2001. *Genesis.* NIVAC. Grand Rapids, MI: Zondervan.

Weeks, Noel. 1978. "The Hermeneutical Problem of Genesis 1–11." *Themelios* 4:1 (Sept.): 12–19.

———. 1988. *The Sufficiency of Scripture.* Edinburgh: Banner of Truth.

Wenham, Gordon J. 1987. *Genesis 1–15.* WBC. Dallas: Word.

Westermann, Claus. 1964. *The Genesis Accounts of Creation.* Trans. Norman E. Wagner. Philadelphia, PA: Fortress.

———. 1984. *Genesis 1–11: A Commentary.* Minneapolis, MN: Augsburg.

White Jr., William. 1974. "Contemporary Understanding of Genesis 1:1–2:3" in John H. Skilton, ed. *The Law and the Prophets: Old Testament Studies in Honor of Oswald T. Allis.* Nutley, NJ: Presbyterian and Reformed.

Whitelaw, Thomas. 1950. *Genesis* in H.D.M. Spence and Joseph S. Exell. *The Pulpit Commentary.* Grand Rapids, MI: Eerdmans. Vol. 1.

Young, Edward J. 1964. *Studies in Genesis One.* Philadelphia, PA: P&R.

———. 1976. *In the Beginning: Genesis Chapters 1 to 3 and the Authority of Scripture.* Edinburgh: Banner of Truth.

Young, Frances. 1990. "Creation Narrative" in DBI.

Zylstra, Mark. 2000. "Re-visiting the Days of Creation . . . Again." Oct. 20. Web. Spindleworks.com.

Subject Index

Name Index

Scripture Index